CRITICAL ESSAYS IN MODERN LITERATURE

The Utopian Novel in America, 1886–1896

The Utopian Novel in America

1886–1896

The Politics of Form

JEAN PFAELZER

UNIVERSITY OF PITTSBURGH PRESS

Published by the University of Pittsburgh Press, Pittsburgh, Pa. 15260
Copyright © 1984, University of Pittsburgh Press
All rights reserved
Feffer and Simons, Inc., London
Manufactured in the United States of America

Library of Congress Cataloging in Publication Data

Pfaelzer, Jean.
  The utopian novel in America, 1886–1896.

  (Critical essays in modern literature)
  Bibliography: p. 181.
  Includes index.
  1. American fiction—19th century—History and criti-
cism.   2. Utopias in literature.   3. Politics in litera-
ture.   4. Social problems in literature.   5. United
States—History—1865–1898.   I. Title.   II. Series.
PS374.U8P43 1985   813'.4'09372   84-40094
ISBN 0-8229-3811-1

Portions of this work appeared in slightly different form in "American Utopian Fiction 1888–1896: The Political Origins of Form," *Minnesota Review* 6 (Spring 1976), 114–17; "Parody and Satire in American Dystopian Fiction," *Science Fiction Studies* 7 (March 1980), 61–72; and "A State of One's Own: Feminism as Ideology in American Utopias 1880–1915," *Extrapolation* 24 (Winter 1983), 311–28.

For Johanna Pfaelzer

Contents

Acknowledgments

I would not have found the impetus, provocation, dialogue, or encouragement for this book in a room of my own. In my first years at the University of California at San Diego, I found them instead in a room next door—the office of my late colleague and friend, Robert C. Elliott, who not only brought his fine formal and historicist presumptions to our field, but also fostered its unusually friendly discourse. Further, in the hearty discussion, thoughtful seminars, and rigorous readings of other colleagues, this project has been focused, argued, and developed. Many have listened and read. Stephen Fender, Margit Frenk, Bram Dijkstra, Richard Terdiman, and Donald Wesling have helpfully commented on various chapters along the way. In particular, Edwin Fussell, Susan Kirkpatrick, and Edward Long have been gentle muses and rigorous editors—encouraging my pursuit of contextual and theoretical questions within the resources of the nineteenth-century utopian tales themselves.

For those of us who are self-defined utopians (probably out of combined commitment, repression, and naiveté), the past few years have finally provided us the pleasure of working within a new and lively critical field. The question of the function of utopianism, reopened by Ernst Bloch after the Second World War, has been recently explored by Darko Suvin, Fredric Jameson, Melvyn Lasky, Frank Manuel, and Fritzie Manuel (among others), who, in documenting the historicity and philosophical impact of the utopian impulse, attest to its longevity and health. In my consideration of how contemporary notions of history inform the narrative structures of the utopian novel, I have also benefited from Kenneth Roemer's important introduction, *The Obsolete Necessity*, which

xi

focused critical attention on nineteenth-century American utopian fiction as a literary vogue.

We know that Virginia Woolf in fact received a great deal more than £500 when her aunt died after falling from her horse when she was riding out to take the air in Bombay. But Woolf's aunt was a metaphoric relative in any case, representing the freedom of time which money brings for creativity and writing. In this crucial area, I have enjoyed the generous support of the regents of the University of California in the forms of an Academic Senate Research Grant, a Regents' Affirmation Action Grant, and a Junior Faculty Summer Fellowship, which gave me the funds to travel, collect materials, ponder, and write.

Many others marked this particular path to utopia. The librarians of the British Museum, the Anderson Room at the University of Cambridge, the Bancroft Library at the University of California at Berkeley, the interlibrary loan and special collections departments at the University of California at San Diego, Brown University, the Library of Congress, and the Charles Kerr Publishing Company were very helpful in gathering materials. Utopian tales cited in bibliographies, publishers' lists, broadsheets, advertisements, referred to in sermons, correspondence, and magazines of the time were tantalizing to discover but difficult to locate without the skilled assistance of such librarians. I also deeply appreciate the careful work of Violet Lippett, Johanna Pfaelzer, and Teri Lamothe who assisted in the final preparation of the manuscript. Finally, I want to thank Jane Flanders of the University of Pittsburgh Press for her graceful persistence.

The Utopian Novel in America, 1886–1896

ONE

Time Yet to Come:
Notions of History and Narrative
Forms

Between 1886, the year of the Haymarket riot, and 1896, when the newly elected Republican President William McKinley reestablished conservative hegemony over a badly faltering economy, more than one hundred works of utopian fiction appeared in the United States. They constituted an unparalleled literary expression of social anxiety and political hope, a cultural event closely corresponding to the militant struggles for industrial, agrarian, and feminist reforms that characterized that turbulent decade.[1] Not only did these utopian tales popularize such reform crusades as the fight for the eight-hour day, urban sanitation, reduced farm mortgage rates, and women's suffrage, and not only did a utopian novel actually launch a national political party; late nineteenth-century utopian novels also announced to a concerned readership that the conditions for an egalitarian future were immanent in American capitalism.

In an era that was uniquely self-conscious about historical dynamics, popular theories of social development became the basis for the narrative structures of utopian fiction. Utopian fictions are in this sense metahistories. But the nineteenth-century utopian novel, as distinct from utopian socialism, utopian communities, or even the "utopian impulse," can hardly be understood as a serious prediction of historical process.[2] The best utopian theorists have always understood Thomas More's pun: *eutopia*—the good place; *utopia*—nowhere. The utopian novel was a literary genre, locked in its own paradox; like any text, it was conditioned by history—time past and passing—while it also purported to represent the future—time yet to come.

This study analyzes the particular image of history embodied in American utopian fiction and explores the impact of this image on narrative form. Until the 1940s, Marxist theorists traditionally argued that utopia represents a tempting but flawed proposition about history—a facile and thus a dangerous guarantee of a serene future. Friedrich Engels found that when such early utopians as Saint-Simon, Fourier, and Robert Owen defined their task "as to manufacture a system of society as perfect as possible," they disregarded the working class as the necessary determinant and agent of social change.[3] By promising the good place prematurely, indeed magically, utopia became a potentially dangerous diversion from the difficult task of forging a new society. Despite the astute observations and the good intentions of these architects of the future, Engels relegated utopia to the "realm of untimely illusion" and in its place he proclaimed scientific socialism which, unlike its utopian parent, was no longer "an accidental discovery of this or that ingenious brain, but the necessary outcome of the struggle between historically developed classes—the proletariat and the bourgeoisie."[4] Engels believed that by failing to generalize from the particularities and peculiarities of immediate reality, utopians divorced the future from the present; essentially idealists, they saw no preconditions for the future except right thinking.

In the twentieth century, however, impelled by the realities of fascism, utopian theorists began again to survey the frontiers of utopia and to reconsider the function of social fantasy. If utopia to Engels was an experiment in communitarian living, or worse, an illusory "kingdom of reason and eternal justice,"[5] to Ernst Bloch it signified the very experience of hope.[6] Fredric Jameson locates that hopeful experience in the various "incentives" of current ideology, which are commonly posed as promises of eternal life, images of a transformed body, or pictures of easy sexual gratification. Because of these incentives, the utopian is at one with the ideological and the ideological is at one with the utopian.[7]

After considering well over a hundred texts, I have come to believe that the incentives of utopia can represent either a stimulus to or a digression from praxis, depending on the conception of histori-

4

cal process within the fictional activity of the text. Popular notions of American history define the categories of this study. Many utopian tales, written in the United States in the last two decades of the nineteenth century, cast contemporary theories of social expansion in narrative forms that provide literary resolutions to the historical tensions of those turbulent years. In an era of militant protest against the injustices caused by too-rapid economic expansion and industrialization—at Haymarket in Chicago and Homestead in Pennsylvania, in Colorado and West Virginia—utopian authors imagined safer possiblities for social change through a number of literary devices: drugs, time-travel, shipwrecks, mesmerism, and century-long naps that transported dissatisfied citizens into serene futures. By suggesting that conscious activity, individual or collective, is not necessary to wrest the future from the present, these aesthetic solutions do represent an ideological incentive in Jameson's sense. History's promise is automatically fulfilled. Although many late nineteenth-century utopians hoped (and most dystopians feared) that a socialist future might be inherent in the technological progress and class tensions of the epoch, they still assumed bourgeois attitudes toward change, believing in laissez-faire economics, social evolution, determinism, and the progressive tendencies of democracy and industrialization. Whatever their imaginary political structure, utopian fictions of this era anticipated a future based on a shared premise: that capitalism contained the seeds of its own perfection.

In fact, these tales had a deeply radical potential that has little to do with their tactics for change or their recipes for an ideal future. Rather, these stories created a disjunction—a space in the mind of the reader—between the familiar present and the imagined future, between history and possibility, between satire and utopia. Yet, as Ernst Bloch suggests, "the future is always concealed in that which exists."[8] The utopian future uncovered in these novels represented a set of radical social and economic alternatives in narrative forms that identified and abstracted possibilities arising from the historical tensions of the late nineteenth century. In the 1880s and 1890s, utopian writers echoed social theoreticians, Populists, trade unionists, and feminists who announced that solutions to the problems wrought by industry, immigration, and urbanization were now available. Utopian narratives of the late nineteenth century depict societies whose characteristics are derived from the tendencies inherent in laissez-faire economic practices on the one hand, but also from the tendencies toward collectivity on the other. As Marx wrote,

Humanity always sets itself only such tasks as it can solve; since, looking at the matter more closely, it will always be found that the task itself arises only when the material conditions necessary for its solution already exist or are at the least in the process of formation. . . . The productive forces developing in the womb of bourgeois society create the material conditions for the solutions of that antagonism.[9]

But were these novels really meant to be read as maps to heaven? Social solutions and aesthetic solutions are distinct, if dependent, systems. Terry Eagleton reminds us that texts process

ideological conflict under the form of resolving specifically *aesthetic* problems, so that the problem solving process of the text is never merely a matter of its reference outward to certain pre-existent ideological cruxes. It is, rather, a matter of the "ideological" presenting itself in the form of the "aesthetic" and vice-versa—of an "aesthetic" solution to the ideological conflict producing in its turn an aesthetic problem which demands ideological resolution, and so on.[10]

Which is to say that social ideology is shaped by aesthetic concerns, and aesthetic concerns always work with raw material, history. The aesthetic structures of nineteenth-century American utopian novels are, after all, considerably different from the set of formal traditions ultimately inherited from Thomas More's prototype; instead, they stem largely from narrative structures of the contemporary sentimental romance, which traditionally celebrates a reconciliation of natural and social growth.[11]

This reading of utopian fiction of the late nineteenth century explores how the utopian incentive—the promise of historical fulfillment and the realization of the good place—shaped contemporary narrative forms. If authors of nineteenth-century utopian novels actually thought that they had "stumbled" (as Edward Bellamy put it) upon the road to socialism, if not to perfection, our task would be only to evaluate the degree of correspondence between prediction and what actually has occurred—that is, to assess the accuracy of their political predictions. But such a reading would ignore the mediations of contemporary belief systems and the mediations of aesthetic traditions as well: in these fictional anticipations of imaginary postcapitalist societies, time itself emerges as the "experience of hope," structured through literary resolutions of political tensions. I suspect that although these novels aimed at the fictional realization of social remedies, the literary formalization of the utopian hypothesis, "What if the world were good?" was ultimately more liberating to the consciousness of the nineteenth-century reader than the specific cure.

This study argues that popular theories of social development defined the narrative categories of American nineteenth-century utopian fiction: I have classified them into industrial-progressive, agrarian-pastoral, conservative, apocalyptic, and feminist utopias, as well as dystopias, their parodic counterparts. The distinct literary structures and the peculiar relationship of these works to their historical moment derived from the state of industrial revolution in the United States during the last two decades of the century. Configurations of the utopian societies were conscious responses—expressed as idealizations, distortions, inversions, or exaggerations—to actual conditions of industrial and economic disarray.

The Historical Context of Utopian Solutions

The years during which this popular wave of utopian fiction appeared are often characterized as a long series of economic depressions that slowly capped an era of unprecedented and unregulated economic growth. This period of intense labor unrest and industrial violence more or less began with the Great Railroad Strike of 1877 (the first national strike), persisted through the Haymarket riots of 1886, the Homestead strike of 1892, and the ongoing violence in the Pennsylvania, West Virginia, and Colorado coalfields. The panic of 1893, caused by the completion of the nation's basic steel and railroad requirements, put an end to the era of easy investment and massive profit. Millions of Americans were unemployed, and those who still worked took repeated cuts in their already very low wages; many textile workers, for example, earned only sixty cents a day.[12] By the mid-1880s, railroad expansion, the growth of heavy industries, and the government's support of monopolies and trusts had consolidated the industrial revolution that had been stimulated by the demand for arms, railroad cars, uniforms, and canned foods during the Civil War. Meanwhile, immigrants from Wales, Ireland, Germany, Eastern Europe, and China created a new American working class wrenched from native traditions of culture and polity. Moreover, those who came to America after the Civil War encountered a society struggling to adjust to the rapid displacement of its own indigenous population, on the move from village to city, farm to factory, east to west, south to north. Inevitably, the nexus of cash (the receipt of wages and the purchase of commodities—but not enough of either) displaced the personal relations and social autonomy of an agrarian-artisan culture, a loss restored in pastoral utopias. Activities that had once been localized—financing enterprises, marketing of crafts and agriculture, dispensing news—were now controlled by distant and unknown investors.[13] It is not surprising, then, that this period from the 1870s to the 1890s should also show the first significant success in organizing the American industrial work force, in the formation of large farmers' groups and in the growth of women's organizations.

The popularity of this generation of utopian fiction lies partially in its incorporation of various explanations for the recurrent industrial depressions and suggestions for their cure. Progressive, pastoral, and feminist utopias subscribed to class analyses and cooperative remedies, while conservative, dystopian, and apocalyptic utopias realized the promises of "trickle-down" theories, which held that the community prospers when industry prospers. According to these theories, through a cycle of increased employment, production, and consumption, investors' profits would filter downward to the lower classes. Other theories stressed the need for government support of the economy. During this period of falling prices, American industry sustained the momentum of economic development through coalitions with the federal government, which had grown in size and complexity as a result of supervising Reconstructionist economic and political policies in the South and by maintaining fiscal stability for industry in the North. Government investment for expansion in the West and overseas would continue to underwrite capitalist enterprises; for example, in order to stimulate the construction of the transcontinental railroad following the Civil War, the federal government gave the railroad companies land grants equal to the area of Texas.

The idealized alliance between business and government that appears in conservative utopias, as well as in those progressive utopias that argue for the nationalization of industry, was an extension of the current trend toward incorporation (in trusts, pools, holding companies, and monopolies) that signaled a new concentration of wealth and power. In 1893 the U.S. Census Bureau estimated that 9 percent of the nation's families owned 71 percent of American wealth, through monopolies controlled by such families as the Vanderbilts, Harrimans, Goulds, Carnegies, Rockefellers, and Morgans. Laissez-faire theory notwithstanding, monopolization depended on an increasingly explicit partnership between business and the branches of a growing national government. For example, although Congress passed the Sherman Anti-Trust Act in 1890, the law was rarely enforced after its test case, *United States* v. *E. C. Knight Company* (1895). The Knight Company had purchased four sugar refineries that gave it control of 98 percent of the national sugar production.[14] When the Supreme Court allowed the purchase to stand, it was seen to have invalidated the antitrust act for business, although the Court soon applied the principle of "combination in restraint of trade" to labor unions.

Despite the popularity of laissez-faire explanations of late nineteenth-century economic patterns,[15] the federal government actively intervened in the "free" marketplace with financial and military as well as judicial supports for industry, thus forging a forceful weapon against labor movements. In the Haymarket Square riot of 1886, the Chicago court, under pressure from McCormick Harvester, sentenced seven anarchists to death for their mere presence at a strike rally where a bomb exploded. In 1892, Utah Copper and the Carnegie Steel Company ended a long strike at the Homestead Works only when hired Pinkerton guards fired at employees. The Pullman strike of 1894 stopped all railroad traffic between Chicago and the West, until President Cleveland sent in the cavalry and field artillery, under the pretext of protecting the mail.

Responding to corporate fears that the closing of the frontier might presage a dwindling domestic market, the federal government intensified a policy of overseas expansion (fulfilled in the global and occasionally galactic American empires described in conservative utopias). This movement began as early as 1863, when Secretary of State William Seward arranged the purchase of Alaska. After acquiring Samoa and Hawaii in 1898, the United States opened protected shipping lanes to Japan and China, a route to Asia completed by its annexation of the Philippines, acquired in the victory over Spain in 1898. The next year, the United States announced its interest in the China trade with the publication of Secretary of State John Hay's Open Door Notes.

A popular rationale for these economic policies—whether Gilded Age or utopian—came from the misapplication of the emerging biological and zoological sciences. The growth of industry, it appeared, was another example of the inevitable and beneficient laws of evolution. According to Yale sociologist William Graham Sumner, competition encouraged and enforced changes that were desirable for progress as well as necessary for survival. Using the positivist arguments of the English sociologist Herbert Spencer, Sumner extended Darwin's model of the survival of the fittest to economic classes, and easily concluded that immigrants, criminals, and "the poor" were undeveloped, dangerous groups that deserved to stand outside the boundaries of reciprocal social relations. The poor could easily be distinguished from the industrialists by physical traits that revealed their degenerative or atavistic nature.[16] Cesare Lombroso, an Italian criminologist popular in America, discovered that criminals were an inferior species, characterized by physical traits reminiscent of those of apes, lower primates, and savage human tribes.[17] The American criminologist Henry M. Boies asked the government to "exterminate the incapable, those who are by nature unable to maintain themselves without assistance; the physically, mentally or morally defective; cripples, deformed, deaf, blind, imbecile, weak-minded, diseased, insane or criminal."[18] Social Darwinism thus synthesized the pessimistic economics of David Ricardo and Thomas Malthus with Charles Darwin's explanation of natural selection, to conclude that the industrious, temperate, and frugal worker—British or American-born—was the "fittest" for survival. In an era when up to 18.4 percent of American workers were without jobs and when low wages kept most immigrants and city dwellers living in slums, poverty was interpreted as an act of aggression.[19] But all was not lost, because the fittest would transmit their innate superiority to succeeding generations, creating a genetic inheritance which even Edward Bellamy promised would eventually produce a healthy social environment. Thus society itself was seen as a "superorganism, changing at geological tempos."[20] The future, optimstically foretold in several conservative utopias, was eternal capitalism which would evolve as the inevitable and natural fulfillment of benevolent forces of competition.

However, alongside the "trickle-down" and laissez-faire solutions for improving the welfare of the state were various theories of social cooperation that formed the political basis for "progressive utopias." These cooperative solutions sought to replace private property with social property, private ownership with public ownership, and competition with various forms of cooperation. A rhetoric of communalism appeared in the labor movement, the women's movement, the farmers' movement, as well as in attempts to preserve the antiracist legislation of the Reconstruction years.

The period from the 1870s to the 1890s marks the first major success in the organization of American industrial and farm labor on a national scale. In 1869, a small group of blacklisted garment workers in Philadelphia organized the Knights of Labor, which grew into a national union after the depression of the seventies. Under the banner of "one big union" welcoming women and blacks, the Knights of Labor reached a membership of 700,000 in 1886, was active in calling for the eight-hour day, abolition of national banks, nationalization of the railroads, and an end to alien landownership. When the membership in the Knights fell under the tepid leadership of Terrence Powderly, the American Federation of Labor emerged in 1886, organizing only skilled labor. Promising that the benefits won by his men would filter down to other workers, Samuel Gompers and the A.F. of L. sought to bargain collectively for the eight-hour day, a six-day work week and the elimination of child labor.[21]

In promising a future of prosperity and justice for women, progressive and feminist utopian authors joined a vocal if diverse movement for women's reforms. Influenced by the membership and goals of the Abolitionist cause, the new women's movement was the result of the restructuring of women's economic roles in an industrial society. In the 1890 census, four million women, or

11

nearly 20 percent of the work force, listed "occupations," but their economic lot was not improved by working outside the home. In 1886 in the garment industry, women worked sixty hours per week at the loom or sewing machine for wages of from $6 to $10. It is not surprising, then, that women from a variety of ethnic backgrounds eagerly joined the Knights of Labor, which opened assemblies for female clerks, teachers, waitresses, as well as textile and other factory workers. In the South, women enlisted in the Knights' assemblies for servants, laundresses, and cooks—groups traditionally difficult to organize because they work at separate places and live in their employers' houses. In Arkansas, the Knights established an assembly of women farmers. Still, the largest collective activity for social reform was the women's suffrage movement. Through diverse membership and tactics, organizations for female suffrage demonstrated the national concern with correcting the financial deprivation and political exclusion of women.

In the decades following the Civil War, farmers constituted a third group seeking a collective redistribution of the national wealth, popularizing in their political platforms the agrarian myths that would form the basis of pastoral utopias.[22] In the late 1860s, in flight from postwar unemployment, immigrants and native-born Americans alike moved westward into land opened by the railroads. Two-thirds of the population lived in rural areas in the 1890s. However, land booms in Argentina, Canada, and Australia contributed to an international decline in agricultural prices that lasted through the 1890s. Meanwhile, most of the profits of American farmers went to Eastern banks, absentee landowners, and urban industrialists who owned the railroads, manufactured the farm equipment, and processed the raw materials which were resold in the West—at a high profit to the transporters and manufacturers.

Meanwhile, in the New South, where there were few large cities, agriculture accounted for seven-eighths of the total economic output; however, by 1880, 70 percent of the farmers— primarily black—were tenants and sharecroppers whose produce was owned by white landowners or the country store. The rise of Jim Crow laws and the decline of Reconstruction in the seventies disenfranchised the black majority—over 75 percent in many areas. Perhaps because of the South's extreme poverty, the clear distinction between owner and tenant, and the biracial alliances among tenant farmers, in the South was to be found the most radical area of agrarian revolt. In the third rural area, the Rocky Mountain states, there was just one "crop"—silver, devalued when the United States went on the gold standard. Here the pressure for monetary reforms began.

The Populist struggle started in the 1880s when several regional farming orders or "alliances," including separate black alliances, formed as antirailroad groups in the West and as marketing cooperatives in the South. Through the new organizations, farmers soon controlled state legislatures, which quickly passed laws to impede mortgage foreclosures and to ensure the fair grading of grain. By 1890, the Western alliances began to organize into the national Populist party, which quickly came to dominate local committees of the Democratic party. The national and state elections of 1890 produced three Populist governors, two senators, several members of Congress, and majorities in eight state legislatures.

In 1896, the farmers lost control of their young movement and the coalition soon died. While the Populists had eventually agreed on reforms for landownership, transportation, and the monetary supply, they had divided on the issues of women's suffrage, immigration restriction, prohibition of alcohol, and alliance with the Democratic party. The panic of 1893 encouraged a naive agreement among farmers that money itself was the cause of hard times, and the farmers yielded to the silver miners, who frowned on larger social and political issues, and demanded only the free coinage of silver. When the Democratic party adopted the "free silver" plank in 1896, the Populists' sole issue was in the hands of William Jennings Bryan, the Democrats' nominee for president. In the most costly presidential campaign to date, Bryan was soundly defeated by Republican William McKinley, who promised to restore the economy with expansionist foreign policies. The publication of utopian fiction waned after his election.

The Politics of a Literary Genre

By subverting the perception of historical change as eternal necessity, the utopian novel in its very form became its own hopeful content. The political configuration of utopian fiction cannot be understood only through its recipes for an improved future—its

13

inclusion, exclusion, representation, or misrepresentation of new social relations, and its inversion of current forms of economic and social stratification; the political defiance inherent in utopian novels needs to be understood as part of the aesthetic structures themselves. In the literary act of picturing the future, utopian fictions transcend the dominant consciousness of their times. In the literary act of realizing the future, utopian fictions envision a horizon of change and stimulate notions of social and political alternatives. Granted, in the processes by which they deliver the future, writers of late nineteenth-century utopian fiction often share the assumptions of the social determinists; still, they create a realm that assumes the subversion of the present. First, the reader may fantasize about the political, economic, or social arrangements of a new society, but soon observes that the alternative world also proposes an enriched way of being, and develops human capacities that are suppressed in cities and factories. The textual activity of utopian fiction defies the dominant sensibilities of the era. Rebellion is part of the inner logic of the genre itself.

Thus, in the creation of new societies, utopian literature inevitably functions as an experience of estrangement. In his discussion of science fiction, Darko Suvin calls the innovation that is superimposed on the familiar reality "the novum," a term borrowed from Ernst Bloch. The novum, which can deviate in various degrees from the familiar or the empirically known reality, defines the "internal determination" of utopian and science fiction. In science fiction "the essential tension . . . is one between the reader, representing a certain type of Man of our times, and the Unknown, introduced by the novum . . . the postulated innovation." Suvin suggests that this innovation can vary from a gadget to a "spatio-temporal locus" which cannot in a work of fiction be tested *in vitro* or *in vivo,* in the laboratory or by observation in nature. Instead, it must be developed as a "mental experiment" following accepted scientific logic.[23]

But Suvin does not go far enough. What happens when the novum is an entire society? In late nineteenth-century utopian fiction, the novum must refer to the entire alternative and redeemed society that is developed from historical actualities, and it must also refer to political premises that are internally logical, regardless of the magical literary device used to deliver the hero to the new world. Hence there is a cognitive split. The imagined society has a logical political history which is empirically determined, even though the visit itself, the matter of the narrative, is not.[24] The narrative device that ushers in utopia is rather an image of current patterns: technological invention, monopolistic commercial practices, imperialism, and the extension of the common weal. In this sense, utopian fiction is a mimetic mode that reproduces familiar experiences, extrapolating them from current and past realities.

Thus an important distinction between utopian fiction and science fiction is that in utopian fiction, in one way or another, change must be accounted for, whereas in science fiction the novum just appears. And yet, paradoxically, the literary devices of utopian fiction negate the central axiom of history: change itself. Generally, utopia is achieved instantaneously, through literary gimmicks, a political sleight-of-hand that relies on two literary modes: a realistic or plausible representation of the new world and a fantastic representation of the visit itself. Only in the few utopias that describe apocalyptic transformations do we see the dynamic process of social metamorphosis, and even in those, history is generally cloaked in a religious metaphor.

But utopian fiction is also, and unavoidably, realistic. Its fictional rendering of political history derives from the author's analysis of the origins of the contemporary social malaise. The conditions of nineteenth-century American life generate the dream of an alternative society which, unlike the new worlds of science fiction, exists in a familiar location. Most of these utopias are discovered in Boston, New York, Chicago, or San Francisco, where the voyager comes upon architectural souvenirs from the nineteenth century that help to verify and authenticate the past. Unlike fantastic fiction, with which it is often confused, utopian fiction pictures things that may someday be. The fantastic, according to W. R. Irvin,

is based on and controlled by an overt violation of what is generally accepted as possibility; it is the narrative result of transforming the condition contrary to fact into "fact" itself. . . . Whatever the material, extravagant or seemingly commonplace, a narrative is a fantasy if it presents the persuasive establishment and development of an impossibility, an arbitrary construct of the mind with all under the control of logic and rhetoric.[25]

15

The utopian future, by contrast, while materially impossible, is seemingly predicated on logical principles that give it the aura of possiblity. The utopian society, if not the voyage thence, must be credible and, consequently, not fantastic. Eric Rabkin calls the defining characteristic of the fantastic "a quality of astonishment that we feel when the ground rules of a narrative world are suddenly made to turn around 180°."[26] But in reading utopias we feel familiar and we experience recognition.

Utopian fiction is only momentarily "fantastic," that is, only until the historical inevitability of the utopia is explained to the visitor. During this delay, the reader experiences what Tzvetan Todorov calls the fantastic dilemma: "The fantastic occupies the duration of this uncertainty. Once we choose one answer or the other, we leave the fantastic for a neighboring genre, the uncanny or the marvelous. The fantastic is that hesitation experienced by a person who knows only the laws of nature, confronting an apparently supernatural event."[27] The sense of the fantastic persists only as long as the uncertainty lasts. Once we come to a decision or a recognition, the fantastic evaporates and we pass into the genre of the uncanny which has a natural explanation, or the marvelous which does not. Thus, the notion of reality must be present for the fantastic to exist at all. Applying Todorov's schema, utopian fiction would cease to be fantastic, and change into the uncanny (still within the boundaries of the mimetic) as the historical determinants of the utopian world are revealed. Further, fantasy and utopian works have significantly different effects on the reader. The fantastic plays with the norms of reality to contradict, subvert, oppose, question, or reverse them—to expose them as false. The fantastic confronts us with situations that do not conform to the ground rules of the world, rules that we empirically assume; it calls into question our very modes of perception. Such dislocation cannot but stimulate feelings of terror, fear, and uncertainty, along with wonder and curiosity. Utopian works, by contrast, stimulate feelings of optimism and possibility.

My description of utopian fiction, which hinges on this general notion of historical possibility, derives from Darko Suvin's claim that cognition, as well as estrangement, is a necessary condition of our response to science fiction. But in addition to being based on cognitive or scientific empiricism, the utopian novum (the novelty or innovation)[28] requires a historical logic, a historical empiricism as well. Because the utopian future derives plausibly from the old society, the logic of the narrative ratifies the utopian axiom that the seeds of the future are immanent in the present. The paradox of nonexistence—*outopia*—hinges on the possibility of existence.

Nevertheless, the utopian future in the nineteenth century was regarded as finite. Unlike the modern utopia described in *The Dispossessed* (1974) by Ursula LeGuin,[29] which argues for permanent revolution, earlier utopian texts explicitly discounted notions of future political evolution, although they did not outlaw inventions or galactic discoveries. This denial of change—perforce a denial of history—reflects a fear of change. But without a concept of historical change, it was impossible for utopian authors to use the narrative structures of the novel of the 1870s and 1880s. James's *The American* (1877) and Howells's *The Rise of Silas Lapham* (1885), for example, are predicated on the moral and at times financial growth of characters as they interact with society. But as Georg Lukács notes in discussing the fictional consequences of socialist realism, "If . . . the elimination of this antagonistic character [that is, social contradiction and class struggle] is seen as something immediately realizable, rather than as a process, both the antagonism and contradiction, the motor of all development, will disappear from the reality to be depicted."[30] With the exception of apocalyptic utopias, utopian novels of the late nineteenth century similarly lack antagonism, contradiction, and process, and therefore they leave the reader to search elsewhere for the motor of America's development. Lacking change, utopias seem to mark the end of history.

Indeed, it is this absence of change that generates our "estrangement" in reading utopian fiction, for it negates the nineteenth-century experience of a world in flux:[31] Unlike the real world, nothing much changes in utopia. And because everything is predetermined, we observe no dialectic between character and environment: character no longer affects plot or is affected by it. As a result, we lose our usual identification with the protagonist. We certainly do not have to worry about him (he is usually male) once he makes it to utopia, for there everything by definition is good. In addition to this happy tautology, the utopian form itself defuses the reader's emotional engagement through a rhetorical pattern in which commentary and analysis alternate with plot. An episodic narrative further weakens our involvement. Since there is no need for the author to attach our fears and aspirations to central characters, many citizens of utopia briefly appear, exhibiting only those traits that ratify political doctrine. As in a Brecht play or a Godard film, we read events, institutions, and relationships as parables.

Further, utopian fiction evokes "estrangement" because its satiric and normative functions require us consciously and continuously to refer to our experience outside the textual world: utopia is an extended metaphor. Thus the reader of a utopian tale can formulate a description of the author's politics, even if no summary statement appears in the text itself. I use the term *apologue*[32] to describe utopian tales in which internal literary structures point to and establish a normative statement about historical process and political prediction. Within the utopian apologue, two distinct kinds of rhetoric represent assumptions about history: the fable and the manifesto. The fable is a sequence of events fashioned into a story, usually influenced by the traditions of romance. The manifesto interprets the narrated events and explains the utopian context to the protagonist-visitor, who, like the reader, is an outsider. Unlike the realistic novel, then, utopian fiction no longer establishes morality through dramatic interaction of characters. Instead, in the utopian manifesto, the burden of analysis passes to a guide (inevitably wise, powerful, and smug) and his marriageable daughter, who interpret the new institutions and gadgets to the traveler (inevitably naive, young, deeply critical of his own society, ready to be convinced). The action halts while the guide describes the events that impelled the new society from the past into the future perfect.[33] Toward the end of the tale, the utopian initiation often stops for the visitor to return to the late nineteenth century—whether in a dream or through a magical telescope. As he travels backward in time, the rhetoric shifts into a naturalistic vocabulary that contrasts the sordid details of urban life in the Gilded Age to the placid social organization of utopia.

In the manifesto, utopian authors describe the 1880s or the 1890s in order to validate the social remedies portrayed in utopia. Because of such undiluted social commentary, literary critics often classify utopian fiction as a species of satire. Robert C. Elliott, for example, argues that utopian works and satire differ only in the "proportion of positive and negative elements," there being an "understated positive element in satire" that establishes a norm.[34] Satire, however, lacks the extended representation of alternatives to what is criticized, the illustration of which occupies most of the utopian narrative. The reader of *Gulliver's Travels* or *A Connecticut Yankee in King Arthur's Court,* satires that picture imaginery societies, cannot formulate a normative statement for Jonathan Swift or Mark Twain. Furthermore, satire operates through humor. While utopian authors represent their own time as rather dismal in order to juxtapose it against the serene future, the satirist portrays—and often exaggerates—the present in order to ridicule it. The present is always an available referent in utopian fiction, if only by implication, a tacit alternative that contradicts the utopian projection.

Nonetheless, utopian authors of the late nineteenth century also represented the progressive potential of their era; most of their projections into the future fulfilled the hopeful tendencies of democracy, technology, and current ideas of social and economic reform. Thus utopian works are the antithesis of satire, which, as Hayden White observes, is informed by an archetypal theme that is "the precise opposite of the Romantic drama of redemption; satire is, in fact, a drama of diremption [disjunction], a drama dominated by the apprehension that man is ultimately a captive of the world rather than its master."[35] White also observes how "the satirical mode of representation signals a conviction that the world has grown old."[36] Satire would thus preclude the utopian reconciliation of political opposites and would deny the victory of the visitor's conscience in the world of new experience.

One feature of nineteenth-century American society that these utopian novelists often retain in their imaginary futures is advanced technology. In all but the small group of pastoral utopias, technology alleviates a basic threat often associated with socialism: scarcity. In most nineteenth-century utopias and dystopias, applied science, even more than idealized politics, delineates the possibilities of the future. By the mid-1890s, according to David Noble in *America by Design,* the "systematic introduction of science as a means of production presupposed and in turn reinforced industrial monopoly. This monopoly

19

meant control, not simply of markets and productive plants and equipment but of science itself."[37] Industrialization stimulated scientific investigations in the fields of energy production, transportation, mining, and manufacturing; most utopian writers understood rather clearly that the social orientation of technology, indeed, of information itself, was controlled by the new monopolies. And the age was fascinated with its new science. Crowds attended scientific lectures, large audiences supported popularized scientific journals, and literary magazines included science fiction stories. By the 1870s science fiction was a well-established genre.[38]

But technology in utopian fiction goes well beyond fascination with industry's new tools or products. Science in progressive utopian fiction represents the population's need and ability to control the environment, and thus it inverts the dystopian fear of domination of the culture by technology. Furthermore, as H. Bruce Franklin suggests, our twentieth-century experience with science distorts our perception of earlier utopian and science fiction: with a lived experience of technology that outstrips the wildest nineteenth-century predictions, we tend to look down on earlier utopian societies as unimaginative or naive.[39] But the introduction of technology produces a deeper contradiction in scientifically advanced utopias: technology by definition is temporal and mutable, yet it arises in utopian societies that are atrophied in their perfection. But scientific wonders are a traditional part of utopian fictions, which borrowed nearly as many scientific devices from the romance as from the world of emerging technology. Long before Julian West fell asleep for a hundred and thirteen years in *Looking Backward* (1888), Rip Van Winkle had already introduced "time travel" into American fiction; C. B. Brown, Poe, and Hawthorne added "biloquism," hallucination, mesmerism, drugs, extended sleeps, cryogenics, elixirs of life, and magical injuries. Psychic phenomena, wondrous inventions, lost worlds, telepathy, and voyages in time and space had long been familiar to romantic and Victorian readers.

It is the literary tradition of romance rather than the referential markings of satire that shapes the narrative patterns of utopian fiction. In *Metahistory*, Hayden White observes:

The romance is fundamentally a drama of self-identification symbolized by the hero's transcendence of the world of experience, his victory over it, and his final liberation from it. . . . It is a drama of good over evil, of virtue over vice, of light over darkness, and of the ultimate transcendence of man over the world in which he was imprisoned by the Fall.[40]

What better way to achieve transcendence of the experienced world than through its fulfillment in utopia, where an entire society is imagined to have mastered the environment and where the individual human consciousness is finally able to overcome the forces of fear, and occasionally, of death itself. As tales of technological invention and personal transformation, utopian novels celebrate the reconciliation of the social world and the natural world.

Ultimately, faith in utopianism (and most likely faith in socialism) rests on a belief in the perfectibility of our social behavior. Nineteenth-century utopian writers shared in the contemporary repudiation of original sin, popularized by liberal theologians such as Henry Ward Beecher, who, in an updated version of the idea of salvation through good works, modified Protestantism to assure middle-class parishioners that the Christian struggle was manageable. Society, rather than original sin, determined a person's capacity for good and evil. Utopia is the space where individuals cease to act solely in self-interest. This somewhat naive faith in humanity further distinguishes the utopia from the satire, which borders it on one side, and from the pastoral, which borders it on the other. Conventionally, satire operates through ridiculing humanity, while the pastoral protects it from the sordid influences and temptations of culture by hiding the body politic in an imaginary garden, away from the court and the city. Characters who inhabit most utopias are not the rustic citizens George Kateb calls "untouched natural growths fresh from their maker's hands."[41] Instead, in industrially progressive utopias citizens realize their capacity for perfect behavior through the influence of highly developed educational and economic structures. Even the pastoral utopias are not islands of repose and sensuality, but rather societies with highly circumscribed moral codes where virtue derives from the interaction of character, nature, and benevolent social

21

institutions; the human capacity, indeed the human appetite for evil is not ignored. Nevertheless, these nineteenth-century utopias preceded Freud's assumptions of instinctual aggression. In the utopian construct, poverty, ignorance, and hunger are what promote hostility and competition; the stimulus for evil is external to character. In utopian fiction the forces of good or evil need not battle for possession of the soul or social conscience. For the elimination of evil, the society rather than the citizen must change.

It was this optimistic attitude toward human nature that formed the basis for Christopher Caudwell's critique of H. G. Wells's utopianism. Caudwell calls Wells's notion that the individual is "naturally free" and functions best when allowed to express and satisfy his desires the basic "bourgeois illusion." Where real societies restrain instincts, utopian societies ostensibly permit individual expression. But Caudwell contends that the very notion of absolute liberty as put forward by utopians was really "the bourgeois value of their time, hypothetized as eternal."[42] Further, he argues, utopians ignored the paradox of their times: demands for reform and for freedom itself were successful only to the extent that they were collective. Consequently, utopians failed to understand that the freest individual is the most isolated, and thus has the fewest chances for change.

The changed possibilities for personal activity called forth different conceptions of characterization. Where nonutopian authors might turn to accident, competition, or fate to forge the moral growth of character, utopian writers had to consider the unfamiliar effects of social equality. Is equality necessary for human individuality and idiosyncracy? Might equality promote uniformity? Would socialism bring homogeneity? Utopian authors often avoided the entire dilemma with a literary device, simply by introducing threats from the preutopian world. Yet perhaps their toughest problem was how to reconcile the promise of political equality for women with female characters descended on the maternal side from women in the gothic and sentimental novel who were modest, pious, and compliant.

This study investigates the relationship between the literary structures of late nineteenth-century American utopian fiction and the tendencies of late nineteenth-century American history. It explores how historical change is represented in utopian literature.

As an "ideological critique of ideology,"[43] utopian fiction derives its critical power from its capacity simultaneously to project and subvert contemporary discourse about history. Utopian fiction thus has its own dialectic that transcends what Eric Rabkin terms the "mythic function" of literature—that is, the degree to which it perpetuates inertia, conserves traditional values, and resists new possibilities. While the literary devices that carry the traveler from the present into the future may well be diversionary tactics that distract the reader's attention from more likely agents of social change, these texts also picture values that are radical and transformative. For, as Bloch reminds us, fantasy perforce derives from familiar ingredients; nineteenth-century utopian novels identify and recognize insistent social possibilities.

Ernst Bloch sees significant "oppositional tendencies" in all fantasies or "wish-fulfillment" ideas—whether mythic, religious, or Marxist. Utopian romances contain two political alternatives: they can be "distracting, gilded con-dreams of pulp literature in which an impossible stroke of good fortune befalls some poor devil, and in which the happy ending is unhappy deceit."[44] The romance "distracts" a reader who experiences satisfaction by utopian proxy—an act of false consciousness. But in some utopian tales Bloch observes "no mere distraction and voyeuristic palliation, but a vital stimulus and direct relevance. The brave little tailor conquers with cunning, that Chaplinesque weapon of the poor, and wins the beautiful princess."[45] Whether the work provides distraction or stimulus depends for Bloch on how the hero gets to utopia—by fortune's intervention or his own activity. Thus he attacks visions that describe "plenty without labor" but admires utopias that "evoke longing" and represent social changes relevant to their own historic moment. As a criterion for evaluating both the satirical and motivational value of utopianism, political praxis is unnecessary. Robert C. Elliott distinguishes myths from utopias using criteria similar to Bloch's. In myth, he argues, labor is absent or invisible, while "in utopia the work of the world goes on, rationalized, cleaned up—often to the point where the sewers hardly smell; . . . the work is there, nevertheless, as a necessary condition of Utopia's existence."[46] Like Bloch, Elliott finds that the utopia's effect depends on how utopia is built—by dreams, magic, or human labor. Utopia, he thinks, might even happen some day, but only when "man no longer merely dreams of a divine state in a remote time. He assumes the role of creator himself."[47]

But what is the role of the creator? Utopia is generally presumed to be teleological; history is a predetermined passage toward a finite state which marks the end of change, regardless of human will or activity.[48] Karl Mannheim in his seminal work *Ideology and Utopia* observes that in utopia "events which at first glance present themselves as mere chronological cumulation take on the character of destiny."[49] And Northrop Frye would concur, suggesting that utopia records the "end at which social life aims."[50] The telos orders the mythic and romantic events.

Addressing this significant contradiction, Frederik Polak charges utopian fiction with the paradox of presenting activity within passivity; utopianism has a "passive essence—optimism, which rests its case on the laws of social dynamics, and an active influence—optimism, which strives toward the goal of hidden utopia."[51] In nineteenth-century conservative utopias the laws of history—represented as the inevitability of technological growth, the expansion of the state, laissez-faire economics and Social Darwinism—automatically create the perfect state and the reader becomes passive; utopia is inevitable. But when progressive utopians such as Bellamy suggest that we "strive" for the potential utopia, the reader is invited to analyze history, detect its utopian currents, and imitate the model. As Bloch would find, it is "all the worse if the revolutionary capacity is not there to execute ideals which have been represented abstractly. . . . Nonetheless action will release available transitional tendencies into active freedom only if the utopian goal is clearly visible, unadulterated and unrenounced."[52]

This work studies the contradictions of utopianism: how an apparently progressive literary vogue contributed to the period of political reaction following McKinley's election in 1896. By representing, for the most part, individuals freed before they created the conditions through which freedom could be realized, these tales perpetuated the myth of upward mobility, inevitable progress, and sanitized the process of social change. Utopia was predicated on the assumption that the dreams of a single person ought to be realized in society as a whole; utopia exists on the author's terms alone. Technology, democracy, and the army would automatically solve the problems of working-class and unemployed people who were demanding economic relief and social equality—the passive essence.

At the same time, these imaginary societies secularized images of the future. Extracting and developing political tendencies from their own historical moment, they fulfilled the socialists' expectations that property would someday belong to the community as a whole. Meanwhile, the tales popularized demands for social security, universal suffrage, universal education, trade unionism, and limited emancipation for women. Capable utopian citizens countered the nihilistic predictions of the naturalists—the "active influence." By focusing on the development of society as a whole, and by representing prosperity as a collective process, utopian fictions also attacked the ideology of competitive individualism.

This study also examines how the aesthetics of the utopian novel fulfilled the genre's purported intention of representing as yet unlived history. Herbert Marcuse once called despair the "retreat into a world of fiction where existing conditions are changed and overcome only in the realm of the imagination." But cannot this same inversion produce hope? Is it not possible that in this hybrid, flawed, and at times absurd genre aesthetic content and form have briefly become one, so that even if the content of the fantasies is formulaic and the narration stylized, the genre itself provides an act of "aesthetic desublimation"? Marcuse also wrote, "The truth of art lies in its power to break the monopoly of established reality (i.e., of those who established it) to define what is real."[53] In picturing the future of society, nineteenth-century utopian tales attacked the competitive individualism and the awesome sense of powerlessness precipitated by the rise of industrial capitalism. In utopian fiction, fantasy is at once an individual and a social experience. While the predictable images of the inevitable future sublimate the reformist impulse and reconcile the reader to the difficult exigencies of the time, the act of fantasizing about the future—that is, the form itself—shatters the notion of determinism and reinforces a creative and rebellious subjectivity.

TWO

Edward Bellamy and the Progressive Utopia

*Who be more desirous of new mutations and alterations than they
that be not content with the present state of their life? Or, who be
bolder-stomached to bring all in a hurly burly (thereby trusting to
get some windfall) than they that have now nothing to lose?—*
Thomas More, Utopia

*I*n 1887, Edward Bellamy wrote *Looking Backward, 2000–1887*
and published it quickly in January 1888, promising a distraught
public—alarmed by a severe economic recession, violent strikes,
and corruption in business and government—a safe journey to a
clean, orderly, and egalitarian future. *Looking Backward* is the story
of Julian West, an effete young aristocrat who recalls that in 1887
he was "rich and also educated, and possessed therefore all the
elements of happiness enjoyed by the most fortunate in that age.
Living in luxury, and occupied only with the pursuit of the pleasure
and refinements of life, I derived the means of my support from the
labor of others, rendering no sort of service in return."[1] In his
wealthy life there was neither achievement nor social consequence
because his inheritance, a "tax in perpetuity upon the product of
those engaged in industry" (p. 9), supported an ethos of class without community. For Bellamy, the economic and social hierarchies
of nineteenth-century Boston represented a dangerous world of illusion, perhaps even the illusion of surplus value itself; Julian inhabits
a mysterious world of money without work, enjoying what he calls
the magic of "warmth without combustion" (p. 10).

But a new strike in the building trades, delaying the completion
of his new mansion and delaying, too, his marriage to the wealthy

and lovely Edith Bartlett, precipitates Julian's journey into a social-ist future with a more accurate perception of social realities. "I remember distinctly how exasperated I was at [the strike], and the objurgations as forcible as the presence of the ladies permitted, which I lavished upon workmen in general and those strikers in particular. I had abundant sympathy from those about me" (p. 10)—an abundant sympathy readily acquiescing in the material basis of Julian's life. He remembers,

As one of the wealthy, with a large stake in the existing order of things, I naturally shared the apprehensions of my class. The particular grievance I had against the working classes at the time of which I write, on account of the effect of their strikes in postponing my wedded bliss, no doubt lent a special animosity to my feeling toward them. (P. 27)

Writing from a socialist world in the year 2000, Julian remembers when only a common relation to property defined social cohesion.

By the mid-1880s, many American working people with noth-ing to lose were quite willing to "bring all in a hurly-burly," as More put it, for despite the promises of Grover Cleveland, Wil-liam Graham Sumner, and Philip D. Armour, neither evolution nor packaged meat was doing much for the standard of living. Sewage ran through the streets, ten-year-old children stitched ar-tificial flowers for twelve hours a day in dimly lit factories, in one Chicago precinct a newborn baby had only two chances in five of surviving the first year of life, and a workingman was charged 25 percent interest on a bank loan. Between 1880 and 1900 in industrial cities, where over 68 percent of the population had been born abroad, there were an incredible total of 38,303 strikes.[2]

The year 1884 marked yet another dip in the erratic economy of the Gilded Age. People lucky enough to have jobs were laid off one week in four, while at least one-quarter of the work force lived in tenements. Religious, political, and labor groups soon pressed for relief. In New York and Chicago, the early socialist movement sought legislation to ensure clear drinking water, public baths, sani-tation inspections of slums and factories, and a balanced budget. The Knights of Labor, the first major national organization of workers, grew from a membership of 28,000 in 1880 to 700,000 in

1886, including 60,000 black members. In a successful strike against Jay Gould's Wabash Railroad, they legitimized collective bargaining. By 1886, businessmen were forming private military clubs and the Senate enlarged the National Guard.

On May Day 1886, 340,000 demonstrators all over the country paraded, demanding the eight-hour day. Two days later, in Chicago, in attempting to disperse a meeting at Andrew Carnegie's McCormick Harvester Works, police killed several strikers. The following day in various parts of the city, where 50,000 people were already on strike, political and immigrant groups met in protest. The anarchists, who included many German immigrants, filled Haymarket Square. When the police arrived to disperse the crowd, a bomb exploded, killing one person and wounding several others. No culprit was ever found, but within a few days the state of Illinois arrested eight well-known anarchists; seven were quickly convicted and sentenced to death. Such progressive thinkers as Walt Whitman, Mark Twain, and William Dean Howells were confounded. What now to do with the "bolder-stomached"?

Julian's response is to sleep out the fearful century. His descent into the night world of romance quite literally begins when he has himself mesmerized in a remote underground vault to avoid his insomnia, an affliction that for Bellamy indicates egocentricity and guilt. While the vault, the sleeplessness, and the hypnotic trance recall many a tale by Poe and "The Birthmark" by Hawthorne, Bellamy's favorite author, the fact that the walls of the vault were laid in hydraulic cement and the door lined with asbestos assures us that this romance will be tinged with wondrous new technology. Although the house above him burns down and everyone thinks he is dead, thanks to the hermetically sealed doors Julian safely sleeps through the rest of the nineteenth and the entire twentieth century, awakening 113 years later in the home of a prestigious socialist, Doctor Leete and his daughter Edith. It is still Boston, but redeemed and glorified in the year 2000. The true triumph of good over evil begins.

As is so often true of utopian apologues, Bellamy divides his personal version of socialism between two narrative modes, the fable and the manifesto. And as so often happens, the fable follows the standard romance tradition. Conventionally enough, it begins with a "happy accident" which makes a break in Julian's consciousness. His long trance provides the necessary interruption in the continuity of his identity. The breach also dislocates Julian from the defenses of his inheritance, his wealthy sweetheart, and his house. He asks the utopian Edith, " 'Has it never occurred to you that my position is so much more utterly alone than any human being's ever was before that a new word is really needed to describe it?' " (p. 417). The traditional psychic alienation of romance is, in this text, a direct consequence of Julian's social alienation. His descent into the underground womblike vault initiates a release from the repressive as well as the oppressive ties of the nineteenth century, suggesting the romantic alliance between death, sexuality, and rebirth. It is autumn, a time of wisdom and maturity, when the spell is broken and Julian awakens. He is tired and ill, a common problem with travelers in utopia, suggesting his pain—perhaps even a birth pain—at leaving his safe if sinful homeland. Although he is still in Boston, the thought of a socialist system, an advanced technology, and even a new political vocabulary daunt our hero, who begins his quest for right thinking as a familar figure from romance: a lonely traveler in a strange land.

As an emigré from capitalism, Julian stands outside the history of social transformation. Overly impressionable as a tourist, rather immature in his loves and loyalties as a youth, and vulnerable as a displaced person, he has been unintentionally thrust into utopia. Exiled from his own century and somehow wounded in his voyage—his wound suggesting the painful loss involved in leaving his own society—he is discovered by a liberated lady (like the princess in a fairy tale) and her wise and authoritarian father (like the benevolent king) who will initiate him into the Nationalist utopia. The utopian present will teach him to transcend the past. Without the pretense of psychological causality or motivation, experiences will happen *to* him until he earns the utopian grail, a new political identity. In the fable, ritual rather than activity formalizes Julian's commitment to Nationalism; his love for Edith symbolizes his naturalization as a citizen of utopia. We never doubt that Julian (a literary descendant of the reformed rake of Restoration drama, the domestic novel, and the dime novel) will be persuaded, for our familiarity with the romance tradition assures us that he will win a transformed consciousness.

The Utopian Novel in America

Two forces contribute to the moral and political development of Julian West: love (in the fable) and re-education (in the manifesto). As soon as Julian has drunk two glasses of socialist claret, Doctor Leete secludes our willingly voyeuristic and naive hero in his study. Here the fatherly humanitarian teaches him how state ownership saved Boston from its violent self. Bellamy thus interrupts our concern with Julian's moral growth and our interest in his inevitable romance with Edith II; he disregards his own successful formula by which fiction was held to be useful for "the working out of problems, that is to say . . . to trace the logical consequences of certain assumed conditions"[3] and he reverts to Socratic dialogues and guided tours. Ironically, Bellamy's solution, "Nationalism" (the nationalization of industry), embodies all too well a core feature of late nineteenth-century capitalism, monopoly, abandoned to its centralizing appetite by laissez-faire theory. Ultimately, Bellamy does accept his era's justifications for social inequality—the rights of private property, Social Darwinism, and the intellectual and social inferiority of women and the working class; Boston in the year 2000 preserves many of the hierarchies that caused Julian's conscience to become atrophied in his first incarnation.

When he is with Edith, Julian confesses his sense of isolation and struggles with his aristocratic allegiances, but when he is with her father he becomes a dry and inadequate foil—curious, ingenuous, and easily convinced, happily launching the wise doctor into yet another explanation of the logic of state socialism. In the fable, Julian exposes the frightened individualism of a lost aristocrat, but in the long manifesto, he is an inadequate spokesman for industrial capitalism.

Julian's first surprise in the new Boston is to discover that every man, woman, and child receives the same income:

"Surely I told you this morning, at least I thought I did," replied Doctor Leete, "that the right of a man to maintenance at the nation's table depends on the fact that he is a man, and not on the amount of health and strength he may have, so long as he does his best."

"You said so," I answered, "but I supposed the rule applied only to the workers of different ability. Does it also hold of those who can do nothing at all?"

"Are they not also men?" (P. 182)

Edward Bellamy and the Progressive Utopia

In the tradition of John Stuart Mill, economic equality for Bellamy rests on a moral claim: no longer does parentage, class, or even accident decide who eats. The welfare state has hired all its citizens and given them a credit card. Rather than abolishing property, the state simply shares it. To each according to his humanity.

But a second justification underlies this ethical sanction for economic equality. In a technological society, Leete explains to Julian (who never worked a day in his life), " 'Many people work on a product, from its historic conception to its current design, manufacture, and distribution' "; its final value is indeed a social creation. Julian's inheritance thus derives from more than his grandfather's investments. Doctor Leete asks:

"How happened it . . . that your workers were able to produce more than so many savages would have done? Was it not wholly on account of the heritage of the past knowledge and achievements of the race, the machinery of society, thousands of years in contriving, found by you ready-made to your hand? How did you come to be possessors of this knowledge and this machinery which represent nine parts to one contributed by yourself in the value of your product? You inherited it, did you not?" (P. 187)

Julian discovers that in utopia equality has also eliminated what Thorstein Veblen called the "honorific expenditure" on waste. Ten years before Veblen coined the phrase "conspicuous consumption" in The Theory of the Leisure Class, Bellamy exposed the illusion of needs. When Edith takes Julian shopping at a distribution center, he instinctively looks for garish advertisements but instead finds only small information cards that help Edith choose her muslin with an eye simply for "taste and convenience": merchandise in itself no longer signifies status.

But even if he does not have to pay for them, many gadgets from the twentieth century tempt Julian. He falls asleep listening to music over a telephone, wakes up to a clock radio, and dials a sermon. He stays dry on rainy days under mechanical unbrellas (awnings?) that cover the sidewalks, and he is spared from carrying Edith's bundles, which are delivered directly to the Leete home in pneumatic tubes. And at a time when the Chicago River caught on fire from the fetid refuse of factories and when the dank fumes from gas lights and coal fires polluted their lungs, readers

31

must have been charmed to learn of utopia's clean, if unexplained, methods of fuel combustion.

Moreover, beyond the gadgets, science in the new society has liberated its citizens from drudgery and fear. Mass-produced clothing has eliminated the sweat shops and home finishing industries where entire families sewed buttons or stitched buttonholes all night long. Now machines have replaced heavy manual labor, and the same pneumatic tubes deliver hot meals to the home. Technology is a precondition for morality in Bellamy's utopian Boston, allowing the citizens to merge in "transcendental" solidarity. Through a vision in which prosperity is a foundation for Christian humanism, Bellamy resolved the nineteenth century's concern about the conflict between spiritual growth and technological growth.

At the same time that Bellamy demonstrated how the new sciences could solve the problems of housework, climate, transportation, housing, repetitive labor, pollution, and even leisure, he dissolved the tension between the real and the ideal; one simply preceded the other in an elegant model of human progress. By adding technology to the Social Darwinists' paradigm of an evolving society, Bellamy built a lively postindustrial model for human perfection. Yet to appeal to a Christian readership caught in a new tide of religious revivalism, a utopian proposal had to promise spiritual as well as industrial growth. Although Lewis Mumford argues that in *Looking Backward* machines are subordinated to an engineering concept of efficiency rather than to human needs, in fact Bellamy wove technology into his design for Christian socialism.[4]

One Sunday afternoon, Julian listens to a sermon broadcast over the telephone in which one Mr. Barton, a clergyman, announces that the most glorious triumph of Nationalism is the "liberation of man's true nature, which in its essential qualities is good, not bad, that men by their natural intentions and structure are generous, not selfish, pitiful, not cruel, sympathetic, not arrogant" (p. 404). Bellamy thereby rejects that part of Social Darwinism, formulated by Herbert Spencer, John Tyndall, and Thomas Huxley, that took the biological model of natural selection and survival of the fittest and applied it to an apologetics for class struggle and imperialism. Bellamy challenged the new social scientists who saw society as the offspring of our competitive instincts—an explanation that sat comfortably enough with laissez-faire economics and latter-day Calvinism. In the nineteenth century, Mr. Barton explains, Americans

"had been taught and believed that greed and self-seeking were all that held mankind together, and that all human association would fall to pieces if anything were done to blunt the edge of these motives or curb their operation; . . . they believed, that is, that the anti-social qualities of man, and not their social qualities, were what furnished the cohesive force of society." (P. 396)

Instead, Mr. Barton likens human nature in the nineteenth century to a rosebush " 'planted in a swamp, watered with black bog water, breathing miasmic fogs by day, chilled with poison dews at night.' " Where Christians " 'held that the bush belonged to the rose family, but had some ineradicable taint about it, which prevented the buds from coming out,' " Social Darwinists announced that it was " 'a more valuable discipline for the buds to try to bloom in a bog' " because the " 'buds that succeeded in opening might indeed be very rare.' " Meanwhile, the bush was dying. But inexplicably, the idea of transplanting the bush " 'found favor. . . . So it came about that the rosebush of humanity was transplanted and set in sweet warm dry earth. . . . The vermin and mildew disappeared, and the bush was covered with the most beautiful roses whose fragrance filled the world' " (p. 407).

In any case, Bellamy does not risk entrusting the safety and organization of his society to ideas about human perfectibility, and relies instead on the military state. In his Nationalist utopia, at the age of eighteen every man and woman is drafted into the industrial army which organizes the entire labor force, from ditchdigger to doctor, at the same time that it indoctrinates its young recruits in the values of order and authority. Twenty-three years of service begin with three years of basic training, "a sort of school, and a very strict one, in which the young men are taught habits of obedience, subordination, and devotion to duty" (p. 96). During those years, this lowest rank performs the unskilled but still necessary labor of the new society. After basic training, each citizen either decides to train for a profession or selects a trade. Without fear of unemployment and without the lure of extra salary, Nationalists choose their careers according to their interests and aptitudes. Art, mechanics, teaching, even "histrionics" are designated positions in the industrial army. Nonetheless, Doctor Leete confesses to Julian that even Nationalism could not erase "the desire of power, of social position" (p. 97), and so the army has adopted a system of ranks, insignias, and special privileges—first grade wins a gold merit badge. There is just one alternative to military service: "A man able to do his duty, and persistently refusing, is sentenced to solitary imprisonment on bread and water until he consents" (p. 257).

Bellamy was not the first utopian to organize society along the lines of an army. As Harry Levin (perhaps echoing Northrop Frye) has pointed out, "the paradoxical aim of most utopists is the organization of anarchy,"[5] and Louis Blanc and other eighteenth-century utopians introduced the military as a symbolic alternative to social chaos. Bellamy, who had always wanted a career in the military, presents the utopian army as a practical agency for the organization and education of an ideal society.[6] In "Why I Wrote *Looking Backward*" he recalls that as he worked out the details of the industrial army: "I perceived the full potency of the instrument I was using, and recognized in the modern military system not merely a rhetorical analogy for a rational industrial service, but its prototype, furnishing at once a complete working model for its organization."[7] The socialist society of *Looking Backward* thus presumes a military state and in fact is run by retired generals. David Bleich suggests that Bellamy's utopia achieved a transcendence over labor that anticipates the social vision of Herbert Marcuse: in *Looking Backward* "life becomes art. . . . Work and play are identified. . . . Alienated labor is replaced by libidinal work relations."[8] But although simple sharing and an efficient technology have shortened the work day and freed the workers for sports, music, and education, the competitive and compulsory forces of the industrial army are hardly libidinal and the divisions into ranks and tasks seem familiarly alienating. The harmonious pattern Bleich identifies appears only in pastoral utopias, such as William Dean Howells's *Through the Eye of the Needle*, where workers gracefully glide through the fields singing chants in praise of the harvest. Bellamy seems unaware, in fact, of how life in an egalitarian society would alter human consciousness.

How different is Julian's indoctrination from Georg Lukács's description of growth in the realist novel: "Only in the interaction of character and environment can the concrete potentialities of a particular individual be singled out from the 'bad infinity' of purely abstract potentialities, and emerge as the determining potentiality of just this individual at just this phase of his development."[9] But utopian fiction, by definition, precludes such growth: characters cannot make choices affecting either their society or their own psychological development. Julian does not need to make decisions that would determine the social growth of the community. Instead, *Looking Backward* achieves its effect by accumulation, piling up enough details to convince Julian, and by extension the reader, of the perfection of a Nationalist world. We wait for Julian to attain self-knowledge and fall in love with Edith only because these acts emblemize his new posture as a utopian initiate. Indeed, initiation is the main activity for tourists visiting utopia. (How to keep the story exciting is another problem.) Julian, like other utopian travelers, appears static, both because of the programmatic goals of the genre and because of Bellamy's nondialectic representation of historical process and personal change.

The absence of any relation between character and environment makes for a schizophrenic view of character—particularly of female character. On the one hand, the women in Bellamy's utopia benefit from his admiration for Frances Willard, the Women's Congress of 1873, and the suffrage movement. Bellamy's allocation for unskilled labor certainly reflects his awareness of the plight of the American working woman of the 1880s: in the garment industry, for example, a seamstress worked ten hours a day and then went home to seven hours of housework. In domestic service, a woman worked a ninety-hour week for four dollars plus room and board.[10] But in the year 2000, all women earn the same income as men; they have their own branch in the army and obey only female generals and judges. The highest governing council reserves one permanent seat for a woman, who may veto any issue relating to her sex. Choosing either the public commissary or her own dining room, Edith eats meals cooked in centralized kitchens and sends her dirty clothes to the centralized laundry. Most surprising, if she chooses to do her own housework, she is paid. At a time when married woman were not allowed to own property in their own names, Bellamy announced that wives should "in no way be depedent on their husbands for economic security" (p. 256). After Frances Willard read *Looking Backward,* she wrote to Bellamy's publisher, "Some of us think that Edward Bellamy must be Edwardina . . . i.e., we believe that a big-hearted, big-brained woman wrote this book. Won't you please find out?"[11] In the 1890 census, four million women listed as occupations such new jobs as typing, operating telephone switchboards, and selling in the big new department stores; these were added to the more traditional women's jobs such as sewing, laundering, teaching, and working in cotton mills or as domestics. However, Bellamy's ideas about women and work reflect a qualified feminism. He restricts women to a few jobs because, in his view, they are "inferior in strength to men and further disqualified industrially in special ways" (p. 257). Yet, inconsistently with the premises of Nationalism, the state "allows" married women to work.

In believing that economic factors alone were responsible for women's inequality, Bellamy perpetuated patriarchal images of natural female inferiority and created socialist female characters who conformed to the standards of the cult of True Womanhood, who were pure, pious, domestic, and submissive.[12] Thus, only women who have been both wives and mothers reach high ranks in the industrial army because "they alone fully represent their sex" (p. 257). Doctor Leete tells Julian that the best function for utopian women is to inspire utopian men; they are men's "incentive to labour" (p. 257), and men only "permit women to work because it makes them more attractive and fulfilling companions" (p. 256).

It is hardly surprising, given the inspirational powers of the ideal woman, that Julian finally becomes a socialist not so much because of Doctor Leete's persuasive lectures on the merits of Nationalism, but because he is loved by a utopian lady. Perhaps Julian recovers so easily from his jet lag of 113 years because Edith II looks, acts, and most importantly, sounds so much like Edith I. Julian never sees her at work—he never even bothers to ask what she does in the industrial army. Instead, he watches her set the table, arrange flowers, tend the garden, and go shopping. As Edith assures him, she's just an "indefatigable shopper"—quite the Victorian lady.

From the first, Leete insists that socialism has done nothing to disrupt the old gender distinctions. Indeed, he asserts, the new society is less feminist than the old, tainted as it was by the suffragettes, by an assembly of women farmers seeking admission to the Knights of Labor, and by Amelia Bloomer printing patterns for ladies' "Turkish trousers" in her small women's paper, *The Lily.* The doctor reminds Julian that

"the lack of some such recognition of the distinct individuality of the sexes was one of the innumerable defects of your society. The passionate attraction between men and women has too often prevented a perception of the profound differences which make the members of each sex in many things strange to the other, and capable of sympathy only with their own." (P. 362)

Sympathy only with their own? In *Looking Backward,* the women repeatedly offer sympathy to the men. As Edwin Fussell observes, whenever Leete and the contiguous males stop talking long enough for Edith to open her mouth, out comes the magic word: "Her beautiful face was full of the most poignant sympathy. . . . The tender human sympathy which thrilled in the soft pressure of her fingers had brought me the support I needed. . . . 'Indeed I will not go away,' she said, with a little quiver of her face, more expressive of her sympathy than a volume of words. . . . He [Leete] said that it would be better not to show too much sympathy with you at first. . . . 'But you will not try to contend with it alone again, at least,' she persisted. 'Promise that you will come to us and let us sympathize with you and try to help you.' "[13] Circumscribed by Bellamy's characterization (if not by economic role) in her nurturing role, Edith mothers Julian into a socialist consciousness.[14] Like her sisters from the sentimental novel, she must be either better or worse than her lover.

What Julian really needs help with is his guilt—fortunately, now only his guilt by association—for his nineteenth-century money and his nineteenth-century sensibility. Bellamy long held that all people have a dual consciousness, representing both an "impersonal" or altruistic side, and a "personal" or egocentric side.[15] An "impersonal" state of mind reflects a nice balance between self-interest and social commitment, while a "personal" state promotes either

37

vanity or paranoia. The inflation of the personal side also produces guilt, which chains one to the past until released by an image of "impersonal" love.[16] The love between Julian and Edith signifies the time traveler's romantic transcendence of history.

In *Looking Backward,* Bellamy first explored the political implications of an overactive "personal" side. Julian's membership in the old aristocracy stimulated his "personal" traits by blinding him to the poverty and needs of most of humanity. Wandering in an "impersonal" society without the map of class in the year 2000, Julian faces a terrifying loss of identity:

There are no words for the mental torture I endured during this helpless, eyeless groping for myself in a boundless void. No other experience of the mind gives probably anything like the sense of absolute intellectual arrest from the loss of a mental fulcrum, a starting point of thought, which comes during such a momentary obscuration of one's identity. I trust I may never know what it is again. (P. 105)

Perhaps only Dostoyevski or Sartre could have finished this scene, for Julian's "intellectual arrest" is a story of historical guilt. His is the conscience of a class that refused to see what it had created until confronted by its opposite in utopia. Up to the moment when Julian freely chooses Nationalism, he is caught between two realities: "The idea that I was two persons, that my identity was double, began to fascinate me with its simple solution of my experience" (p. 105). His schizophrenia appropriately exposes his perception of two ways of seeing that will not unite in a single analysis.

Lodged in the world of romance, however, Julian cannot understand nor undertake the sorts of activity that could embody historical change. No matter how dramatic it appears to be, activity in romance reveals a sequence of events closer to moral "states" than to novelistic action.[17] The plot of *Looking Backward* is not a function of Julian's heroic deeds because Julian is not an actor. Rather, Julian is a "registering apparatus" who learns to tell the difference between good and evil, which, in Bellamy's view, are static principles rather than historical conceptions. Fredric Jameson has found that in postindustrial literature, where evil appears as the state or category of "otherness itself," romance provides a "powerful deterrent against deviancy or subversion."[18] However, when Bellamy and other nineteenth-century utopian authors appropriated the conventions of the romance, these static traditions contradicted their need to account for change. Bellamy resolved the tension between historicism and romance by resolving the disjunction between the hierarchical nineteenth century and the egalitarian future. In the fable, they are interchangeable.

Bellamy proclaimed, "We make no war on individuals; we do not censure those who have accumulated immense fortunes," recognizing that guilt alone would never impel the wealthy classes toward socialism. Instead, as in Julian's case, it arrests the development of social conscience. Guilt binds Julian to the realities of nineteenth-century capitalism. Bellamy's genius—and this may partly explain the popularity of *Looking Backward*—was finally to absolve Julian, explaining that he was a product of his times, limited by the narrowness of the choices available to a wealthy young investor in 1887.

But the sentimental heroine, even with her traditional literary devotion to social victims (from slaves to prostitutes to drunks), is a good match for Julian's existential guilt. Not that he complains when all she can offer is more of the same. Edith: " 'Promise that you will come to us, and let us sympathize with you.' " Julian: " 'All you need do is to be sorry for me, as you seem to be now' " (p. 114). As a woman, she "symbolizes the humanity of the race," reduced, by convention, to one female virtue. This is in the end what saves Julian from his guilt and permits him to enlist in utopia. The fable in *Looking Backward* concludes in the garden where Edith gathers flowers, and Julian is at her feet: "Kneeling before her, with my face in the dust, I confessed with tears how little was my worth to breathe the air of this golden century, and how infinitely less to wear upon my breast its consummate flower. Fortunate is he who, with a case so desperate as mine, finds a judge so merciful." And so the tormented aristocrat from another century ends his story in the arms of a liberated lady. But neither has traveled very far from 1887. As so often happens in romance, Julian returns to a familiar state of identity. And what could be more familiar than the arms of the woman, the mother, the flower of sexual purity, the moral umpire, the secularized virgin of enlightened technology? Thus in the process of repudiating capitalism, time has lost its destructive force for Julian; through Edith he has begun a passage toward rebirth, toward political liberation. Pictured as a utopian woman, the future can convert the past.

Nevertheless, the passage that is supposed to establish the conversion of Julian calls into question the very project of utopianism. In a dream Julian returns to the Boston of 1887. As Northrop Frye has found in traditional romances, the romantic hero or hunter, in pursuit of a new version of his self, becomes his own prey, creating the conventional twin or dark-light motif.[19] In the nineteenth-century utopian romance, where the hero seeks a political self, the doubling effect is realized through the presentation of two worlds. Before initiation is complete, the utopian hero must return to his first world, through a magical mirror, fantastic telescope, sleep, drugs, or simply memory, in order to recognize the inversions of the new society. Restored to the nineteenth century, Julian for the first time notices poverty, disparities of dress, headlines announcing the employment of young girls in the coal mines, and advertisements defacing every window and pavement. He now confesses,

No more did I look upon the woeful dwellers in this Inferno with a callous curiosity as creatures scarcely human. I saw in them my brothers and sisters, my parents, my children, flesh of my flesh, blood of my blood. The festering mass of human wretchedness about me offended not now my senses merely, but pierced my heart like a knife, so that I could not repress my sighs and groans. I not only saw but felt in my body all that I saw. (P. 458)

In a Whitmanesque fusion of subject and object, his perception of others transcends mere vision; Julian's sojourn in utopia has penetrated the isolation of his class.

Overwhelmed by the sights of waste and loneliness in the city, he dines at the home of wealthy friends, where the women are sumptuously dressed and the table glitters with silver and china. Here Julian lectures his own class on cause and effect, waste and poverty, and utopia: "With fervency I spoke of that new world, blessed with plenty, purified by justice, and sweetened by brotherly kindness, the world of which I indeed but dreamed, but which might so easily be made real" (p. 466). But instead of showing enthusiasm, the women are disgusted, and the men call

40

him a "madman," a "fanatic," an enemy of society. Ostensibly, the book ends happily; Julian wakes up in his utopian bed. But within the text the experiment has failed. Julian is powerless to use his vision of a just and attractive future to effectuate a significant change in the consciousness of the middle class of his own time.

The romance form itself also limits the transforming function of utopian fiction. In describing Shakespeare's *Tempest*, Frank Kermode writes,

In romance there survived that system of ideal correspondences and magic patterns which in actuality could not survive the scrutiny of an informed and modern eye. . . . In actuality the issue is always obscured, but in art the ideas can develop as it were of themselves, with ideal clarity, as if to show that a formal and ordered paradigm of these forces is possible when life is purged of accident, and upon the assumption that since we are all willy-nilly platonists we are perfectly able to understand the relevance of such a paradigm.[20]

Like the magical kingdom of romance and like a Platonic model, Bellamy's Nationalist society exists only for our admiration and contemplation. Julian's acceptance of Nationalism inevitably follows his archetypal discovery of its truth and beauty. Healthy citizens, functional architecture, even sunny weather demonstrate the new society's virtues to the nineteenth-century aristocrat who learns that the beauty of Boston's utopian citizens and buildings is a reflection of its institutional order. But humanity has again renewed itself through a literary device.

Bellamy, however, did better than Julian. Not only did *Looking Backward* sell over a million copies in its first ten years of publication; the book itself, to Bellamy's surprise, launched a movement of state socialism, the Nationalist party, which by 1894 had over 140 chapters, 50 newspapers and journals, and over 10,000 members. Between 1888 and 1900, the financial as well as the political success of *Looking Backward* encouraged over a hundered other authors to turn their own blueprints for the future into books, pamphlets, and newspaper serials; not since *Jane Eyre* had there been a text more widely imitated in American popular fiction.[21]

It is hard not to suspect that one reason for the astounding popularity of this hybrid text was its promise of equality without class conflict. Throughout the book Julian wonders what forestalled the violence of the 1880s: " 'All I can say is that the prospect was such when I went into that long sleep that I should not have been surprised had I looked down from your housetop today on a heap of charred and moss-grown ruins instead of this glorious city' " (p. 69). But Doctor Leete reassures him that Nationalism arrived peacefully: monopolies grew and consolidated automatically, evolving into " 'the one capitalist in the place of all other capitalists, the sole employer, the final monopoly . . . The Great Trust' " (p. 78). Thus, in Bellamy's view, socialism inevitably succeeds and grows out of capitalism. Doctor Leete tells Julian that similarly the riddle of the labor question just answered itself: " 'The solutions came as the result of a process of industrial evolution which should not have terminated otherwise. All that society had to do was to recognize and cooperate with that evolution, when its tendency had become umistakeable,' " a process all too consistent with the hands-off inclinations of laissez-faire economic theory and the determinism of Social Darwinism. Despite his faith in the "rosebush" of human nature, Bellamy can imagine no role for human activity or choice in creating the future.

Fearing the charred ruins that might have resulted from class violence, Bellamy ignored the notion of class altogether, and called for a movement that would appeal to all. Nationalism would promote the "solidarity of the race and the brotherhood of man" as long as it was run by teachers, generals, ministers, and professionals. Although Leete describes the working people's satisfaction with Nationalism, Julian encounters only one worker in utopian Boston, a waiter who is really a college student on vacation. Given the portraits of working people in Bellamy's other writings, this is not surprising. For example, in his essay, "How I Came to Write *Looking Backward*," Bellamy pities the nineteenth-century laborer as a helpless brute. He "feels in some dumb, unreasoning way oppressed by the frame of society, but it is too heavy for him to lift. The institutions that crush him down assume to his dulled brain the inevitable and irresistible aspect of natural laws."[22]

These institutions also assume the inevitable and irresistible reality of natural law in Bellamy's brain. In his famous allegory of the coach and riders in *Looking Backward,* Bellamy portrays the inexorability of economic and social decay under capitalism:

I cannot do better than to compare society as it then was to a prodigious coach which the masses of humanity were harnessed to and dragged toilsomely along a very hilly and sandy road. The driver was hunger, and permitted no lagging. . . . Naturally [the places at the top] were in great demand and the competition for them was keen. . . . For all that they were so easy, the seats were very insecure, and at every sudden jolt of the coach persons were slipping out of them. . . . Was not their very luxury rendered intolerable to them by comparison with the lot of their brothers and sisters in the harness? . . . Oh, yes; . . . when the vehicle came to a bad place in the road, . . . the desperate straining of the team, . . . the pitiless lashing of hunger, the many who fainted at the rope and were trampled . . . made a very distressing spectacle. (P. 12)

The members of the ruling class are mere passengers on the economic coach, competing for their position, constantly insecure because of its potential loss, and in no way responsible for the bumpy ride. And by separating the members of the society (the riders) from the society itself (the coach), Bellamy creates an implausible image of economic determinism in which no one has produced or prospered from the current crisis, which is just an incident on the road.

After workers, Bellamy most mistrusted socialists and insisted that they be kept out of the Nationalist clubs. He rejected any variant of the word *socialism* as a title for his movement, on the grounds that the term was associated with immigrants, workers, and un-Americanism in general. In 1888 he wrote to William Dean Howells,

In the radicalness of the opinions I have expressed I may seem to out-socialize the socialists, yet the word socialist is one I never could well stomach. In the first place it is a foreign word in itself and equally foreign in all its suggestions. It smells to the average American of petroleum, suggests the red flag, with all manner of sexual novelties, and an abusive tone about God and religion, which in this country we at least treat with decent respect.[23]

Instead, Bellamy wanted "respectable men" to lead the Nationalist party because, as he wrote his military friend, Colonel Thomas Higginson, he wanted the social issue "taken out of the hands of blatant, blasphemous demagogues" and placed "before the sober and morally-minded masses of American people. Not until it is so presented by men whom they trust will they seriously consider [the social issue] on its own merits."[24]

How much Bellamy knew of socialism is difficult to assess. His editorials and reviews are markedly impersonal; his correspondence is uncollected. Further, many of his papers, letters, and large sections of his journal burned in a fire at the home of an early biographer, Arthur Morgan. It is certain that for a year, he read literature and political economy at Union College, but we do not know which texts. Then there was a year of study and travel in Germany where he possibly encountered the writings of Bebel and Liebknecht which were then being circulated and disputed; and Marx, Bakunin, and Proudhon were working out the principles of the First International at this time. On his return, he entered a two-year apprenticeship with a law firm, but quit the profession after his first case, which involved the eviction of a widow. In 1871 Bellamy moved to New York, where he worked for the reform-minded *New York Evening Post,* writing exposés of tenement housing, sanitation conditions, and corruption in Boss Tweed's city government.

But within a year, Bellamy returned to his home town of Chicopee Falls, Massachusetts, to become a reviewer for the *Springfield Union;* we know that after this time he read George Sand, Bulwer-Lytton, Thomas Hardy, and George Eliot. And while they had little direct influence on *Looking Backward,* he approvingly reviewed works by Alexander Pushkin, Maurice Kingsley, Joseph Arch, and Charles Bradlaugh. Still, Bellamy was never clear about the sources for his political theory. Given its popularity, he ought to have been familiar with *Progress and Poverty* (1879) by Henry George, which called for a huge single tax as the route to redistribution of the national wealth. He ought to have known *The Cooperative Commonwealth* (1884) by Laurence Gronlund, which told how to legislate capitalism out of existence.[25] But as Bellamy insisted, "I have never been in any sense a student of socialistic literature." He claimed not to know "more of the various socialist schemes than any newspaper reader might."[26]

Yet if only as a reform journalist, Bellamy probably was aware of the growth of socialist activity in America after the Civil War. The National Labor Union, which had lobbied for the eight-hour

day, decided to challenge private enterprise by forming "producers' cooperatives," dividing the profits among the workers in a
factory. The International Working People's Association merged
with the Socialist party and, led by such anarchist leaders as Albert
Parsons and August Spies, began to argue within the trade union
movement for the abolition of the wage system as well as the
abolition of government. The anarchist movement itself, which
had roots in the First International, was quickly growing among
German immigrants expelled from their homeland by the antisocialist legislation enacted after 1848 and later by the anti-Semitic
policies of Bismarck in the 1870s. In 1870, the Marxist General
Council shifted from London to New York and forged connections
between the old First International and the Knights of Labor. The
arrival of thousands of French radicals after the suppression of the
Paris Commune in 1871 also stimulated the spread of socialist
ideas in the United States.[27] Even the Grangers began to advocate
collective ownership of the land.

Nonetheless, Bellamy has given us two alternative explanations
for the genesis of *Looking Backward,* both of which ignore these
relevant political currents. According to the first, he disclaimed a
reform motive altogether, whereas in the second he admitted to a
limited reform purpose, but largely as a result of the impact of
economic problems on his home town and his family. In the May
1890 issue of the *Nationalist,* Bellamy wrote:

In undertaking to write *Looking Backward,* I had at the outset no idea of
attempting a serious contribution to the movement of social reform. The
idea was of a mere literary fantasy, a fairytale of social felicity. There was
no thought of contriving a house which practical men might live in, but
merely of hanging in mid-air, far out of reach of the sordid and material
world of the present, a cloud palace for an ideal humanity.

But, he recalls, as the story grew, he suddenly realized that he had
"stumbled over the destined cornerstone of the new social order,"
and he changed the romance from "a mere fairy tale of social
perfection" to "a vehicle of a definite scheme of industrial
reorganization."[28] (Bellamy's explanation echoes Engels's famous
critique of utopian socialism as an ahistorical "accidental discovery of this or that ingenious brain."[29]

In 1894, however, writing in the *Ladies' Home Journal,* Bellamy offered a more autobiographical account that gives some clue as to how the son of a wealthy Calvinist minister came to write one of the most influential texts of American socialism. Here he describes how his childhood in the quiet New England village of Chicopee Falls gave him an idealized view of society. Although Chicopee Falls grew during Bellamy's youth into a major textile town in which an immigrant population waged bitter strikes against the mills, his placid social view persisted until his trip to Germany in 1868, where he noticed the conditions of industrial poverty for the first time. When he returned from Europe, he recognized that there was an "inferno of poverty beneath civilization" in America as well, and he concluded that poverty was the result of a form of slavery that had not been abolished by the Civil War. But ultimately, he explained, it was his fears for his children's future that encouraged him to address this economic problem in literature: "In the fall or winter of 1886 . . . I sat down to my desk with the definite purpose of trying to reason out a method of economic organization by which the republic might guarantee the livelihood and material welfare of its citizens on a basis of equality corresponding to and supplementing their political equality."[30] Denying that he introduced the romantic fable to "command greater attention," he explains that he had always used fiction for "the working out of problems, that is to say, attempts to trace the logical consequences of certain assumed conditions."[31] Through his characters, Bellamy tested the social and psychological implications of political theory.

Although Bellamy thereby saw the fable of Julian and Edith as indistinguishable from the novel's historical analysis, from the first critics saw the two elements as structurally distinct—at best a "sugar coating" on a political pill. Some critics, such as James Hart, have suggested that it was mainly the fantasy that was responsible for the popularity of *Looking Backward,* because of the public's large appetite for escapist literature.[32] But, as Granville Hicks claims, "Readers picked up the book as seekers of amusement and laid it down converts."[33] Or as William Dean Howells put it in his 1888 review for *Harper's Monthly:*

46

Here is a book which in the sugar-coated form of a dream has established a dose of undiluted socialism, and which has been gulped by some of the most vigilant opponents of that theory without a suspicion of the poison they are taking into their system. . . . They have accepted it as the portrait of a very charming condition of things instead of shuddering at the spectacle in every fibre.[34]

Bellamy repeatedly denied that he had meant to write a radical novel. When he tried to account for the sales of *Looking Backward,* he suggested that a novel of propaganda produced an effect "precisely in proportion as it is a bare anticipation of what everybody was thinking and about to say."[35] *Looking Backward* made no speculations that were "greatly in advance of public opinion"; the book was effective because it "seized on currents already present in society."[36] He knew that it was timely. When Benjamin Ticknor was considering its publication, Bellamy wrote him, "If you tackled it, how soon could you bring it out? I am particularly desirous that it should see the light as quickly as possible. Now is the accepted time, it appears to me, for a publication touching on social and industrial questions to obtain a hearing."[37]

Perhaps some of the popularity of *Looking Backward* derived from its image of technology. In an age of unbridled industrial expansion, *Looking Backward* offered a comfortable view of machinery. The zipper, the sewing machine, packaged meats, and canned foods had already demonstrated the labor-saving possibilities of the new machinery, descriptions of which Bellamy generously distributed throughout his book. William Morris, often something of a Luddite, attacked *Looking Backward* for its mechanistic materialism and called it a "Cockney's paradise." Thomas Higginson similarly characterized Nationalism as a "statue with feet of clay and limbs of iron, and a forehead of brass . . . with a cigar in its lips and a wine cup in its right hand."[38] What Morris and Higginson apparently did not recognize was that this was an era when 400,000 tourists would pay fifty cents apiece to enter the 1893 Chicago World's Fair where they discovered a machine to freeze champagne into sherbert, a Krupp cannon weighing 130 tons, a long-distance telephone to New York, a hybrid delicacy called grapefruit, and an enormous revolving wheel especially designed for the fair by George Washington Gale

Ferris. William Dean Howells (who in 1894 abandoned machinery in his pastoral utopia of Altruria) confessed that at first he saw Bellamy's gadgets as "sorry patches on the rags of our outworn civilization, or only toys to arouse our greed and vacancy," but he later understood that the inventions themselves were "part of Bellamy's democratic imagination." Bellamy, he saw, promised "things for lives hithero starved of them."[39]

Contemporary sales patterns indicate, however, that the unusual popularity of *Looking Backward* (during the 1890s it was surpassed only by the Bible in book sales) is best explained by its politics. The success of *Looking Backward* represents an unusual chapter in the history of book publishing. Three hundred thousand copies were sold in the first two years, and over the next decade, a million copies were sold in the United States and England.[40] It was distributed by retailers and jobbers in the cities and by traveling salesmen who sold it door to door in rural areas. Significantly, American sales were highest in the Western states and the Mississippi basin, areas where the farmers' movement had strength. The Populists, the Women's Christian Temperance Union, the National Council of Women, and the Grangers all urged their members to buy *Looking Backward*. Copies that could not be sold were given away. Reform-oriented magazines such as the *Ladies' Home Journal,* the *Indianapolis Leader,* even the *People's Health Journal* distributed it free or at reduced rates. Other progressive papers such as the Christian Socialists' *Dawn,* the labor-oriented *Standard,* and the liberal *Arena* and *Lend a Hand* publicized the book.

The highest praise came from the literary left. After Howells's favorable review in *Harper's,* Cyrus Willard, editor of the *Boston Globe,* read *Looking Backward* and announced that the story had totally changed his mind about the possibilities of "cooperation." Laurence Gronlund directed his agents to sell *Looking Backward* instead of his own *Cooperative Commonwealth.* Huntingdon Smith, the American translator of Tolstoi, wrote, "The crowning tribute to the merit of Mr. Bellamy's noble book is that we put it down with the question on our lips, 'why not today?' "[41] H. P. Peebles, a Nationalist from Los Angeles, announced that every social cataclysm had a mastermind: the Israelites had Moses, the Romans had Caesar, the French had Robespierre. "Bellamy is the Moses of today. . . . He has shown us that the promised land exists." Then Peebles adds an interesting coda, "Let us labor and wait."[42] And sometimes the praise was even more extravagant. In Lynn Boyd Porter's preface to his popular proletarian romance, *Speaking of Ellen* (1890), the narrator comes upon a portrait of workers chained in a dungeon:

As I stood there, lost in pity for the unfortunate, a sudden gleam shot across the darkness. A ray of blessed sun penetrated the noisome depths. The confined ones struggled to their feet and took deep breaths of joy! An heroic soul had scaled the outer wall, forced aside a heavy stone. I did not see the man, but someone said his name was BELLAMY. I could not have made that bold ascent, but by new light I saw many things.

I learned that the prison had a door whose bolts, tho' rusted in their sockets, were not immoveable.[43]

But in fact Bellamy did little to move the rusted bolts. It was perhaps inevitable that admirers of *Looking Backward* should demand a practical route to utopia, and in 1888 Bellamy joined with a few friends to form the Nationalist party, which soon organized hundreds of local propaganda and discussion clubs but apparently had little, if any, impact on the reform issues of the day. One problem for this organization seeking to build a mass movement was its choice of leadership; as early as July 1888, Bellamy congratulated the founders of the original Boston club for their decision first to convert "the cultured and conservative class . . . the special end for which *Looking Backward* was written."[44] Local groups tended to be led by such figures as Edward Everett Hale, a philanthropist and novelist, John Lovell, a publisher, and Clarence Darrow, the famous lawyer. When Sylvia Bowman, biographer of Bellamy, reviewed the membership lists of the clubs, she found that few Nationalists had Irish, German, or Jewish names, and that few trades were represented in the members' occupations. Bowman concludes, "It is easily understood why it was said that Nationalism had put the silk hat on socialism."[45] In 1891 when Bellamy tried to launch the Nationalist campaign for municipal control of power plants (the party's only political drive), he found that the Theosophist movement, a religious organization of millenarian reformers, had gained control of the local Nationalist club, and his efforts to revitalize the party failed. By the mid-1890s, the organization was bankrupt. Disheartened by its failure, Bellamy wrote a second utopian novel, *Equality,* in which he held that because capitalism controlled the schools, the churches, and the press, as well as industry, social change must start with propaganda and re-education.

Over one hundred and twenty contemporary authors seemingly agreed. Although only nineteen joined with Bellamy in predicting a socialist future, *Looking Backward* influenced them all. While most of these utopian authors attacked Bellamy, many borrowed his literary devices and some even used his characters. None of them, however, was up to Bellamy's achievement of a coherent political alternative and none of them, including his own *Equality,* created a setting as convincing as his picture of Boston in A.D. 2000—a vision that persuaded so many readers through the logic of his fictional development. Many of these progressive utopias shared Bellamy's naive faith in the political effectiveness of utopian fiction. In *That Island* (1892) by Samuel Crocker, Nationalism triumphs through the distribution of two million copies of a utopian novel, while the hero of an anonymously published work, *The Beginning* (1893), writes a utopian novel to prove his new social conscience to a reluctant heroine. Zebina Forbush in *The Co-opolitan: The Story of the Cooperative Commonwealth of Idaho* (1898) and Bradford Peck in *The World a Department Store* (1900), among others, asked for money to put their utopian solutions into practice. Although none of the other progressive utopias sold as well as *Looking Backward,* they helped popularize the idea of a major redistribution of property: the future societies equalize wages and abolish inheritance, interest on loans, and sometimes money itself. And although no nineteenth-century utopia could predict the achievements of modern scientific research (Albert A. Merrill in *The Great Awakening* [1899] promised the horseless carriages in his twenty-second-century city would go fifteen miles an hour) no matter how far into the future they date their new societies, all progressive utopias envisioned a humanized technology—such as the collective ownership of tractors or the invention of a labor-saving dishwasher, which could help realize the institution of the four-hour work day.

The socialist premise of *Looking Backward* also stimulated attacks on the novel. Writing in the *Yale Review,* William Higgs denounced Bellamy for suppressing individual freedom, abolishing private property, destroying competition, and worst of all, weakening Christianity by eliminating the very need for charity.[46] W. T. Harris called *Looking Backward* un-American (a recurrent motif) and added, "Perhaps rather one should say that others propose reform, but Mr. Bellamy proposes revolution. They are like physicians who propose to cure the body, while he proposes to get rid of the body altogether."[47] Other critics challenged Bellamy's faith in human nature, declaring, for example, that "man was incapable or unworthy of a larger measure of social felicity than he enjoyed."[48] A reviewer for Chicago's *Inter-Ocean* proclaimed that "the element of self-seeking in our nature is too integral to be eradicated by any altruistic teaching."[49] And the *Los Angeles Times* review concluded that Bellamy's scheme was doomed because "self-aggrandizement is the natural tendency of human nature."[50]

Despite the short life of Nationalism, *Looking Backward* has had a lasting influence. In 1938, fifty years after its first publication, 5,000 copies were sold that year in the United States alone. And in the 1930s, when Charles Beard, John Dewey, and Edward Weeks independently listed their choice of the twenty-five most influential books written since 1885, all three ranked *Looking Backward* second only to *Das Kapital*. Albert Levi claims that "*Looking Backward* has probably produced more native American socialists than any reading of Marx, Engels, Lenin, or the customary European sources."[51]

Edward Bellamy died in 1898 without becoming disillusioned with utopian principles, although his last journal, the *New Nation*, had ceased publication in 1894. Meanwhile, the Populists had absorbed many of the Nationalists' goals, and Bellamy's party shared the farmers' defeat when William Jennings Bryan and the Democrats took up their demands and then were soundly beaten by William McKinley, who promised to end the current depression by revamping the navy and developing new markets in Latin America. But in the year in which Bellamy was dying of tuberculosis, he told the English journalist William Stead that his cause did not "share the debility of its servants" and added that he was devising a new plan to bring about socialism by packing the Supreme Court.

THREE

William Dean Howells
and the Pastoral Utopia

*"Ha, I dare say," answered the banker, as he tossed the waiter a
dollar, and we rose and strolled out into the Plaisance. "If all men
were unselfish, I should agree with you that Altrurianism was best."*

*"You can't have unselfishness till you have Altrurianism," I re-
turned. "You can't put the cart before the horse."*

*"Oh, yes we can," he returned in his tone of banter. "We always
put the cart before the horse in America, so that the horse can see
where the cart is going.—William Dean Howells,* A Traveller from
Altruria, *p. 215*

A *Traveller from Altruria* (1894) is the story of Aristedes Homos, a
visitor from the pastoral utopia of Altruria who discovers on a visit
to America that he is in a topsy-turvy land of misperceptions and
inversions, of realities that controvert ideals and put the cart of
human nature before the horse of social conditions. As Aristedes
Homos says, America is a land that is "the complete inversion of
our own and in which I seem to get the same effect of life that
boys sometimes get of the landscape by putting down their heads
and looking at it between their legs."[1] And this is what Howells
would have us do. He has sent a visitor from utopia who, unlike
Julian West, cannot understand what he encounters. He does and
says the democratic thing, and he is an embarrassment. The less
he understands, the more do we. Then he takes us back with him
to Altruria, which in its homey simplicity and rural democracy is
the "complete inversion" of the United States.

Homos is so relaxed and healthy that he does not even look like
an American. When he gets off the train at a luxurious New En-

gland resort, where he is to spend his vacation, his host recognizes him because he is the only passenger who is not hot, worried, and anxious. And then, to his host's dismay, Homos helps the porter toss his trunk into the wagon:

"Do you know," he said, "I fancied that good fellow was ashamed of my helping him. I hope it didn't seem a reflection upon him in any way before your people? I ought to have thought of that."

"I guess we can make it right with him. I dare say he felt more surprised than disgraced. But we must make haste a little now; your train was half an hour late, and we shall not stand so good a chance for supper if we are not there pretty promptly."

"No?" said the Altrurian. "Why?"

"Well," I said, with evasive lightness, "first come, first served, you know. That's human nature."

"Is it?" he returned, and he looked at me as one does who suspects another of joking. (P. 9)

"Evasive lightness" describes both the structure and the tone of Howells's tale. Aristedes Homos has disembarked from his train along with wealthy bankers and merchants who commute to the country on hot summer weekends to be reunited with their wives and children and to enjoy the restorative effects of "nature." But Howells's purpose is to use Homos to "precipitate the best within us," and the best will be the recognition, by contrast with Altruria, of our early American moral principles, our historic connections with the land, and our democratic "altruism," which we have subverted. Howells suggests that we know we have betrayed our beginnings; now we need to cover up the lie. And so, by behaving inappropriately and asking just the wrong questions, Homos stands us on our heads so we can clearly see what we have done. And about time. Howells, too, is aware of Haymarket lurking at the gates of the garden.[2]

This, then, is the world of satire, not the world of political prescription. Homos's fellow travelers are very different from the cool aristocrats, gluttonous in the face of the starvation of the poor, whom Julian West meets in his dream-return to the nineteenth century. The society lady and the economics professor and the banker and the minister and the novelist who have gathered at the hotel to instruct Homos in the manners of the Americans are hard-working and thoughtful citizens who simply cannot perceive the contradiction between their democratic ideals and their habits of work and play. After Mr. Twelvemough, a rather effete society novelist, lectures Homos on the "honor of work" in America, the utopian rushes off to help a waitress lift a heavy tray and arrange a sumptuous meal. And Twelvemough cringes: "I wished to tell him that while a country schoolteacher who waits at table in a summer hotel is very much to be respected in her sphere, she is not regarded with that high honor which some other women command among us; but I did not find this very easy, after what I had said of our esteem for labor, and . . . I was thinking how I could hedge" (p. 213). While both the novelist and the visitor from Altruria go on to praise the glorious Declaration of Independence, Twelvemough hedges in order to repress the contradictions that the presence of the utopian visitor has raised. Accurate perception, he senses, would undermine the rationalizations that sustain his class allegiance.

Rather than satirize a peculiar institution, Howells uses the innocent perceptions of the utopian observer to explore middle-class myopia in a world of mirrors that Howells senses is about to crack under the pressures of contemporary problems—epitomized in the Haymarket trials and the Homestead strike—and the current financial "cyclone." The function thus of Homos's journey is to help the American middle class "get the light." "There is everything to hope from this [recognition]," says Howells, "for it means that if change comes at all, it will not come superficially and it will not come violently" (p. 191). One thing that this "comfortable class" would have to notice is the existence of class itself, but the bourgeoisie vacations at a resort—itself a metaphor for the upper middle class—which is so isolated from the rest of society by virtue of its elite clientele, the great expense of staying there, and its exclusive rituals that other social classes seem invisible. Twelvemough observes: "It has sometimes seemed to me as if our big hotel there were a ship, anchored off some strange coast. The inhabitants come out with supplies and carry on their barter with the ship's steward, and we sometimes see them over the side, but we never speak to them or have anything to do with them' " (p. 96).

But Homos sees that the hotel is bounded on one side by a dead forest, an ugly "scar" of scorched stumps—the trees sold for profit and the land for commercial development. On the other side of the resort are farms, worked by an angry rural class now impoverished by land speculation, high transportation costs, and inflated mortgage rates—all profits for the wealthy urbanites who frequent the resort, thinking they have gone to the "country." As Twelvemough contentedly observes the hotel's guests, he notes, "Everyone was well-dressed and comfortable and at peace, and I felt that our hotel was in some sort a microcosm of the Republic" (p. 24).

Even the novels that Twelvemough writes help the middle class to construct its own version of reality. Twelvemough—the sort of artist Howells particularly attacked in the 1880s for disguising such social realities as class distinctions enforced through differences in language and the daily routines of business and play—announces to Homos:

"I am a writer of romantic fiction, and my time is so fully occupied in manipulating the destinies of the good old-fashioned hero and heroine, and trying always to make them end in a happy marriage, that I have hardly had a chance to look much into the lives of agriculturalists or artisans. . . . We have a theory that they are politically sovereign, but we see very little of them, and we don't associate with them. In fact, our cultivated people have so little interest in them socially that they don't like to meet them, even in fiction. . . . I always go to the upper classes for my types." (P. 30)

But when Homos asks the novelist how workingmen spend their leisure time, Twelvemough notes, "I hung my head in shame and pity; [his question] really had such an effect of mawkish sentimentality" (p. 34). Twelvemough has simply internalized the emotions of the sentimental novel at the expense of whatever real feelings he might otherwise have possessed. Hence, the novelist evades the utopian's sincere questions through repartee, ridicule, or interruption: " 'The question is unanswerable.' " Or, "I found all this very uncomfortable, and tried to turn the talk back to the point I felt curious about" (p. 54).

Isolated and bewildered by the guests at the hotel, the socialist visitor explores the nearby village, which forms a possible link for him between the values of the United States and the values of Altruria. There Homos discovers that the latent utopian potential in the American character is to be found among farming people. But even the rural village reveals the exploitative connections between the city and the country. Riding in a carriage with Mrs. Makely, a society lady, and Twelvemough, his host, Homos encounters Reuben Camp, an angry young farmer who tells the hotel guests that the quiet village is in fact a lonely and depopulated community. Poverty has forced his neighbors to overwork their land until the soil is barely worth cultivating. Impoverished by the competition from the new "immense agricultural operations," many Yankee farmers have abandoned their farms, lured by the myth of prosperity in the Western territories where, they soon discover,

"there ain't any public domain that's worth having. All the good land is in the hands of the railroads, and farm syndicates, and speculators; and if you want a farm in the West, you've got to buy it; the East is the only place where folks give them away because they ain't worth keeping. If you haven't got ready money, you can buy one on credit and pay ten, twenty, and thirty per cent interest, and live in a dug-out on the plains— till your mortgage matures." (P. 82)

This is the rhetoric of Populism, the farmer's party that grounded its demands for property and currency reform on the myth that the land and its farmers were the repository of traditional principles of stability and equality.[3] Living by the sweat of his brow, the farmer had in fact been caught in an international web of competition, high finance, and railroad mergers. In addition to huge mortgages, Reuben explains, the eastern farmers also pay high taxes for road construction to ease the brief summer season of the "city folks." Only the hotels or farmers who take in vacation boarders can afford decent teams of horses. While following God's injunction to cultivate the land, the farmer has become the victim of a conspiracy hatched in the town. But Mrs. Makely and Mr. Twelvemough are tired of talking about money with a farmer, so they throw a few pennies to the children ("more out of joke than charity"), and they drive away with Homos.

In his description of American agriculture, Howell changed the traditional romantic landscape of pastoral. Only Homos, who is a member of a community in which all citizens, male and female, perform farm labor for three hours a day, appreciates mediated nature—that is, nature that has been worked and altered for human needs, not nature characterized by the wild gorges, stormy vistas, and vast perspectives popular in the romantic landscape paintings of Thomas Cole, Frederick Church, and Albert Bierstadt. Homos's nature is not "landscape" at all. As Raymond Williams notes, "A working country is hardly ever a landscape. The very idea of landscape implies separation and observation."[4] In a 1895 editorial for *Century* magazine, Howells criticized the fashionable taste for the picturesque that ignored the realities of rural poverty:

The underlings are not satisfied when the overlings tell them that it is not only fit that they should be where they are, but that it is very picturesque, and that it promotes sympathy in the overlings. Without troubling themselves to deny that it is picturesque, they invite the overlings to try it awhile themselves, and they will be better able to say whether it is fit or not.[5]

Thus the land in *A Traveller from Altruria* is more than a source of psychological regeneration or a pastoral backdrop to commentaries on love and death. Rural nature satirizes both the political structures of what Howells termed the plutocracy and its consequent ways of seeing. For Howells, land is a natural resource that always has questions of ownership and labor attached to it. Homos asks about the social history of the farmlands he sees in America, refusing to be an observer who merely projects aesthetic patterns onto nature. Twelvemough notes: "The Altrurian was greatly interested, not so much in the landscape—though he owned its beauty, when we cried out over it from point to point— but in the human incidents and features. He noticed the cattle in the fields, and the horses we met on the road, and the taste and comfort of the buildings, the variety of the crops, and the promise of the harvest" (p. 78).

Although, like the painter of idealized landscape, Howells ignores the primary processes of agricultural labor—plowing, planting, irrigating—and although he pictures the land in harvest fruition, his farmers nevertheless emerge from the landscape to question the accuracy of such a mode of perception. Reuben angrily denounces the tourist who cheaply purchases an old farm to visit "a few months in the summer, when he could enjoy the sightliness of it and see me working over there on my farm while he smoked on his front porch" (p. 82). The aesthetic parasitism of the rich exposes the economic.

But Howells's best hope is the middle class, which holds the key to the future because it alone has a sense of the past. As Homos observes, " 'Of course the vast majority of Americans are of the middle class, and with them you can still find the old American life, the old American ideals, the old American principles; and if the old America is ever to prevail, it must be in their love and honor of it' " (p. 190). But while they preserve these possibly anachronistic democratic principles, middle-class Americans also suffer in their newfound status. In an article called "Equality as the Basis of Good Society," Howells wrote that social and economic inequity "never was a gain to the superior except in some advantage of food, clothing, and shelter. It never made him in any wise a finer, purer, juster man; and it very often made him arrogant, luxurious, bestial."[6] The guests who gather on the hotel verandah on hot summer evenings to indoctrinate Homos are not the debauched aristocrats who terrorize New York in Ignatius Donnelly's *Caesar's Column.* Yet even the intellectuals, the clergy, and the women, whom Howells usually counts on for accurate perception, do not see what is going on. But Homos still insists, " 'It is to such of these as perceive the fact [social injustice] that the good cause can look for help' " (p. 192).

The guests at the hotel, however, do not "perceive the fact," because they do not recognize their own contradictions. For example, in describing the role of servants Twelvemough confesses: " 'We have found that the logic of our convictions could not be applied to domestic service.' " Or, in justifying the individual rights of the farmer who sold his timber, Twelvemough argues, " 'You know that in America the law is careful not to meddle with a man's private affairs, and we don't attempt to legislate personal virtue.' 'But marriage,' [Homos] said; 'surely you have the institutions of marriage?' 'I was really annoyed at this' " (p. 22).

But as the utopian confides, he has come to America to try to understand these "colossal contradictions," and he presses on. He admires the moral and intellectual superiority of American women and innocently suggests, " 'The influence of women in public

58

affairs must be of the greatest advantage to you.' " He admires the Americans' preoccupation with leisure and their enjoyment of vacation resorts—"refuges," as Twelvemough calls them, for "our weary toilers." When Homos questions whether miners and iron moulders and printers prefer to go to resorts of their own, Twelvemough is speechless and turns him over to other guests at the hotel for an explanation. But they compound the contradictions. The feeblest response to Homos's inquiries comes from the minister who tepidly advocates brotherly love, insisting, " 'I have had some of the very best people—socially and financially—with me in the wish that there might be more brotherliness between the rich and the poor among us,' " but who admits that there are no working people in his congregation (p. 126). The professor of laissez-faire economics also expresses his concern for the working poor: " 'The day of over-production is sure to come, when their work must stop unless the men that give them work are willing to lose money' " (p. 35).

Worst of all, the women—guardians of morality and custodians of culture—also represent the conflict between the real and the ideal; to Howells they are, not surprisingly, most to blame for class myopia. Homos is told that middle-class American women are "cultivated"; freed by servants from housework, they study art and music and Browning and psychology and political economy while the men skim the morning papers. But Homos learns that they have no part in "public affairs." At the hotel, they are represented by Mrs. Makely, a "cultured American woman . . . necessarily quite ignorant of her own country, geographically, politically, and historically." Howells sympathetically records the hidden social and psychological risks of the cult of True Womanhood. American women are cultured but ignorant, freed from labor but always tired, dominating but powerless. And lacking real authority or useful activity, Mrs. Makely is manipulative and indirect, ostensibly nurturing but fundamentally arrogant and insensitive. Rude to the farmers, condescending to the seamstress, Mrs. Makely loudly defends the hotel's taboo forbidding lonely female guests to dance with farmers. When she finally invites Homos to give a speech on Altrurian socialism—to raise money for charity—she makes the tickets expensive in the hope that the local farmers will not attend, once again discouraging communication between social classes.

Throughout the story, Homos hints at Altrurian solutions to the problems of caste and class, but he withholds details of the political, social, and economic institutions of his utopian island—perhaps appropriately for Howells, who was ambivalent about socialism and unclear about how social change might safety occur. Like his heroine Annie Kilburn, Howells had explored various strategies for radically rearranging American society. Between 1894 and 1896, when Howells completed *A Traveller from Altruria,* the first part of the trilogy, and wrote most of *Through the Eye of the Needle,* the third, he was active in the Populist party. Although Twelvemough demeans the Populists as "just a lot of crazy hayseeds who don't want to pay back the money they have borrowed," the farmers' party was a formidable legislative force in the early 1890s, and had elected three governors, two senators, and several members of Congress (including Ignatius Donnelly, who soon after wrote the apocalyptic utopian novel *Caesar's Column*). However, narrow goals, such as the free coinage of silver, diverted the Populists' attention from the consensus issues of land and transportation reform. William Jennings Bryan and the Democratic party, fearing that the coalition of northern farmers, black sharecroppers, and western miners might form the radical electoral party that Howells and Bellamy so craved, successfully wooed many western Populists with promises of currency reforms. By 1896, Howells was "bewildered" by the turns in the Populist party, which was becoming divided on the issues of women's suffrage, immigration restriction, and prohibition, and he wished they "had kept to the middle of the road."[7] But he was also dubious about the Republican campaign which Mark Hanna was organizing for William McKinley—not only the most expensive presidential campaign in American history but also one that openly funded terrorist acts against black Populists.

Even as early as 1888, Howells was confounded by the tension between his Populist allegiance and his commitment to private property. As he explained in an early letter to Hamlin Garland: "Your land tenure idea is one of the good things which we must hope for and strive for by all the good means at our hands. But I don't know that it's the first step to be taken; and I can't yet bring myself to look upon confiscation in any direction as a good thing. The new commonwealth must be founded in justice even to the unjust."[8]

William Dean Howells and the Pastoral Utopia

Justice for the unjust is the theme of Howells's story. When the garrulous Mrs. Makely finally persuades Homos to give one speech on his homeland, he agrees to lecture on "the history of accumulation," or the change from capitalism to "Altrurianism," a history which of course retells the story of American industrial capitalism up to the early 1890s and then proceeds in imagination from there. Altrurians, Homos explains to a large crowd of farmers, railroad workers, and hotel guests, had tasted cooperation; like Americans, they enjoyed it in their political parties, in their labor unions, and most particularly in their families. Even so, economic fears had forced them to think and act competitively. Technology, too, had undermined the traditional community as machines released hands and minds

"to an activity unheard of before. Invention followed invention; our rivers and seas became the warp of commerce where the steam-sped shuttles carried the woof of enterprise to and from with tireless celerity. Machines to save labor multiplied themselves as if they had been procreative forces; and wares of every sort were produced with incredible swiftness and cheapness." (P. 147)

Finally, the Altrurians saw that this immense power "which called itself prosperity . . . blasted the landscape with the enterprise that spoiled the lives of men" (p. 148). A bitter cycle of strikes, lockouts, unemployment, and starvation followed; meanwhile, trade unionists and industrialists alike forgot to use the "despised and neglected" vote. When the leaders of the Altrurian workers recalled this archaic tactic for bringing about change, they "ceased to counsel strikes, or any form of resistance to the Accumulation that could be tormented into the likeness of insurrection against the government" (p. 153). Instead, they simply urged workers to vote to nationalize the already centralized communications and transportation industries. As in *Looking Backward,* monopolization simplified the road to state ownership. Swiftly and peacefully, the Altrurian public soon voted itself the ownership of the mine, the small businesses, and the farmlands as well. This easy electoral solution described in his fiction belied Howells's deep confusion about the power of the vote. As he wrote in the *North American Review:*

At the end, as in the beginning, it is [the impoverished American] who is responsible, and if he thinks himself unfairly used, it is quite for him to see that he is used fairly; for, slowly or swiftly, it is he who ultimately makes and unmakes the laws by political methods which, if still somewhat clumsy, he can promptly improve; . . . if we have a plutocracy, it may be partly because the rich want it, but it is infinitely more because the poor choose or allow it.[9]

That Homos never explains just how the poor Altrurians stopped colluding with their plutocracy may reveal the influence on Howells of Laurence Gronlund, who first introduced the novelist to the principles of democratic socialism. In *The Cooperative Commonwealth* (1884), Gronlund pointed to the socialist tendencies within American institutions—in public education, in trade unions, and in the vote—and he formulated for Howells the central contradiction that underlies the satire of the Altrurian romances: the coexistence of political democracy and wage slavery. Gronlund seems to have persuaded Howells, in an argument that follows the lines of Social Darwinism, that European and American society were evolving organisms, automatically growing toward cooperation. America's geographical isolation would further protect this evolutionary trend. Howells exaggerated this isolation in his novel by locating Altruria on a distant isle.

Howells opposed violence on any side as a strategy for social change. He was disturbed by the Homestead strike, during which hired Pinkerton guards brutally attacked the strikers when they successfully fought them off. Howells wrote his father,

I suppose you have been excited, as I have been, by the Homestead affair. It is hard, in our sympathy with the working class, to remember that the men are playing a lawless part and that they must be made to give up the Carnegie property. Strikes are only useful as a means of diagnosis; they are not a remedy; they are merely symptomatic of the fact that the trouble must go on as long as competition goes on; they are themselves an essential part of competition. . . . I must come back to my old conviction that every drop of blood shed for a good cause helps to make a bad cause. How much better if the Homesteaders could have suffered the Pinkertons to shoot them down unarmed. Then they would have the power of martyrs in the world.[10]

William Dean Howells and the Pastoral Utopia

Violence was unnecessary in Altruria. In the end, the motive for the change from plutocracy to Altrurianism was neither simply economic nor simply political. It was a response to the overall reduction in the quality of people's lives caused by industrialism. Even after nationalization, Homos admits,

"We came to realize in the depths of our steamships were those who fed the fires with their lives, and that our mines from which we dug our wealth were the graves of those who had died to the free light and air, without finding the rest of earth. We did not see that the machines for saving labor were monsters that devoured women and children and wasted men at the bidding of the power which no man must touch." (P. 147)

Not only does this passage disturb the traditional image of Howells as "the quiet rebel" who recognized only "the smiling aspects" of American life, but it also forecasts his utopian belief that work should be tied to art and labor to structures of feeling. For his theoretical critiques of capitalism, Howells turned to Hamlin Garland and Henry George; for a model for political change, he turned to Laurence Gronlund. But for a design for utopia, for his own sense of an ending, appropriately enough he turned to Tolstoi and William Morris and caught a glimpse of the kind of society Herbert Marcuse would later term libidinal and aesthetic.

Throughout his visit to the resort, Homos insists that "America implies Altruria." The industrial and bourgeois present is only a prelude to a recycled Jeffersonianism, hiding for the moment on the island of Altruria, but potential in America. Altruria is a literary border country that lies between the nineteenth-century city and the eighteenth-century country. Waiting for Mrs. Makely and Mr. Bullion and Professor Lumen and poor confused Mr. Twelvemough is more injustice, machinery, waste, isolation, and decadence; behind them lies human possibility. But somewhere over the rainbow is again the old rural community, a metaphoric country that recalls the American capacity for creativity and self-control, the respect for simplicity, equality, family solidarity, and resourcefulness that got lost on the yellow brick road.

Before Homos returns to utopia, he goes to New York to visit the new friends he met at the hotel. In this portion of the trilogy

63

(published as a whole in 1907), entitled *Through the Eye of the Needle,* the encounters between utopian and capitalist occur in the city, and are described in a series of letters written by Homos to a friend back in Altruria. Social injustice is everywhere apparent. The noise of the elevated train drowns out a mother's last conversation with her dying child; servants carry groceries up the back stairs while their employers ride the elevators; food is wasted at twelve-course Thanksgiving dinners where bored ladies display dresses they will wear only once. As Homos's New York hosts generously display the social rituals of the plutocracy to their genial democratic visitor, they unconsciously reveal their deviations from their principles and traditions.

The epistolary structure here has a nice twist; as readers of the letters, we too are assumed to be Altrurian socialists. American readers had already endured the subject-object experience in the visitors' literature of Tocqueville, Dickens, and Frances Trollope, where the audience watched itself as a curiosity, an amusement, a familiar "other." But this time the correspondent is an agrarian socialist whose naive bewilderment at apartment-house loneliness is normative as well as satirical. In other words, not only do we see ourselves from the outside in order to reevaluate our political choices and social judgment, but also we see that this ridiculous historical moment is part of an inevitable process going back to our political and social roots. This self-reflective narrative thus extends the estrangement effect as we watch our national history move into the future.

Among other things, *Through the Eye of the Needle,* a "study of the plutocratic mind," is Howells's record of his own middle-class and urban ambivalence. Homos wanders amid the haute bourgeoisie of New York, exploring "that measure of loneliness" which Americans' "warped, and stunted, and perverted lives certainly show," observing the "ridiculous contradiction" of thwarted human potential. It is a story not only of progress and poverty but also of isolation within the crowd. Homos begins, "If I spoke with Altrurian breadth of the way New Yorkers live, my dear Cyril, I should begin by saying that the New Yorkers did not live at all" (p. 275). The American community has broken down.

Thus the city of New York determines as well as reflects life in plutocracy, daily reproducing patterns of individualism and isolation. Indeed, in Fredric Jameson's phrase, the city becomes a "sign for the experience of the human community."[11] When Homos searches for his friends in expensive clubs for bored and lonely executives, he recognizes that the American sense of community has also been destroyed for men who advocate competition and individualism. Howell's satire of the bourgeoisie points to what Raymond Williams terms the breakdown of the "knowable community" in the migration from country to city. New York is "unknowable" for Homos partly because of its crowds and its confusing streets. In the city, one is a stranger surrounded by an alien geography and "neighbors" whom one has never met. Homos is also baffled by the jobs he discovers in New York—by the apparent "necessity" of activities that he never even imagined existed.

In New York Homos falls in love with a wealthy widow, Evelith Strange, whom he meets at a formal dinner party. When she first talks with Homos, she confesses that despite her Christian conscience, she has chosen the life of an idle socialite out of frustration at the uselessness of good works. " 'Charity,' " she explains to Homos, " 'is like trying to soak up the drops of a rainstorm.' " But " 'if you think of the misery around you, that must remain around you forever and ever, as long as you live, you have your choice—to go mad, and be put into an asylum, or go mad and devote yourself to society' " (p. 336). Now, feeling guilty and imprisoned in her mansion, Evelith depends on the decadent pleasures of her own class.

Homos soon notices that Evelith suffers from "the essential vice of a system which concenters a human being's thoughts upon his own interests, [and] from the first moment of responsibility, colors and qualifies every motive with egotism. . . . All egotists are unconscious," the argument goes, "for otherwise they would be intolerable to themselves" (p. 334). This view is reminiscent of Bellamy's categories of personal and impersonal characters. It is partly to save her from herself, then, that Homos proposes to marry Evelith and take her to a world without social classes, a world free of the divisiveness that she has internalized. But, she wonders, can she repudiate her class for the green world? And what will she do with her money while she is there? " 'Why,' " she reminds Homos, " 'Tolstoy himself doesn't destroy his money, though he wants other people to do it. His wife keeps it and supports the family' " (p. 358).

In deciding whether or not to renounce her wealth and return with Homos to Altruria, Evelith confronts and overcomes Howells's own ambivalence about class privilege, his own tension between belief and practice. In 1888, Howells wrote to Henry James:

I'm not in very good humor with "America" myself. It seems to be the most grotesquely illogical thing under the sun. . . . After fifty years of optimistic content with "civilization" and its ability to come out all right in the end, I now abhor it, and feel that it is coming out all wrong in the end, unless it bases itself anew on real equality. Meantime, I wear a fur-lined overcoat and live in all the luxury money can buy.[12]

By asserting that human beings have an instinctual drive for equality, Howells goes much further than writers of other utopian novels. Nevertheless, he goes on to argue that this drive could only be satisfied within one's own class:

The patrician wishes to be with his equals because his inferiors make him uneasy; the plebeian wishes to be with his equals because his superiors make him unhappy. . . . Inferiority and superiority were intolerable to men, and so they formed themselves into classes so that inside of these classes they might have the peace, the comfort, of equality; and each kept himself to his own class for that reason.[13]

Which came first? For Howells, it seems as though class originates in class consciousness. In this conflict, Howells, like Evelith, is aware of the parallels with that of Tolstoi, although he feels inadequate to his mentor's decision to put away worldly things. "As much as one merely human being can help another I believe that he [Tolstoi] has helped me; he has not influenced me in aesthetics only, but in ethics too. . . . The way he showed me seemed impossible to my will, but to my conscience it was and is the only possible way."[14] Howells never felt comfortable with his own economic status, and he took the title of the third book of his trilogy from Christ's admonition against personal wealth in the Book of Luke: "How hardly shall they that have riches enter the kingdom

66

of God! For it is easier for a camel to go through a needle's eye than for a rich man to enter the kingdom of God."

While Edward Bellamy leapt over 113 years of history in a single text and landed gently in a socialist technocracy at the edge of the twenty-first century, a small group of Christian reformers which included Joaquin Miller and Mary Agnes Tincker slipped back into the garden to escape the arid mechanization as well as the economic inequalities of industrial life.[15] But unlike the writers of progressive utopias who achieve their political goals in the idealized future, pastoral utopians do not suggest that everyone take up farming. Rather, they repudiate the present, reverse historical time, and attach their desire for an attractive community to an agrarian moment in American history. Descended from classical pastoralism—a literary tradition concerned with the psychological and aesthetic function of rural perfection rather than a description of the rural place itself—the pastoral utopias guide us to a new way of seeing which makes possible the perception of innocence. They actualize the subjective capacities of human character rather than the objective realizations of political tendencies and technological potential.

Protected by artifice, free from historical anxiety, and mimicking the safe consciousness of childhood, travelers to a pastoral utopia can criticize their world from inside the walled garden. Like the valleys of the Renaissance pastoral that stand in contrast to the decadent court, these regressive communities derive their definition from their antithesis, the city. The contemporary world frames or encloses the ideal world; utopia neither succeeds nor replaces reality. Unlike progressive utopias which occupy distant planets or futuristic cities, pastoral utopias can be found on the map. Homos and Evelith flee New York for the Greek island of Altruria; Joaquin Miller's everyman hero abandons Oakland, California, for the City Beautiful in Egypt; and Mary Agnes Tincker's heroine hides from the debased cognocenti of Venice in San Salvador, a secret village in the Pyrenees.

When Homos finally persuades his reluctant bride to leave America, he brings her, with her mother, to the utopian world of first principles where Evelith discovers a rural Jeffersonian federation of small villages, and her wealthy mother discovers that she loves to do the dishes. "You know," Evelith explains in a letter to

67

her American friend, Mrs. Makely, "She was of a simpler day than ours, and when she was young, she used to do her own work, and she and my father always washed the dishes together after they had company. I merely said, 'Well, mother!,' and she laughed and colored and said she guessed she should like it in Altruria, for it took her back to the America she used to know" (p. 383). And as soon as she exchanges her corsets and tight shoes for an Altrurian toga, Evelith proceeds to earn her bread "only in one currency, in the sweat of [her] face" and is immediately delighted with her new feeling of participitation and production. Utopia has given her a second chance. Where Homos learns that in New York an American wins social recognition "upon condition that he has left off working with his hands for a living," Evelith finds that in Altruria utopians seek out tasks that are productive, even in their free time: after farming, the men make shoes, the women sew, collect recipes, and together clean their houses. Shared work is the connective tissue of the utopia. Not only does Evelith no longer feel guilty or indolent or bored, but she also discovers a special link between what she wears, or what she eats, and what she does. Food and clothing are made, used, and occasionally, if there is a surplus, stored or traded. Howells responded to Tolstoi's view of the "divisive and repressive nature of money" by simply eliminating it in Altruria.

A second influence of Tolstoi on Howells was his call for a life "in which the bonds linking man to nature will not be cut, that is, a life under the open sky, in the sunshine and in the fresh air, where one can commune with the earth, with plants and animals."[16] In Altruria, nature represents a balance of the material, social, and spiritual needs of its citizens. Where progressive utopians had a functional view of nature—seeing nature as a resource which human activity could modify, control, and use—the pastoral utopians saw nature as a regenerative garden where the spirit thrives, the mind heals, and the citizens revert to instinctual patterns of human behavior, undeformed by social pressure.

The pastoral utopia frees the human consciousness from society and promises that in a life close to nature, traditional patterns of authority and freedom, work and play, responsibility and self-interest, individuality and community will automatically flower. In *Through the Eye of the Needle* Howells characterizes men and women by their fundamental personality traits, by their relations with each other, and most particularly, by their relations with their natural environment, pushing the narrative toward allegory. In finding a temporary geography of nurturance, repose, and structured permission, the pastoral utopia tends to actualize an illusion of social harmony, eliminating the tensions between the self and the world that so tormented Evelith in New York. Altruria expands on the original pastoral juxtaposition of guileless shepherd and courtier, innocence and experience; it juxtaposes forms of social organization: the image of rural ecology and artisan simplicity is set against the mud, noise, poverty, disorganization, and competition of New York.

Thus in Altruria, nature is not wild, tumultuous, or gothic—nor even particularly romantic. In touring the countryside, Evelith discovers: "The old railroad beds on which we travelled are planted with fruit and nut trees and flowering shrubs, and our progress is through a fragrant bower that is practically endless, except where it takes the shape of a colonnade near the entrance of a village, with vines trained about white pillars and clusters of grapes (which are ripening just now) hanging down" (p. 389). The great outdoors is pruned, controlled, and humanized. Indeed, the Altrurians have even changed their climate by cutting off a peninsula to let a warming current enter a bay.

Unlike Marx, who proclaimed the contemporary "idiocy of rural life," Howells and Gronlund saw agricultural communities as the culmination of the historical drive toward socialism. In 1891, Gronlund argued:

The present relation of city to country is an abnormal one. Every civilized country, with its overgrown cities, may be fairly compared to a man whose belly is steadily increasing in bulk, out of all proportion to the body, and whose legs are constantly growing thinner. This evolution is as yet perfectly legitimate. Our large cities and towns are the necessary fruits of our industrial system, and are destined to become the needed and inevitable centres for the coming changes; in their hands will chiefly lie the threads of destiny. But, then their purpose will have been fulfilled. Then the evolution will necessarily have to go back in the contrary direction. Population will have to take its march back into the country.[17]

Howells in fact abolishes both the country and the city, organizing his island into identical villages that combine the rural values of community and outdoor work with the cultural benefits of towns. Instead of industrial cities, Altruria has many "capitals," accessible civic centers that provide neither housing nor factories but offer instead artistic events and town meetings. The productive life of Altruria takes place in the hamlets, but to prevent the isolation and decay that are also part of American rural life—which he knew all too well as a boy—Howells places a capital within easy reach of every village. These small capitals imitate the participatory values of the countryside. They are the seats of the government, which is directly representative; Evelith must go to her capital not only to vote on all legislation, but also to attend criminal trials in which the public audience decides the verdict.

Robert Hough, along with other critics, has suggested that Howells selected his native Ohio village for the model of his ideal state, and observes that Howells's socialism is "essentially a barn-raising, housewarming kind of cooperation between neighbors."[18] Certainly, Howells applauded Edward Bellamy for recognizing in his own futurist state that Americans are "a village people far more than . . . a city people." He thought that Bellamy correctly appealed to "this average, whose intelligence forms the prosperity of our literature and whose virtue forms the strength of our nation."[19] Although Howells insisted that his utopian models were the family, Christianity, and ancient Greece, his particular brand of socialism depended on his faith in human nature. In a long critique of Social Darwinism, Howells argued against "mistaking our conditions for our natures and saying that human nature is greedy and mean and false and cruel, when only its conditions are so. We say you must change human nature if you wish to have human brotherhood, but we really mean that you must change human conditions, and this is quite feasible."[20] Here he announced that human beings possess an instinctual need for order and an inborn tendency toward cooperation which just might perpetuate the tenuous "balance" of classes and forestall violence. More than technology, monopolization, or equal suffrage, Howells predicted that these human drives would be the real forces for political change and social harmony.

In contrast to America, Altruria respects the helpful, creative, and rational qualities of human nature. Of all the utopian populations in the nineteenth century, only the Altrurians healed the split between what we are and what we make and use, a view of daily life that Howells borrowed from William Morris. Howells found that Morris, unlike Bellamy, asks his reader to "go through the streets of any city and consider the windows of the shops, how they are draped with cheap and vulgar and tawdry gimcracks, which men's lives have been worn in making, and other men's lives in getting money to waste upon, which are finally to be chased out of our houses and swept into our dust bins."[21] Howells credited Morris with showing him how machinery deprived a worker of the right to create useful and beautiful objects slowly and lovingly. After reading Morris, he despaired of a utopia in which the hope of material things "formed the highest appeal to human nature."[22] Seeing the consequences of advanced technology, Howells preferred to do without those "sorry patches on the rags of our outworn civilization . . . toys to amuse our greed and vacancy."[23] Instead, as Evelith writes to Mrs. Makely, the Altrurians "have disused the complicated facilities of the capitalist epoch which we are so proud of, and have got back as close as possible to Nature" (p. 385).

In Altruria, free time, self-direction, and even patriotism ensure that there is not "a furrow driven or a swath mown, not a hammer struck on house or ship, not a temple raised or an engine built" without "an eye to beauty as well as use" (p. 158). Because every worker is an artist in Altruria, vocational categories, along with classes, have disappeared: " 'We do not like to distinguish men by their callings; we do not speak of the poet This, or the shoemaker That, for the poet may very likely be a shoemaker in the obligatories, and the shoemaker a poet in the voluntaries' " (p. 161). Whereas Bellamy's utopians were honored by ribbons, ranks, and distinctions, Altrurians resist specialization; from design to consumption, they restore the unity of work characteristic of artisan life before the Civil War.

As in the United States, life was not always simple in Altruria. During its early Period of Accumulation, Homos explains, the Altrurians " 'continued to live in populous cities; . . . we toiled to heap up riches for the moth to corrupt, and we slaved on in making utterly useless things merely because we had the habit of making them to sell' " (p. 155)—a cycle of production and consumption that tied the island to a profit economy. When the island at last returned to handicraft labor, the Altrurians' needs changed as the distinction between work and art, between work and play, broke down. By the time of Evelith's visit, after the Altrurians finish their daily three hours of farming, after they have made their shoes and cooked and gardened, they sing and dance and write poems. So, in addition to abolishing the scientist and farmer and even the shoemaker, Altrurians have also abolished the "job" of artist, while dedicating their state to the artist's "spirit."

The utopia of radical simplicity seems to have raised fewer fictional problems for Howells than the leap into the year 2000 raised for Bellamy. Because pastoralism is as much about changed consciousness as about rearranged institutions, the narrative is less split than *Looking Backward*. Without futuristic technology, Howells avoids elaborate fictional devices in delivering his characters to utopia; a shipwreck satisfies. As a pastoral society, Altruria is more contained; where technology implies an expansive economy, not likely to be tucked away on an island, in its artisan simplicity Altruria comfortably shares the map of the more or less known world with America and England. To establish the contrast between the utopian and nonutopian world, a simple letter replaces Julian West's confusing nightmare, where neither he nor the reader is quite sure which century he lives in.

Like Bellamy, however, Howells needed two literary styles in which to conceptualize two geographies and two time zones. In describing the Americans—the hotel guests, the nearby farmers, the apartment house residents in New York—Howells reproduces details of posture, motivation, and language in much the same way as in his realistic novels. He continues to be a brilliant ironist. Evelith Strange writes to Mrs. Makely from Altruria:

Do you still keep on murdering and divorcing, and drowning and burning, and mommicking, and maiming people by sea and land? Has there been any war since I left? Is the financial panic as great as ever, and is there much hunger and cold? I know whatever your crimes are, your heroism and martyrdom, your wild generosity and self-devotion, are equal to them. (P. 430)

William Dean Howells and the Pastoral Utopia

With the placid arrogance of the newly converted, Evelith manages to review the great American contradictions and belittle Mrs. Makely with the wonderful pun on the word "equal." At his best, Howells's narrative strategies also mirror his social vision. For example, at the hotel, Homos watches the guests watch the farmers watch a dance through a hotel window—a brilliant image of the perception of social barriers.

In his pictures of New England, Howells also realistically describes village life, including farm mortgages and rents, planting times and mowing times, and neighborhood visits within an economically depressed community. Altruria, by contrast, seems a bit vague—not that Howells intended fully to specify and elaborate an alternative society. But his style changes in describing the homogenized, classless culture of Altruria. The citizens of utopia lack the defining qualities of his Americans—the social location, idiosyncracies of status, and formal versus vernacular language that are the identifying marks of class. Aside from Homos, of whom we see little in Altruria, Howells develops none of the citizens of utopia as characters. Perhaps no more than Bellamy could Howells imagine what a difference utopia might make in the conception of human personality. Thus, the ephemeral quality of Altruria also derives from the difficulty Howells had in imagining the future.

Pastoralism simplifies the author's task of moving from the industrial present to the utopian present, or, if one prefers, from the industrial present to the utopian future, residing, at times, in the past. In *A Traveller from Altruria*, Homos merely describes how the islanders suddenly recognized the possibilities of the ballot and voted to nationalize private industries. In *Through the Eye of the Needle*, where change is more a matter of personal conversion than historical transformation, a series of newcomers simply arrive on the island. When Evelith and her mother return with Homos, a freighter drops them off in Altruria; the Thralls, wealthy American industrialists, land in their shipwrecked yacht; an angry group of American seamen arrive in the ship that brought Evelith and Homos. And for all, the experience of living in rural socialism, if only for a few days, converts them to Altrurianism and they refuse to go home. Thus, the return to an earlier way of life reduces the problem of representing future history. In his utopia, Howells simply destroys contemporary urban life—metaphorically posed, of course, as the Altrurian past. One of

73

the old cities does remain, but it is only open to "antiquarians and moralists" for historical study. The rest of the public is forbidden to enter the "pestilential sites" where "ravening beasts and poisonous reptiles lurk in those abodes of riches and poverty that are now no longer known to our life" (p. 160).

Contemporary readers soon condemned Howells for evading the hard realities of political change. An early reviewer in the *Atlantic Monthly* criticized the "practical infeasibility" of Altruria, although he appreciated that Howells avoided the common errors of other socialists who insisted on the revolutionary role of the working class and who assumed the importance of economic guarantees. Not only, wrote the reviewer, did Howells recognize that social change "will hardly result from a movement on the part of one class, or from a specific measure or plan," but also Howells avoided the socialists' tendency to "look for salvation to a widespread material well-being." Instead, Howells correctly appealed "from the intellectual and from the emotional side."[24] A reviewer for the *Nation* attacked Howells for ignoring the lessons of history and the realities of human nature. He suggested that Howells fashioned Altruria after the early Christian communes, even though they degenerated into individualism as soon as the fear of persecution passed. This reviewer criticized Howells for similarly misreading the human factor in suffrage; in Altruria observed the reviewer, "a proletariat which had long been in the voting majority and had persistently elected corrupt and vicious men to control public affairs, suddenly swung about and elected honest and virtuous men, and kept on electing them till even the most hardened of former oppressors praised God that the old order had passed away forever."[25]

Although Howells was an occasional contributor to the *Critic,* that journal viciously attacked his utopian tales for their democratic assumptions—paradoxically echoing the novelist's own fears of social violence:

Mr. Howells dreams of universal peace and goodwill; the mob does not wish to live in peace with its superiors; it looks forward to their humiliation and is resolved, when the time shall come, to drag them below its own level, and to rule in their stead. . . . Mr. Howells sketches a state of utter degradation from which the brutalized poor rise, almost without transition, to the purest altruism; in reality he would find a storm of carnage and bestiality a hundred times worse than was the Reign of Terror.

William Dean Howells and the Pastoral Utopia

The review also decried as unrealistic Altruria's impossible isolation from the global economic network and outside threats, in language suggesting the nativist themes and xenophobia that dominated imperialist utopias of the McKinley era:

> The Altrurians—who are, it should not be forgotten, the Americans of the future—seem to have no need of foreign trade; they manufacture and grow for themselves everything they need. Living on an island, moreover, they need have no fear of unregenerate-individualistic Cossacks or the swarming millions of China.[26]

Howells's utopia did not challenge or engage the reading public as did Bellamy's. *A Traveller from Altruria* and *Through the Eye of the Needle* launched no programs, newspapers, imitators, or clubs, although they did inspire a certain Edward B. Payne to found a short-lived community named Altruria.[27] Only the liberal *Dial* praised Altruria for its satiric criticisms and admired Howells's artful contrast between American ideals and practice. His utopia "awakens the conscience and sets us upon immediate correction of obvious evils."[28] In tepid praise, the *Dial* reviewer added, "In any case . . . no harm is done, so long as the dream is not seriously regarded as a working program to be carried out in detail."[29]

In the 1930s, however, when critics began to seek out a socialist tradition in American literature, there was a revival of interest in Howells's writings, including the Altrurian romances. Newton Arvin, in his search for a "useable past," said of Howells: "No other native writer of his time was so constantly preoccupied with the question of class, and no other watched so responsibly or so anxiously the sharpening of class lines and the stiffening of class barriers in the world about him."[30]

William Dean Howells, however, did not intend to resolve his conflicts as a "theoretical socialist and a practicing aristocrat" in his utopian romances. *A Traveller from Altruria* and *Through the Eye of the Needle* satirize the present rather than program the future. Even Mr. Twelvemough, the society novelist, discovers that Homos is just a "spiritual solvent" who has visited the United States to "precipitate whatever sincerity there was in us, and to show us what the truth was concerning our relations to each other" (p. 99). Howells's concern was not only to call for the free coinage of silver, to nationalize the railroads, to give women the vote, or to abolish the right to inherit property. He used the utopian perspective to record how urban life and class tensions promote hypocrisy and paralyze the conscience of the middle class. Howells's knowledge of actual social conditions was not extensive. Even as late as 1896, Howells wrote (echoing his own words of a decade earlier), "In a land where journeymen carpenters and plumbers strike for four dollars per day, the sum of hunger and cold is comparatively small, and the wrong from class to class has been almost inappreciable, although all this is changing for the worse." Pain, suffering, and disease, he added, are the "tragedy that comes in the very nature of things, and is not peculiarly American, as the large, cheerful average of health and happy life is."[31] It is not surprising that when the angry and impoverished farmers demand a program for social change, Homos only responds, " 'You must let Altruria come to you' " (p. 177).

Altruria came to Howells from memory and literary tradition rather than from history; he calls Altruria a "retrospective condition" which resides in our capacity to remember and return and begin again. However, this capacity could be tapped for a variety of political intentions in the hands of other writers. Like all pastoral modes, the pastoral utopia does not predetermine a political or moral telos. In *San Salvador* (1892), Mary Agnes Tincker, an author of popular Christian novels, indicts the women's movement for inverting traditional relations between the sexes. Her pastoral utopia offers women a chance to "return" to a world of obedience and maternity.[32] In choosing the green utopia, Tincker's female characters regress to their biological roles: childbearing and mothering preserve order and social stasis. What is "natural" for Tincker is female submission. To Joaquin Miller, California mystic, poet, poseur, and sometime politician, the pastoral utopia protects humanity from its worst self, and the City Beautiful is built on the axiom that "man must be saved from man."[33] A pragmatist and contemporary of William James, Miller designs a hierarchical rural community as a principled experiment and tests it against other planned societies. He discovers that utopianism per se fails, as does any theoretical system, when it does not recognize human variables. Only the pastoral utopia takes human nature into account, by protecting its citizens from economic or political systems that ignore or denigrate life instincts—including aggression.

Pastoral utopians thus conceived of nature in somewhat anthropocentric terms. The political and psychological function of nature is to return significance to practical human activity. As poets had been saying since the time of Wordsworth, nature rather than the city permits men and women to enact finite but concrete endeavors—to transform and be transformed to a degree that is limited but comprehensible. Santayana called the parallel movement in philosophy the "new animism." Because pastoral utopians saw the universe as an experiment, they tended to disregard the political tendencies of nineteenth-century history and began de novo on their islands or deserts or mountaintops. But en route to the garden they borrowed from the new sciences a rational empiricism about evolution, social law, and human nature. Therefore, while cherished fantasies for pastoral life may at first glance represent infantile desires for a world without complication or contradiction—indeed, without change—pastoral utopias do in fact bear a dialectical relationship to the city which they repudiate. By stressing consciousness rather than program, writers of the utopian pastoral challenged the promises of industrialism and natural science and exposed the contradictions in late nineteenth-century urban civilization.

FOUR

Dystopias: Parody and Satire

*A*round the time of the publication of *Looking Backward,* another group of approximately twenty writers responded to the growing social unrest by making a "dystopian" critique of current conditions and utopian solutions.[1] Dystopian fiction, formally and historically, structurally and contextually, is a conservative genre. In the late 1880s and 1890s, dystopias written in the United States formalized a defense of expansionism, nativism, and conservative social patterns through satire of social reform movements and through parody of utopian fiction itself. Using these two modes, parody and satire, dystopias not only attacked the goals of the reformers and mocked the sentiments of *Looking Backward* but also challenged the very experience of hope itself. Like utopian fiction, dystopia is, in the phrase of Louis Marin, an "ideological critique of ideology."[2]

The first dystopian text of this cycle appeared in the United States in 1884, but the movement peaked between 1887 and 1894, a period that coincides with heightened activity in the women's movement around the vote campaign and the eight-hour day issue, the emergence of the Populist party as a national voice for agrarian and monetary reform, the formation of the American Federation of Labor, and the popularity of Edward Bellamy's *Looking Backward.* American dystopias relied for their effect on the reader's recognition of two kinds of parallel phenomena external to the text: liberal reform movements and the popular literary tradition of utopian fiction. Writers of dystopian novels held that, as urbanization and monopolization warped the familiar networks of work, neighborhood, and family, utopian solutions to economic problems undermined traditional notions of personal initiative and private property. Dystopias criticized contemporary calls for reform (whether fictional or social) through the inversion and exaggeration of the familiar structures of progressive utopias, referring to and commenting on the original analogy.

The problem of defining dystopias (sometimes termed "antiutopias" or, more scatalogically, "cacatopias") has provoked considerable critical discussion, occasionally providing fruitful tools for classification, more often adding to the terminological babel of the field.[3] Eric Rabkin provides logical categories by dividing the genre of utopian fiction into *eutopia*—meaning "good place" and *dystopia*—meaning "bad place," depending on whether the author approves or disapproves of the imaginary society. Using this formula to distinguish among projections of the future, Rabkin finds similarities between the eutopias of Edward Bellamy and the dystopias of H. G. Wells: both use narrative techniques of the fantastic and both borrow from current technology.[4] Rabkin, however, fails to delineate the narrative codes that notify the reader of the author's approval or disapproval. What literary devices situate us in the fictive geographies of eutopia or dystopia?

Darko Suvin offers a partial solution to the problem by defining dystopia as a society "less perfect" than the author's own. If utopia represents a "quasi-human community where the sociopolitical institutions, norms, and individual relations are organized on a more perfect principle than in the author's community," then dystopia simply involves changing a perfect principle into a "less perfect principle. Making a community claim to have reached perfection is in the industrial and post-industrial dynamics of society the sure fire way to present us a radically less perfect state."[5] Like Rabkin, Suvin speaks to the dystopia's exaggerations of institutions and social forms; hence his definition also accounts only for the *satiric* elements in a dystopian text—those heightened representations of the future which are obviously less attractive or functional than their nineteenth-century counterpart. Suvin fails to explain *parodic* elements of dystopias, the distorted yet parallel literary structures which remind the reader that utopian fiction itself is under attack.

A definition of dystopia that assumes dual referents—the historical and the literary—also explains the intentionality, or what Claudio Guillén terms the "contract" between writer and reader.[6] How do we know if we are to approve or disapprove of the imaginary society? In nineteenth-century American dystopias we recognize intention first through the perspective of the narrator; second, through the author's ironic stance toward a society inferior to the reader's own; and third, through parody, the exaggeration and reversal of the structures of a closely related genre.[7]

Both utopias and dystopias are extended literary metaphors embodying theories about social change. As narrated histories of the future, they extrapolate events, characters, and attitudes from tendencies observed in contemporary life. The two genres share an antiempiricist use of time and a noncognitive, indeed, a noncommonsense representation of both character development and social evolution, reverting to the *voyage extraordinaire* to avoid historical process. Both borrow from romance the mythic trope of quest and discovery. The dystopian narrative, however, does not contain its own meaning, but instead reproduces the obverse of the author's social intentions, picturing an "ideal" society of entropy and mindless obedience, satiation and decadence, ironically justified as more egalitarian, healthy, and attractive than the present one; the political hypothesis of the alternative society reverses the normative system of the utopian author.

In the late nineteenth century, the dystopian hypothesis was invariably politically conservative, mocking the progressive utopians' promises of sexual and racial equality, collective ownership of property, and humane technology, as well as their basic assumption of individual perfectibility. Furthermore, dystopians turned inside out the literary as well as the social models used by progressive utopians, and reversed the configurations of character and plot as well as the patterns of society that establish the setting. Unlike their utopian cousins, the citizens of dystopia are neither plastic nor perfectible; they are incapable of constructing and enjoying a better world.

Rather than represent the tendencies of capitalism and technology that might contribute to the future good life, dystopians (like pastoral utopians) picture an impending historical collapse, a regression to an era—often conceived in Jeffersonian terms—which is preindustrial, preimmigrant, and preurban. Reversing the central utopian axiom, they assert that American history is not inherently progressive.

Dystopias: Parody and Satire

Approximately twenty popular dystopias appeared in the United States in the last two decades of the nineteenth century. Three examples will demonstrate how dystopias function both satirically and parodically, projecting reality into a metaphoric elsewhere while internally referring to and commenting on utopianism per se: Anna Bowman Dodd's *The Republic of the Future: or, Socialism a Reality* (1887); Arthur Dudley Vinton's *Looking Further Backward* (1890); and Charles Elliot Niswonger's *The Isle of Feminine* (1893).

In *The Republic of the Future*, Anna Dodd mounts a Social Darwinist attack on utopian socialism (such as might be found in Laurence Gronlund's popular utopian-socialist tract, *The Cooperative Commonwealth*, published in 1884). By mocking the utopian conjunction of socialism, feminism, and technology, Dodd anticipates the themes of later dystopias and science fiction. *The Republic of the Future* appeared in 1887, the year of the Haymarket riot and subsequent trial, accompanied by tremendous antisocialist propaganda in party platforms and the press.

Reversing the narrative pattern of utopian fiction in which the reader follows the social indoctrination of an ingenuous visitor, Dodd's cynical narrator refuses to be reconciled to the new society and maintains his political and aesthetic isolation, often by force. In the year 2050 A.D. Wolfgang, a nobleman from the capitalist state of Sweden, travels to New York Socialist City in a submarine pneumatic tube; we read his letters to Hannewig, a friend back home. In adopting an epistolary form, Dodd resolves unique problems of perspective for the dystopia. By moving geographically rather than temporally, and by making Sweden resemble the reader's familiar present while the "future" develops in the United States, Dodd avoids a common dilemma of utopian and dystopian fiction: the narrational illogicalities caused by contrasting present and future. With this narrative device she compares political decisions with their eventual historical consequences. Through the letter form she establishes a fictional reader, Hannewig, who shares the beliefs of the text's assumed empirical reader: both live under capitalism and thus share common criteria with which to measure the new state.

Wolfgang begins with a catalogue of mechanical gimmicks rather than an analysis of the political innovations he finds in the

81

new country, establishing early on a position of objectivity. He is merely an observant tourist charmed by the air balloon which has carried him to his hotel, where he registered as a guest from the window of his floating omnibus (a futurist prediction of drive-through facilities which startled modern audiences when Julie Christie and George C. Scott checked into a motel in the 1968 film *Petulia* without getting out of her Porsche). The first-person narrator leaps the cognitive hurdles of this futurist genre; the narrator is not the time-bound author. By simply dating the first letter "December 1, 2050 A.D.," Dodd avoids an immediate explanation of how the transition from capitalism to socialism was accomplished. Other literary devices help to establish the *in medias res* effect. The first letter begins:

At last, as you see, my journey is safely accomplished, and I am fairly landed in the midst of this strange socialist society. To say that I was landed, is to make use of so obsolete an expression that it must entirely fail to convey to you a true idea of the processes of the journey. Had I written—I was safely *shot* into the country—this would much more graphically describe to you the method of my arrival.[8]

Wolfgang's reference to the anachronistic language of the past confirms that he is indeed in the future. His unfamiliar pseudo-scientific terms, such as the Pneumatic Tube Electric Company, further support the illusion of the future and transport us to the world of "the uncanny," the world that might someday be.[9]

Wolfgang's deadpan descriptions of his trip under the sea also immediately establish Dodd's ironic perspective:

Beyond all else, however, in point of interest, was the spectacle of the wholesale cannibalism going on among the finny tribes, a cannibalism which still exists, in spite of the persistent and unwearying exertions of the numerous Societies for the Prevention of Cruelty among Cetacea and Crustacea. . . . A Sub-marine missionary who chanced to sit next to me, told me that of all vertebrate or invertebrate animals, the fish is the least amenable to reformatory discipline.[10]

The narrator's comic disdain at fish cannibalism and the reference to submarine missionaries confirms Wolfgang's comparative rationality and parodies the utopian project of global improvement, while seriously introducing the dystopian commitment to a laissez-faire approach to social and economic relations. Despite mankind's zealous pretensions to "reformatory discipline," the creatures of nature resist human interference. Dodd's message is that New York Socialist City has been foolish at best to assume the perfectibility of any species and to interfere with competition between the "tribes"—ideas that provided a central rationale for early imperialistic policies as well as for maintaining the economic status quo in the United States.

Wolfgang's travels confirm his suspicions about the new state. Dodd mocks what she takes to be the central criteria of socialism: uniformity and utilitarianism. Not only has the Hudson River been filled in with apartment houses and office buildings, but also Wolfgang notices that "each house is precisely like its neighbor; each house has so many rooms, so many windows, so many square feet of garden, which latter no one cultivates, as flowers and grass entail a certain amount of manual labor, which, it appears, is thought to be degrading by these socialists."[11] Economic equality has forged a tedious society: "The result of the plan on which this socialist city has been built, comes, of course from the principle which has decreed that no man can have any finer house or better interior or finer clothier than his neighbor."[12] Socialism has homogenized the culture.

In a world of automatic elevators and mechanical bedmakers, Wolfgang finds a terrifying social anomie and writes Hannewig that abundant technology and a facile satiation of physical desire have produced citizens "who wander about with hands in pockets, on the lookout for something that never happens."[13] The New Yorkers have even abolished food. Rather than cook, they fill prescriptions for bottled pellets of food substitutes delivered regularly in the "culinary conduits" that run through the city. Meanwhile, the women send their children to day-care centers. And persuaded by the demands of the women's movement, long and elaborate meals, servants, even flirtation, have been abolished in utopia. Indeed, in the largest vote recorded in the city, socialist women outlawed art until mechanical dusters for ornate picture frames could be invented. As technology fulfilled the socialists' demands for a two-hour work day, people began to die for want of hard labor. Others spent their new leisure "drifting aimlessly into theaters, museums and clubs."[14] Lassitude and equal rights even molded men and women "into two men" with many identical features—such as "weak" receding chins.[15]

Dodd feared that her imperfect citizens could not control the new technology. Historians such as David Noble observe that by the mid-1890s, instead of solving problems, technology in the United States had come to reinforce the existing social order, particularly in industries where a "systematic introduction of science as a means of production presupposed, and in turn reinforced, industrial monopoly. This monopoly meant control, not simply of markets and productive plants and equipment but of science itself."[16] Industrialism had eagerly absorbed new scientific developments in the process of creating new technologies and new investments. While even progressive utopians such as Bellamy recognized that technological change could also undermine the social order, the nineteenth-century optimistic view was that labor-saving and socially integrated technologies held out the promise of a society not marked by overproduction, wasteful competition, mindless labor, or physical drudgery.

But for Anna Dodd, technology is a metaphor that articulates her fear of socialism. Inverting the conventional picture of the utopian future, she projects how machinery, designed and produced under the socialist slogan, "By the people for the People,"[17] develops its own volition and transforms people into passive machine tenders. In New York Socialist City scientists have become dictators who destroy human individuality and idiosyncrasy by enforcing identical standards for houses, clothing, and meals. And what is worse to Wolfgang, in supplying all New Yorkers with the same share of money and food, the new technological society has destroyed competition and personal initiative. The imaginary city depends on the machine and the machine replaces the individual. Soon Wolfgang is distressed to hear himself asking robots for things he does not want. Technology, he observes, has "defied" the laws of evolution that are meant to perpetuate inequality and struggle. Restless and bored, he concludes that the old struggle for survival was better than the new curiosities. Where progressive utopians foresaw the possibility of humane technology and described the benefits of clean urban transportation, dishwashers, and birth control, Dodd predicted only nihilism and decay. Observing a life without tragedy or conflict—similar to Bellamy's controlled future—Wolfgang finds that "because they live without competition, indeed without fear, [the New Yorkers] have the look of people who have come to the end of things, and who failed to find it amusing." He concedes that socialism limits frustrations but he wonders, "What can happen after the consummation of all dreams and desires?"[18]

Thus while utopias neutralized political anxiety by representing easy roads to change, nineteenth-century dystopias stimulated political anxiety by representing the risks of change. Like Bellamy, Dodd recalls the phantoms of the historical present. But rather than comfort her readers by picturing an imaginary resolution to current problems, Dodd reminds them of the dangers of contemporary solutions offered by an imaginary coalition of German, Irish, and Russian socialists and anarchists, "the foreign elements . . . who had imported their revolutionary doctrines with them."[19] She describes the "War of Blood" over property that broke out in 1900 as a result of Henry George's critique of the unequal distribution of land. When the "communards," poor soldiers that they were, realized that they would lose in a conventional battle, they leveled the city with explosives and seized control of the government. The new revolutionary government spawned New York Socialist City, enshrining Henry George in the Temple of Liberators. And the revolution is celebrated with an annual sacred reading of George's *Progress and Poverty*. Unlike Bellamy, who optimistically discovered progressive tendencies in contemporary economic movements (even in monopolies), Dodd disdains the imminent future. In *The Republic of the Future* historical process becomes the negation of the utopian negation of current problems through the inversions of literary parody.

Fredric Jameson notes that "anti-utopianism constitutes a . . . decodable and unambiguous position. . . . The enemies of Utopia sooner or later turn out to be the enemies of socialism." He also observes that the "play of topical allusion is structurally indispensable in the constitution of the Utopian text as such and provides one of the distinctive traits necessary if we are to mark the utopia off from its generic neighbors in the realm of fantasy or idyll." In utopian fiction, contemporary reality is not just an "image . . . but rather something borne within and vehiculed by the text itself."[20]

Like Suvin, Jameson refers to the satiric function of dystopias—historicism within the text makes a statement about the world outside the text. Dystopia, like satire and utopia, relies on the readers' recognition of "indispensable" parallels between history and text; Dodd's revolution, for example, should be read as a thinly disguised metaphor for the anarchist riots in Chicago in 1887. Nevertheless, the fiction that mediates history as well as history itself is an implied structure in the dystopian text. Dystopia refers to utopia as well as to history; and in the late nineteenth century the subgenre grew quickly after the publication of *Looking Backward* in 1888.

In *Looking Further Backward* (1890) Arthur Vinton used Bellamy's narrative frame to warn readers of the dangers of the new ethnic composition of the American working class. Vinton availed himself of the very characters and setting of *Looking Backward* to "predict" the consequences of recent Chinese and Eastern European immigration, thereby playing on nativist fears while also attacking utopian socialism. Vinton's tale shows how the parodic supports the satiric function of dystopia.

The primary topical allusion in *Looking Further Backward* is immigration. During the economic panic of 1873, with thousands of people unemployed, American railroads encouraged the immigration of 150,000 Asians to serve as low-paid laborers. That summer there were anti-Chinese riots. These in turn provoked anti-Chinese legislation as well as a wave of popular literature and cartoons that depicted the immigrants as drunken strikebreakers who reduced American living standards, and worst of all, who bred in greater numbers than Anglo-Americans. Within a few years reform movements also reflected these prejudices. The American Federation of Labor in effect excluded blacks and Chinese by admitting only skilled workers. Similarly, after the Supreme Court granted the vote to "male citizens of African descent" in 1868, the women's suffrage movement divided on the race issue, with a large faction pushing the vote for white women ahead of more broadly democratic goals: black women were even segregated from whites in suffrage parades.[21] Meanwhile, the popularized versions of Darwin's theories of evolution claimed that a divine purpose sanctioned the triumph of the "higher" races. A prominent minister, Josiah Strong, even urged American missionaries to remain in the cities in the United States rather than going afield, because "our safety demands the assimilation of these strange populations."[22]

This nativist sentiment organizes the fable and manifesto, the narrative pattern, and the political critique of Vinton's *Looking Further Backward*. It is now the year 2023 and Julian West, Bellamy's traveler from the nineteenth century, has resided quite miserably in Boston since the close of *Looking Backward*. Nationalism, he has discovered, has not worked out as Doctor Leete had promised. The trusting socialists have naively welcomed immigrants, have foolishly encouraged women's equality, and most seriously, have abolished the standing army. Instead of bringing progress, Bellamy's policies have created a decadent and pacifist state controlled by bureaucracies of frivolous women. China has invaded the United States, demanding $100 million in ransom. When the Chinese generals refuse to accept the Nationalist credit cards, a currency based on the labor theory of value, Boston surrenders. The New Yorkers, however, rebel and the Chinese bomb Manhattan, killing four million people. But the ultimate Chinese plan is to "subjugate through numbers"; they round up and manacle several thousand Bostonians whom they ship to slave camps, while they import an equal number of "fertile" Chinese men to repopulate th⌐ United States. Within the year New England is renamed "the North Eastern Divison of the Chinese Province of North America."

Julian, who has become a professor of American history in the Nationalist State University, is replaced by General Wong Lung Li, the narrator. The novel is comprised of a series of lectures to Julian's former history class reviewing the progress of the Chinese invasion. The history professor/dictator as narrator provides an ironic perspective on the economic and military vulnerability of Nationalism, a narrative perspective that establishes the reader as an uninformed student. The format of the history lecture justifies the recounting of the invasion, and Li's political position justifies his analysis. He begins the first lecture by calmly announcing, "I come before you as a stranger . . . an instructor placed over you by force of arms . . . a director of your thoughts. . . . I have come to endow you with the glorious civilization of China."[23]

As a professor and conqueror, Li has special access to historical information. Yet his dictatorial references and tone immediately warn us that his stance is dangerous. His unreliability as narrator contributes to the genre's unusual demands regarding point of view. This complex narrative perspective gives Vinton three vantage points from which to justify his attack on socialism: the colonized present, the recent socialist past, and the earlier capitalist era before Julian's original nap (the assumed reader's actual historical moment).

The fable also unfolds in Li's lectures, for he has discovered his predecessor's diary, which he reads to the class. In Julian's diary, he alone recognizes the threat of the Chinese invasion and delves into his Victorian soul to recover lost skills of self-reliance with which to defend himself and his family. Unlike Julian, his Nationalist wife and children naively depend on the protection of the government and refuse to act on their own behalf. The diary reveals how Julian finally persuades his family of their danger and arranges for them to flee from Boston in an abandoned railroad handcar. Vinton's tale inverts the story of Julian's first initiation in *Looking Backward* when he transcends the individualist values of the nineteenth century and repudiates capitalism.

The Victorian aristocrat who awoke after a century's sleep to Bellamy's utopia is in Vinton's novel the only American capable of critical thinking and resistance.[24] Rather than guilelessly accept Nationalism, Julian rediscovers his old laissez-faire principles: "I have instinctively turned to the remembrance of those earlier days of my life, when it was everyone for himself, and when men, knowing this, looked to their own ability, and never thought of casting responsibility for personal success or safety on a paternal government."[25] But in their flight from utopia, the Wests discover that socialism has indoctrinated the people in passivity and obedience. Julian cannot escape with his children without getting a note from their teacher. While he retrieves his hoard of nineteenth-century gold to help in his escape, docile socialist railroad workers obediently transport arms and gunpowder to the Chinese. Julian's difficulty in rousing his family and neighbors points to Vinton's main objection to Nationalism: its axiomatic faith in self-reliance and the benevolence of human nature.

Determined to raise an army of resistance, Julian visits the nation's president who is suffering from nervous paralysis, tormented by dreams that Nationalism has destroyed his ability to act. In dystopian fiction the hero either arrives straight from capitalism or he anachronistically holds nineteenth-century values. This Julian, unlike Bellamy's naive visitor who thirsts for indoctrination, retains his critical capacities. He alone can lead the new army.

Rather than a troubled seeker or initiate, the visitor to dystopia is often himself the savior of those in the new country. Moreover, Julian's preservation from the perils of socialism bears visible parallels to Christian salvation. A member of an aristocratic and religious minority, a conservative rebel, an atavistic hero who leads the attack on progress, Julian represents the "saving remnant." In flight from Boston along the deserted railroad, he recalls "another flight more than two thousand years ago when another father and mother fled under their dim light to save their offspring."[26] Vinton implies that the only hope for humanity lies with a wealthy, conservative, and godly minority. As in many dystopias, the hero dies in an apocalyptic contest, leading the one major battle against the Chinese.

Wong Lung Li explains that Nationalism destroyed the possibility for resistance to invasion by repressing its citizens' involvement in and criticism of their government. Nationalist newspapers, for example, financed by subscription rather than advertisements, eliminated articles critical of the government that might offend patriotic subscribers. Citizens had passively accepted an oversized government ruled by "gossiping women." But as each of the coastal states falls to the Chinese and the socialists' economic controls lapse, capitalism automatically reappears. After the Chinese abolish the credit card system described by Bellamy, a barter economy develops, soon replaced by paper currency, profits, and private property. The lazy, the indigent, and those who somehow fail to accumulate property give Christians the chance to be charitable again. Workers meanwhile turn to their employers rather than to the state for their wages. The story ends with a warning in the final passage from Julian's diary: the Chinese have gained control of all but a small area of the midwest, and the hero predicts that "it's just a question of time till they close in."

Looking Further Backward also contains an antifeminist message. In contrast to the male hero's instinct for capitalism, females in American dystopias easily succumb to socialism's temptations.

By caricaturing women and by showing the dismal consequences of female rule, Vinton parodies Bellamy's promise of women's equality. This view is characteristic; many dystopians predict that the utopian projection of feminism would destroy the family, the democratic system, and those "enticing" differences in human character between the sexes. Based on exaggerated and contradictory literary stereotypes of women, the female citizens of dystopia are passive/aggressive, intuitive/logical, possessive/self-sacrificing, materialistic/spiritual, frigid/lustful. The norm is male.[27] Dystopian authors are particularly susceptible to images that characterize women in extreme terms because parody, a basic component of the dystopian novel, is based on overstatement.

Writers of futurist fiction were in the unique situation of portraying women for whom there were few accessible models in literature or life; in the United States in the 1880s and 1890s there were few women who were allowed to play the political roles caricatured by the dystopians.[28] And without a concept or image of the totality of a female character with intellectual, financial, political, sexual *and* domestic concerns, these authors divided the woman's personality allegorically among a number of women; consequently, there are often more female than male characters in both utopian and dystopian fiction.[29] Indeed, dystopian authors often went further than Bellamy and his disciples in facing the social and psychological implications of the women's movement. To the writer of dystopian fiction, who reflected prevailing values of the time, female industrialists and politicians not only threatened male supremacy but defied their biological role as well. The literature of the Gilded Age defined the male hero by his relationship to the worlds of business, society, and nature, and defined a woman by her relationship to men—as mother, wife, daughter, or mistress. Nineteenth-century culture tended to idealize the family (the world of women) as a retreat from the tense world of politics or business, rather than its mirror. Perhaps the snide tone of dystopian authors regarding feminism reveals an awareness of the potential social consequences of the suffrage movement, the labor movement in which women played a role, the new women's colleges, and the outspoken sexual demands of Victoria Woodhull, even fear that the stereotype of the domestic and passive woman might perhaps become extinct.

90

Dystopias: Parody and Satire

In Dodd's *The Republic of the Future* Wolfgang learns that in socialist New York women are engineers, firefighters, and mechanics who give their babies to the state to raise. "All family life has died out," although children are allowed to spend Christmas day with their parents. Gender education begins early, undermining what Wolfgang sees as the basic drives of human biology: the girls get whips and the boys get dolls for Christmas. Wolfgang also notices a "decay of erotic sentiment" which he traces to women's refusal to wear corsets, to be contained by bustle and bust. Even socialist men are not attracted to unchaperoned women who roam the streets of New York in baggy trousers, women who are neither wives nor mothers. Enforced "equality" between the sexes has begat the same conformity as economic sharing and mechanization: "Husband and wife are in reality two men having equal rights, with the same range of occupation, the same duties as citizens to perform, the same haunts and the same dreary leisure."[30] Not only does Wolfgang defend the idea of segregating the world of men from that of women (although admitting that the realm of masculine activity is a crowded if somewhat boring corner), but he also assumes that sexual attraction depends on an inferior and confined place for women. He sarcastically concludes, "The perfecting of the women's movement was retarded for hundreds of years, as you know, doubtless, by the slavish desire of women to please their husbands by dressing and cooking to suit them."[31] Women prefer subservience, he is convinced. Despite the new state's insistence on sexual equality, what Wolfgang takes to be natural female inferiority has also destroyed traditional patterns of international diplomacy. After women received the vote, they outlawed war, not for moral or pacifist reasons but simply because women made poor soldiers. Foreign statesmen refuse to negotiate with women diplomats who "still got the best of men with their tempers." Dodd's misogynistic humor underscores the tension of a culture facing serious changes; women's hidden economic value and political power were becoming increasingly apparent as they left the home for the factory and the office.

Arthur Vinton similarly linked feminism and socialism in analyzing the perils of Bellamy's state. We recall that in Bellamy's utopia, Edith is a gentle yet clear spokeswoman for the sexual and

91

economic rights of women in the new society. She not only persuades Julian of the benefits of central kitchens and dishwashers
and the righteousness of wages for housework, but also through
their verbose romance she describes the psychological and genetic
advantages of having women freely choose their mates. When
Edith is reincarnated in *Looking Further Backward,* however, she is
the easy dupe of the state. Despite the nation's unheroic surrender
to the Chinese, Edith blindly trusts the government's capacity to
protect her and she refuses to help Julian plan their escape. With
frustration, Julian finds that although Edith is "physically and intel-
lectually his inferior" she wants him to postpone military action
against the Chinese until American women are drafted. Julian
hopes that when capitalism reemerges in the future, woman "who
had been most unduly exalted under the Nationalist idea, to
equality with man, would sink to the proper state of subordination
and then another element of danger would be eliminated."[32]

The misogynistic rhetoric is more sexual in Charles Elliot Niswonger's dystopia *The Isle of Feminine* (1893), which presents a
parodic form of feminism on an imaginary Caribbean island ruled
by women. By designing a pastoral matriarchy, Niswonger avoids
describing the industrial consequences of female rule, but he
nonetheless proclaims that giving women power in any society
would be disastrous for men. The narrator, Andrew Lowe, is a
New York stockbroker who is shipwrecked on the remote Isle of
Feminine. Young, cynical, and delighting in his own prowess and
bravado, he believes that he has landed in a paradise of maids
until he discovers the men—dwarfed slaves, symbolically cas-
trated and terrorized by a junta of asexual virgins: "Each man's
face wore the stamp of servitude and degradation. I shuddered that
the estate of man should have grown so lowly even in this unknown land."[33] Soon Andy, having become just another man of
"disgusting insignificance," learns to eat, sleep, and speak at the
commands of women.

The perpetuation of female power on the Isle of Feminine hinges
on the women's rejection of sexual intercourse, which confirms the
perversity of female rule. (In two major feminist utopias of this period, *Mizora: A Prophecy* [1889] by Mary Lane, and *Herland* [1915]
by Charlotte Perkins Gilman, chastity is seen as a refuge both from
male-dominated sexuality and from the pain of childbirth. See

chapter 7.) But the island community cannot sustain itself once the virgins find themselves sexually attracted to their American visitor. Rather than become an initiate in matriarchy, Andy teaches Queen Diana, the island's immortal dictator, the principles of democracy, the theology of Protestantism, and the benefits of male domination. In the land he comes from, he tells the queen, "man is superior to woman in intellect and wisdom, and in pity of her weakness is ever pleasing her with pretty sayings."[34] Meanwhile Andy tempts Diana with his sexual charms, and persuades her to exchange her power, beauty, and immortality for eternal Protestant life. And earthly passion. Overwhelmed by Andy's appeal, Diana embraces the New Yorker and immediately her "once heavenly face was shrunken and made hideous by the wrinkles of three thousand years."[35] When the virgins attack Andy for destroying their queen, he carries his favorite maiden, Princess Vesta, to the safety of his old boat; while they enjoy their first kiss, the island disappears. Niswonger has neutralized his fear-attraction to the female ruler, the powerful mother figure, through allegorical destruction.

Dystopian fiction intends a warning. By inverting the progressive utopian's attitude toward time and history, these tales reverse utopian assumptions about the configuration of the future. The significant absence in dystopian literature is a silence regarding history itself, not only the particular reform struggles current in the late nineteenth century or the details of industrial poverty, but also the imminently progressive tendencies of capitalism: the development of technology, the changes in traditional gender roles, and the organization of a conscious working class. While progressive utopias struggle with elaborate literary gimmicks to move history into the future, dystopias end in violent social cataclysms which return America to its presocialist and prefeminist past. These tales climax in cyclic reversals which warn readers of the militant potential of a deprived working class confused by the temptations of socialism, feminism, and new technology. Anna Dodd predicts a scorching battle between "republicans" and "the foreign element" who blow up the urban centers. Arthur Vinton portrays a class and race war in New York as an anticollectivist and anti-Chinese reaction. Perhaps the heaviest dystopian revenge is saved for the land ruled by women: in Niswonger's apocalyptic ending, the princesses get wrinkles while the island sinks into the sea. Apocalypse in dystopia transforms the wish-fulfillment aspect of utopia. The final vision confirms the extended image of a society in which working people are incapable of rationally participating in democratic processes or controlling technological growth. The violent endings of these novels reverse the utopian expectation of a culture (and a narrative) that can persist without development.

Dystopias wrest the present from the future. By the late nineteenth century, dystopian authors were unable to reconcile the idea of industrial technology which is imminently progressive with their reactive and cyclical view of history. The real subject matter of dystopia is the phenomenon of utopianism itself, its literary and political assertion that we can conceive of a future different from and better than the present.

FIVE

Conservative Utopias:
The Future Moves Toward
the Present in Righteous Dominion

"We are living in Utopia; the only Utopia there is or can be; we have gradually conquered the promised land. It is bounded by Magna Carta in the rear, by Invention and Ability on the flanks, and by Evolution in front."[1] With this cheerful diagnosis, David Hinton Wheeler surveyed the borders of *Our Industrial Utopia* (1895), one of the group of conservative utopias that borrowed the format of the progressive utopian apologue to fantasize about the perfection of the already existing order—utopia looks rather like the United States in the 1890s.[2] This minor variant of utopian fiction hinges on an artful job of definition: conservative utopians simply described current relations between capital and labor, men and women, native-born and immigrant, the United States and Latin America, and pushed them along into the twentieth century, there to call them "utopian." As Wheeler explained, Americans were already living in utopia.

But although writers of conservative utopias described contemporary social and economic patterns and saw that they were good, conceptual and narrative problems remained. If Wheeler was already living in utopia, how could he explain the widespread dissatisfaction manifest in his society? How was he to arrest progress, that deus ex machina which had already delivered such a delicious present and which promised so much more of the same? The benefits of evolution, Wheeler pledged, are still ahead, yet they are also here and now. Conservative utopians' commitment to the status quo seemed to foreclose the front gate of history.

95

The Utopian Novel in America

The very intention of conservative utopianism is a contradiction in terms, for who would fantasize about an alternative world when the familiar society itself is virtually perfect? Conservative utopians beg this question and draw up blueprints for the future that generate unwittingly comic tautologies as they evade such current paradoxes as the simultaneous expansion of capitalism and the rise of poverty. Although they do not ignore the restless anger of the 1890s, they reiterate two familiar solutions to the crises of the decade: first, business, unfettered by high tariffs and expensive labor costs, will in due time guarantee prosperity; and, second, the United States will fulfill its racial birthright by supervising the economic development of the Western hemisphere, while at the same time protecting the domestic economy through developing trade, gaining access to global resources, and making large investments in military spending.[3] America-as-utopia simply stops the clock, preserving fin de siècle policies of fiscal expansion and racial dominance. Removing the *ou* (nonexistence) from the utopian pun, authors of conservative utopias define the United States as the best of all possible worlds—in fact, the only possible world.

Rather than occupy the future, the United States, along with its Anglo-utopian allies, Canada and Great Britain, occupies the world, extending the borders of utopia to include Mexico, Africa, Asia, and (just a bit more gingerly) Jupiter and Saturn. Utopian growth appears in space rather than in time. If Edward Bellamy and other progressive utopians looked to the latent socialistic possibilities in industry, monopoly, and the reform movements for clues to the future, the conservative utopians sought in much the same places justifications for the spread of capitalism.[4]

Ernest Tuveson has observed that the United States' role as "redeemer nation" is not so much an apocalyptic prophecy as it is an expression of a "nationalistic theology" which holds that in any given period one nation or people will exercise the *imperium* of civilization, culturally and politically. As early as the mid-seventeenth century, Tuveson argues, American colonization was more than the "pious Errand into this Wilderness"; the settlers, he suggests, took the ideological "next step beyond Reformation . . . the actual reign of the spirit of Christ, the amalgamation of the City of the World into the City of God."[5] By the late 1760s, as a result of the nascent nationalism following the French and Indian wars, William Bradford's notion of the colonies as the New Zion for the chosen people had evolved into the notion of a country destined to regenerate the world. Tuveson traces the emerging myth of manifest destiny—the notion that God had assigned the United States dominion over most of the North American continent—to the early writings of John Adams and Timothy Dwight, where images of conquest and empire reflect the sway of a blessed people over great and wealthy territories. This was not the agrarian, limited utopia of the Jeffersonians.[6]

When the phrase "manifest destiny" first appeared around 1845, it represented an ideology which had developed over two centuries, a millennial tradition that defined the purposes and growth of the new nation. After the Civil War, the myth took on an expansionist tone. In his centennial sermon in 1890, Protestant minister Washington Gladden, a founder of the "social gospel" movement, announced that American history was working out God's eternal plan, which included westward expansion as a central element. By the 1890s, the nation's manifest destiny was engendering "a kind of righteous dominion over the entire world, in which the political would be mixed with spiritual and moral elements. . . . This expectation of empire was part of an ideal of world regeneration."[7] "Righteous dominion" would take the form of material assistance, pacification programs, missionary activities, and repopulation schemes. Implicit in the political theology of manifest destiny, then, is the utopian assumption that America had already begun to realize the promise of the golden age.

In the 1890s, to conceive of America as utopia was simply (and tautologically) to argue that the nation's social and economic institutions were appropriate and immutable because they fulfilled the nation's moral function—designated, to be sure, by these same efficient institutions. History disappears in an ontological defense of the status quo: perfection merely requires the maintenance of contemporary conditions in perpetuity. This presumption of the "present perfect" underlies the aggressive tone and the exaggerated quality of these often bizarre texts. By ignoring such social realities as poverty-level wages, tenement housing, and child labor, conservative utopians were free to extend the munificent present into the inevitable future. Looking backward from the twentieth century, they explained how the nation, the planet, and sometimes even the galaxy prospered because capitalism benevolently tended the welfare of the state. In turn, the state gratefully reciprocated by satisfying the needs of business. In the utopian twentieth century, the government underwrites private property and provides new markets and sources for raw materials in the West and overseas. After the workers discover that profits are the shared goal of labor and capital, they encourage the federal government to boost the economy along by drafting antiunion legislation and arresting strikers—often designated as the "foreign element." Since not much needs to happen in Genesis, the new society is born quickly; usually less than a century passes between the time of composition and the moment described in utopia.

This mode is "conservative" because its predictions are merely extensions of a growing practice in American polity, developing coalitions between government and industry. During the long period of falling prices in the 1880s and early 1890s, American industries sustained the momentum of post–Civil War growth by forging close bonds with the federal government. In response to growing tensions between labor and capital, an alliance between the private and public sectors—legislative, judicial, and even military—brought about industrial stability, creating what Gabriel Kolko terms "political capitalism."[8] In 1877, for example, responding to urgent appeals from railroad magnates, President Rutherford B. Hayes ordered the army to run the trains in order to halt a strike on the Baltimore and Ohio line which had spread to the railroad yards in Philadelphia, Pittsburgh, Chicago, and San Francisco.

Industrialists also sought government assistance in developing overseas trade, arguing that only the expansion of capital would protect jobs and promote prosperity. As early as 1863, Secretary of State William Seward predicted that the United States would always need to add territories for investment and trade. To protect the economy he would make America "the master of the world." But three decades later, when Frederick Jackson Turner "closed" the continental frontier at the American Historical Association meeting in Chicago (1893), investors saw that the United States still trailed behind France and Great Britain in the race for colonies. This provides the theme of a utopian novel written by Arthur

98

Bird, the U.S. vice-consul general in Haiti. In a renovated version of the Monroe Doctrine, Bird predicted in *Looking Forward: A Dream of the United States of America in 1999*:

The Stars and Stripes which never knew, nor ever will know defeat, will, in years to come, gather under its protected folds, every nation and every island in this hemisphere. . . . Our glorious starry banner will rule the entire Western Hemisphere. It will be the emblem of Peace, Liberty, and Civilization, floating over a United America from Alaska to Patagonia. This is America's destiny.[9]

How to achieve the rule of the starry banner was another issue facing utopian planners. One strategy was to pursue England's "spheres of influence" policy which divided the globe among the industrial nations. In Henry Everett's utopia *The People's Program: The Twentieth Century Is Theirs* (1892), the president of the United States announces: "It's my purpose . . . to give the Emperor of Germany absolute power to suppress all war-like difficulties in Africa, and to the Czar of Russia the same power in Asia, while I expect to secure for the President of the United States dictatorship in case of war in either of the American continents. The Queen or King of England is to receive even more extensive dictatorship."[10] Other conservative utopians pictured Europe as old, corrupt, and unworthy, and preferred William McKinley's "open door" policy in which the United States would compete with other industrial nations for new markets and raw materials— an agenda consistent with the tenets if not the practice of laissez-faire economics. Despite such initiatives as the National Association of Manufacturers' opening warehouses in Asia and Latin America, an economic slump persisted throughout the 1880s, encouraging American businessmen to seek a more expansionist foreign policy in the 1890s. In 1897, in response to the Spanish invasion of Cuba, the United States army intervened, partly to protect American investments on the island. The new military expenditures revived the U.S. economy and meanwhile stimulated a rush for colonies—a drive predicted in conservative utopias. Through the terms of the peace treaty negotiated with Spain, America acquired the Philippines in 1898, and annexed Hawaii and Puerto Rico that same year.

The Utopian Novel in America

Although, as McKinley's naval adviser Alfred Thayer Mahon had observed, the morality of expansion was "as little to the point as the morality of an earthquake,"[11] elaborate rationalizations for the American prerogative soon appeared. Josiah Strong, a well-known Congregationalist minister, announced that God had chosen the United States to civilize new territories: "It would seem as if these inferior tribes were only precursers of a superior race, voices in the wilderness crying, 'Prepare ye the way of the Lord.' "[12] In addition to utopian novels, the popular press—in the western novel and in humorous journalism—also justified the righteousness of America's purpose in terms of racial hierarchies. Typically, Asia, Africa, and Latin America were portrayed as "savage" or "barbarian" whereas the United States, Germany, and England were "civilized." In between were the "semicivilized" states—Turkey, China, and India—which were subject either to American or British dominion. In *Looking Forward* (1899), Arthur Bird added sexual rhetoric to notions of racial essentialism in order to defend England's conquest of "those semi-civilized and blood thirsty Turks, with a hideous history drenched in blood, champions of lust and rapine, oppressors of Armenia and violators of chastity."[13]

Hierarchies were not only natural and inevitable but also worthy of perpetuating in the twentieth century. In Amos Fiske's *Beyond the Bourne* (1891) a passenger killed in a train accident reappears, albeit "transubstantiated," in the angels' suburbs on the outskirts of heaven. To his surprise, he discovers that although the Eternal Spirit has given the angels airplanes and solar energy, "working in material substance toward its desired end,"[14] class distinctions are still maintained among them. When the disillusioned traveler wonders why God allows poverty in heaven, a 2,000-year-old man explains that competition and a desire for prestige stimulate the cherubs. Without classes, he adds, " 'What would be the use of continuing this mortal existence upon a material globe? The race might as well be dismantled at once, for it would have no further use for this material field of effort and of training.' " Besides, poverty is inevitable, even in heaven: " 'We cannot relieve the impoverished classes from any part of the burden or the hardships and would not if we could, for we trust God's wisdom and know that what is alloted to them is best' " (p. 167). It is not only futile but also un-Christian to tamper with divine urban planning.

The aged spirit explains, " 'Equal distribution . . . destroys the springs of benevolence—and the motives of mutual helpfulness' " (p. 107).

These utopian tales reveal the contradictions of conservatism— its opposing claims for a laissez-faire economic system calling for a competitive marketplace and a weak federal governnment, on the one hand, and for political capitalism, presuming an alliance of industry and government and thus a powerful state, on the other. Alvarado Fuller in *A.D. 2000* (1890) describes a utopian dictatorship founded on these opposing philosophies. Junius Cobb is an ambitious young officer who invests his money in a long-term savings account and then has himself "inanimated," or freeze-dried. When he is reconstituted a hundred years later— famous from his ordeal and rich from his compounded interest— he discovers that a military utopia has evolved through the eclectic application of laissez-faire economic policies and government in-tervention in commerce. Junius finds that during the twentieth century labor learned to accept its role in the open marketplace, and now the free play of supply and demand sets wages. With prisoners performing the menial jobs, the American worker is "free" either to choose a skilled job or to starve. He is also free, but only as an individual, to negotiate a contract with an em-ployer. Should overproduction force a wage cut, the utopian worker is again free to find a new job. Industries, however, have not competed in quite the same way. While Cobb slept, business has lobbied successfully for protective tariffs and guaranteed pro-fits; small, inefficient industries have disappeared.

Laissez-faire economic practices, Junius learns, have had the same reductive effect on the political process, in which only males "high in social and civil standing" may vote. In the year 2000, Cobb finds only one national newspaper and one political party. Early in the century Congress abolished the jury system because it relied on "ignoramuses . . . men who had not read the events of the day, or if they had, . . . with infantile idiotic minds."[15]

This Hobbesian view of the world fostered authoritarian struc-tures for social organization. In *A.D. 2000*, while American troops are stationed throughout the Western Hemisphere to "diffuse a military spirit among the people" (p. 220), each U.S. state main-tains its own militia and fleet of aerial bombers to control its citizens. South of the Mexican border, only American citizens may own property. Other conservative utopias are also nascent police states, with unusually accurate predictions of the militaristic potential inherent in the new technology. In *A.D. 2050: Electrical Development of Atlantis* (1893) by John Bachelder, a military hero, Captain Jones, organizes a capitalist Atlantis as a haven for refugees from Bellamy's Nationalist society. Bachelder's narrator believes that Nationalism "represented the height of folly, to throw corn to the swine and subsist on the husks ourselves." To protect private property from communists, anarchists, and the Chinese, Captain Jones guards his community with airplanes armed with a new explosive, "eurokite," while, from the ground, huge police towers illuminate the island all night long. For extra security, each citizen of Atlantis has a bedside call button that rings directly at the nearest police station (anticipating a recent invention of today's burglar-alarm companies). Bachelder also predicts the modern precaution of photographing shoppers as they cash checks.

In pursuit of order and conformity, conservative utopias perpetuate misogynistic relations between men and women. Bachelder corrects the mistake of Bellamy's permissive "communistic boomers" who "dethrone manliness."[16] Captain Jones insists on female subservience in Atlantis, and requires that all the women have short blond curly hair, partly—so he claims—to distinguish them from Chinese immigrants. In Addison Peale Russell's early behaviorist utopia *Sub-Coelum: A Sky-Built Human World* (1893), police punish women for drinking, whistling, snoring, bad cooking, and lapses in grammar—habits which are, not surprisingly, disappearing. With all "unchaste" women in prison, sexual vice is virtually extinct. Freed from the scourges of men's "impurities," Sub-Coelum women serve in the moral police force. Like the utopias of Chauncey Thomas and John Macnie, Russell's Sub-Coelum enforces the sterilization of the unfit; blind, deaf, and lazy people can no longer pass these "regressive traits" to future generations of utopians.

Although conservative utopian tales wander into the future, their social ideologies were strikingly familiar to a nineteenth-century audience. Presumed similarities between "present perfect" and "future perfect" allowed these authors to ignore the narrative convolutions of the "novum"—the utopian novelties that permit the estranged reader to ponder simultaneously the innovative world and the familiar world. By reproducing the present in the future, conservative utopians could disregard unwieldy narrative devices necessary to make the future appear logical. With no need to distort time in order to account for historical growth, they could use narrative devices from popular adventure genres—the western, the melodrama, and the sentimental novel.

Walter McDougall in *The Hidden City* (1891) turned to the structures and mythologies of frontier fiction to propel a tribe of backward Indians into an idealized version of the United States in the 1890s. The West is won with Yankee science, several million dollars in Indian gold, the model of corporate capitalism, and a few shots fired from the dime novel. An explorer, Eric Gilbert, comes upon the remote valley of Atzlan, whose early history parallels the story of Atlantis. In the "summer age" of its civilization, it had been a wealthy nation of white citizens, honored for its culture and its civilizing influence over other tribes. When Atzlan was destroyed by fire and brimstone, a remnant of the people had saved themselves by seeking refuge in a cave, but emerged after the storm with different-colored skins and speaking in many languages. A white man and a red woman became the progenitors of the new Atzlan.[17]

Eric Gilbert, the cheerful bearer of the white man's burden, falls from a helium balloon upon a mountain in New Mexico, armed only with a camera, binoculars, a rifle, some surgical instruments, and a wounded pigeon. He sees in the canyon below him a tribe of Indians about to sacrifice a blonde virgin. Eric shoots the fateful knife from the hands of an Indian priest, and terrified, the Indians look up and discover the explorer. This mysterious warrior, they conclude, must be a lost god who (in a handy blending of mythologies) disappeared in the floods of Atlantis, and has returned from the sky. To the Indians it seems as if Eric has come from the upper world, even if we know that it is only a world of rifles and cameras and surgical instruments. The traveler is the bearer of an advanced culture, a fraudulent god who asks for breakfast. McDougall's ironic stance toward the Indians' credulity positions the reader on the side of industrial civilization.[18]

Awestruck by the magic of his binoculars and the power of his .22 rifle, the "innocent people" welcome Eric, who is soon satiated with the offerings of Indian fealty and free tortillas. As he explores the valley of Aztlan and observes the old tribal patterns of agrarian labor—men reaping a poor subsistence crop from unirrigated land, women grinding corn by hand—he decides to use his divine masquerade to elevate the Indians, to render "their condition more in accordance with the times in which the barbarians dwelt" (p. 81). Like Hank Morgan in *A Connecticut Yankee in King Arthur's Court,* Eric plans to "run this town and give it a boom" (p. 308). And he takes the presence of forty white natives, sole descendants of the long-lost white past, as a hopeful sign of latent Indian intelligence.

Thus McDougall altered the traditional mythology of the frontier in which the Indian represented a significant link with the American past. Whereas Cooper, concerned about the absence of custom in American life, saw the Indian as the bearer of older traditions, and Hawthorne and later Whitman viewed the Indian as holding the answer to the historical challenge, "What happened before I arrived?"[19] McDougall's Indians accept the white man's invitation to feast on the innovations of the Gilded Age and surrender to the present. In *The Hidden City* the Indians' only useable past is their secret cache of ancient gold, rescued from old Atlantis.

The forces of good and evil in *The Hidden City* are swiftly defined along the lines of acceptance or resistance to Eric's plans for industrial deliverance. The savages are noble to the degree that they are willing to transform the tribe in the name of progress and to build an industrial city in Atzlan. The good Indians recognize that their traditions cannot save the tribe, which must yield to a modernizing influence.

Earlier in the century, James Fenimore Cooper also acknowledged the impending dominance of white civilization in North America, but avoided making ethical judgments regarding white settlers and native Indians. Each race, he saw, had different "gifts," unique but historically appropriate behaviors that transcend moral evaluations. For Cooper, as illustrated in his characterizations in *The Deerslayer,* for example, a common humanity lay behind these relative gifts, revealed in some Indians and some white men by a respectful attitude toward nature. A few tribes uncorrupted by civilization had preserved an ecological consciousness, an important element in the Americanization of the noble savage motif. But in *The Hidden City,* as the old priests of Atzlan eagerly bite the apple of industrialization, we mark the transition to a new image. Their facile surrender to Eric's gifts reinforces the inevitable triumph of white civilization.

Opposing Eric's plans is the bloodthirsty warrior Chalpa and a corrupt band of young priests who have descended, in the history of fiction, from the evil Pequots in Mary Rowlandson's *The True History of Captivity* (1682), the violent Maguas in Cooper's *Deerslayer* (1841), the lurking Mohawk in Ed Ellis's *Seth Jones* (1860), and the smelly Goshoot in Mark Twain's *Roughing It* (1872). Like his literary ancestors, Chalpa cheats at cards, kidnaps virgins, and threatens the hegemony of the white settler. As is appropriate to the racist paradigms of American popular fiction, Chalpa's skin is darker than that of the other Indians: the issue of race and progress becomes a tautology for McDougall. As Roy Harvey Pearce observes, the moral determinant for fictional Indians is that they reside in "the state of one almost entirely out of contact, for good and for bad, with the life of civilized man; . . . the moral inferiority of Indian society was found to be a product of its historical anteriority."[20]

After the Civil War, the representation in American literature of Indian society as anachronistic helped to justify policies of the Department of the Interior for the acquisition of tribal lands. To protect homesteaders and travelers, and to open land for railroads, settlers, and investors, the federal government supervised a conscious program designed to eliminate the Indians and, later, to force the survivors onto reservations. From the 1860s through the 1880s there were violent wars as the Sioux, Cheyennes, and Arapahoes defended their traditional territories, resulting in the deaths of over one million Indians. Custer's Last Stand occurred in 1876, and the last major battle, the massacre of the Sioux at Wounded Knee, took place in 1890, one year before *The Hidden City* was published.

While lacking the "novum" or the innovative perspective of most utopian novels, *The Hidden City* reveals the "utopian impulse" behind the ideologies supporting U.S. expansion. Conversion to Eric's policies protects the people of Atzlan from destruction and degeneration. Rather than romanticize the pastoral ethic of Atzlan, Eric envisions a "future city, with its water wheels turning merrily, grinding the yellow corn, and pumping water up into the irrigating channels and pipes—ay, and his mind roved on until he saw electric lights, telephone wires, and newspaper offices" (p. 182). None of the traditional tribal leaders questions the benefits of urbanization and technology that Eric promises to deliver. In this story of discovery and conquest, only the "deity" visiting from Montana can start a fire with a sulphur match, reveal great distances through binoculars, and remove cataracts with surgical scalpels. Using his disguise for the greater good, Eric teaches the women how to preserve food and glaze pottery and orders the men to build mills, dams, and even a whole Bessemer foundry for smelting iron. And "like children the Atzlans listened, believing all that they heard, and desirous to emulate the people who had learned so much, they watched all of Gilbert's enterprises with a vague wonder and huge expectancy" (p. 182). Trusting, naive, and obedient, the Indians abandon tradition for the world of industrial enterprise which they do not expect to understand. When Eric starts the flow of water into the new mill, he proclaims, " 'My brothers, when I lift this gate you will begin to live in a new age. The past will no longer be with you.' " In their utopia, the Indians too will participate in the American attraction to historical amnesia.

Even though conservative utopias closely resemble the authors' contemporary society, the processes of change are still mystified. The New Atzlan technology no longer arises from the interplay among need, creativity, investment, and profit. Eric assures the Indians that the transformation from pastoral to industrial society will be easy. But he does not describe how that transformation took place in the past. In the words of an old priest:

"Our brother . . . has told me many things of the fair land he lived in before he came to us. In that land there is no night, for they turned it into day with many suns and moons which they have made themselves. They have great monsters that work for them unceasingly; they can speak to each other afar off, even when they cannot see each other; they make wood and gold and silver talk; they walk upon water and under it, and they fly through the air like birds; they kill their enemies with their eyes and their thunder. We are glad that our brother has come to us." (P. 267)

Science is magic; its explanations are mysterious, its social consequences unexplored. Transformation depends yet again on the dreams of one man alone.

While rebuilding Atzlan in his own image, Eric falls in love with the blonde virgin Lila, whom he rescued on his arrival. Predictably, his romance also takes the form of a rescue, a motif that McDougall inherited from the old captivity narratives and the dime novel. This fictional conceit is the final test in the competition between civilizations, for Chalpa, jealous of Lila's love, kidnaps the ersatz god and chains him in a cave near a rising river. Anticipating Eric's death, Chalpa plans to restore the pastoral order by arranging another ritual sacrifice—of Lila. But before his capture, Eric had released his carrier pigeon, which conveys his plea for help back to civilization. Just in time, a posse rides in from Montana, and immediately the debate over the tribe's correct future course devolves into a shootout between cowboys and Indians. As Eric is watering the roof of his new buildings (in case the Indians shoot burning arrows), a helium balloon wafts over the hidden city flying the banner "The Continent of America." As in other stories of the confrontation of whites and Indians, from the captivity narratives to *The Deerslayer* to *The Virginian* (1902), the dramatic final rescue signifies the persistence and dominance of white civilization.

The "future city" Eric plans for Atzlan resides neither in an alternative time nor in a fantastic location. Except for a few inventions, the perfect society differs little from the known world because, McDougall suggests, American civilization is immanent in all "primitive" cultures and will flourish as soon as they stop living like Indians. As Eric explains, "The race of Indians is dying off the face of the earth because civilization is too powerful for them to resist, and they are too weak to accept its customs" (p. 303). The telos resides in the Gilded Age.

For McDougall, whites and Indians no longer had the reciprocal relationship that may be observed in the works of Cooper, Hawthorne, and Whitman. The tensions between Indian and white that Roy Harvey Pearce finds in earlier narratives of contact, particularly the dialectic that "implies a simultaneity of existence and means that one factor must be treated in relation to its opposite,"[21] disappeared in complacent confidence at the close of the Indian wars. At the end of *The Hidden City*, the old priest lives just long enough to appoint Eric governor of the tribe, " 'to plan new enterprises and put into practice your theory of government.' " In return Eric promises to transform the pastoral valley into a great stock company, run by a board of directors who will determine the future of the "city of unspeakable glory." The posse returns east, taking three wagons of Atzlan gold with which to purchase electricity, mining machinery, and looms for the tribe, "everything in fact that civilization could furnish from its plenteous store." (The leader of the rescue party also promises to invest "a few millions" of gold in solid securities for Eric.) Eric's plan to convert the tribal past into the ideal present is a tribute to contemporary progress; but, true to the utopian convention, the actual force behind this historical development remains hidden.

Eric stays behind to rule Atzlan and use his understanding of two worlds to transfer values from one to the other, a transfer symbolized by his marriage to a (white) Atzlan. But unlike Cooper's Deerslayer, Eric shows no ambivalence about destroying the Indians' world. His final lesson to the Indians is that the price of modernity is the glorious loss of freedom: " 'Most of all, above all, work, work, work,' " he cried. " 'It's the soul, the life of the world, the aim and end of living—Aye—'tis life itself' " (p. 312). Gone is the leisure, the sensuality, and the artisan life of old Atzlan. As Eric watches the wagons moving east with the tribe's gold, he proclaims Atzlan the city of the future, modestly declaring, " 'I have said it, it is good.' "

The utopian potential of colonialism and westward expansion was often conceived in ethical as well as economic terms. In *A Journey in Other Worlds: A Romance of the Future* (1894), millionaire John Jacob Astor represents three historical epochs that justify the hegemony of corporate capitalism. In the year 2000 the United States has completed its global conquest. America now owns most of Africa, which it purchased from European socialists (apparently fiscally naive and foolishly anti-imperialist) who now control their countries. Tired of their "incessant revolutions," Canada, Mexico, and South America have also requested annexation from their neighborly "big brother" who has protected them since the "comfortable days of the Monroe doctrine."[22] Under the beneficent reign of capitalism, the "dark elements" in Mexico, Africa, and South America have fortuitously died out. Meanwhile, three young scientists who work for the Terrestrial Axis Straightening Company have just shifted the planet's axis to give the United

States control of the earth's climate. Bored with their achievements, they leave in an airship to colonize space and prepare to "absorb or run out all the inferior races" (p. 100).

Like much nineteenth-century utopian fiction, *A Journey in Other Worlds* represents the relationships between various sectors of a culture.[23] Astor sketches the political implications of the new developments in transportation, communications, energy, military technology, overseas expansion, and economic investment. In A.D. 2000 American technology reinforces U.S. goals for empire. Scientists from the United States have dammed the Arctic Ocean, creating a temperate climate for its once arid colonies. Steam, drawn from the center of the earth, powers its new industries and solar heaters tap the energy of the Sahara. The "kintograph," a type of "visual telegraph," transmits entertainment produced in New York throughout the hemisphere, while airships, laden with asphyxiation bombs, perpetually hover over the new "dominions." These inventions reveal more than the era's scientific curiosity, epitomized in the popularity of early science fiction stories, displays of industrial inventions at the 1893 Chicago World's Fair, and such publications as the Frank Reade Library, which explained the new mechanics. Freed from the humanistic strictures surrounding the use of technology in progressive utopias, Astor's inventions accurately predict the social configurations as well as particular discoveries of later technology. In the year 2000 color photography, hidden cameras, intercontinental phone service, streets painted with phosphorescent lines, radar speed detectors for carriages, and germ insecticides are valued as social controls.

John Jacob Astor, one of the wealthiest men of his time, was certainly unique among utopian authors. To the extent we can discover anything about them, most writers of utopian fiction tended to be journalists, local politicians, or ministers. As well as being a major shareholder in such large corporations as Western Union, Equitable Life Insurance, and the Illinois Central Railroad, Astor was an inventor in his own right, and patented an improved turbine engine and a new bicycle brake. When the Spanish-American War broke out in 1898, he equipped an entire artillery battery, placed his palatial yacht at the disposal of the navy, and then enlisted himself. In *A Journey in Other Worlds* Astor distributes these diverse talents and characteristics among three adventurers: a wealthy young investor, a geologist, and a colonel in the army.

For his tale of intergalactic conquest Astor used the exaggerated devices of the dime western, a form of frontier fiction that became popular after the Civil War and was written and sold in the East through Erastus Beadle's cheap paperbound series. Astor's adventurers follow the literary trail of Daniel Boone and Kit Carson who, as Henry Nash Smith has observed, fused the western prowess of the gunfighter or trapper with an upper-class defense of eastern values.[24] Packing their rattlesnake medicine, rubber boots, and Kodaks, and hitching their airship to a comet, the adventurers fly first to Jupiter—"the next new world"—where they discover a primordial jungle of giant mastodons, man-eating plants, bulbous snakes, and flying lizards; they christen the planet "Kentucky." Yelping, "Now for the fray!" the colonel lassoes dinosaurs and blood-sucking bats. In the debunking language of the tall tale, the explorers, shooting from a circle (like pioneers surrounded by Indians), "end the careers" of giant ants.

But unlike the travelers to pastoral utopia who enjoy nature as a regenerative source of strength and virtue, the travelers mainly see the mining and investment possibilities of the virgin land: " 'This would be the place to live,' said Colonel Bearwarden, looking at the iron mountains, silver, copper and lead formations, primeval forests, rich prairies and regions evidently underlaid with coal and petroleum." Uninterested in the moral or aesthetic possibilities of Jupiter, the colonel recognizes the planet's Malthusian possibility: " 'Think . . . of the undescribable blessing to the congested communities of Europe and America, to find an unlimited outlet here!' " (p. 262). With the West now closed, Astor finds a new safety valve in the intergalactic frontier.

Leaving the prehistoric planet of Jupiter, the explorers fly to Saturn, where they witness the other side of history, the spiritual culmination of human evolution, in a transcendent utopian world of silent spirits. Through gimmicks borrowed from popular revivalism—automatic writing, mental telepathy, and reincarnation—the spirit citizens of Saturn predict that the United States will control the entire universe. But when the spirits offer the explorers visions of their own deaths, the travelers understand the limits of their worldly desires; we again see the era's pressure to reconcile the acquisitive with the spiritual. In a trance, each traveler witnesses the impending illness of his lover or spouse, the shriveling of his own talent and imagination, and the gruesome decay of his own body. By contrast, utopia is the state of being where desire and duty coincide; the spirits ask them to give up curiosity and greed for the greater social good. The travelers return to earth, determined to plan further explorations, but next time in the name of Christianity.

In *A Journey in Other Worlds* the voyage fulfills both secular and sacred obligations; a journey of scientific exploration and political conquest carries the adventurers to the world of spiritualism itself. The three adventurers travel from genesis to revelation, from genesis to manifest destiny. The conservative utopian novel is a self-reflexive text, observing while reproducing as inexorable the course of American history. As Northrop Frye observes of the quest romance, the conservative utopian journey represents "the search of the libido or the desiring self for a fulfillment that will deliver it from the anxieties of reality but will still contain that reality."[25] The travelers to conservative utopias witness both beginnings and ends; both sides of history signify the present and call it inevitable.

Ignatius Donnelly and the Apocalyptic Utopias

We certainly need a new revolution—a new system—for there seems to be no life left in the old one.—Nathaniel Hawthorne

In *A Connecticut Yankee in King Arthur's Court* (1889), Hank Morgan, a nineteenth-century foreman at the Colt Revolver Factory, having just sold telephones, toothpaste, and Sunday School to the Knights of the Round Table, boasts,

My works showed what a despot could do with the resources of a kingdom at his command. Unsuspected by this dark land, I had the civilization of the nineteenth century booming under its very nose! It was fenced away from public view, but there it was, a gigantic unassailable fact—and to be heard from yet, if I lived and had luck. There it was, as sure a fact, and as substantial a fact as any serene volcano, standing innocent with its smokeless summit in the blue sky and giving no sign of the rising hell in its bowels.

Unlike Hank Morgan (who himself betrays a certain doublemindedness about his achievements), other American utopians did suspect the "unassailable facts" of their own remedies and doubted that consumer cooperatives, nationalized railroads, public education, and the women's vote would guarantee a prosperous future.

As early as 1890, a small group of utopian authors concluded that only apocalypse would deliver utopia; they alone, among utopian authors of this period, attempted to represent historical process.[1] But they could not, with Hank's (ironic) assurance, promise a safe passage from hierarchy to equality, from chaos to social

112

order. To writers of apocalyptic utopias, the 1890s were the worst of times; despite the pleasant dreams of some literary folk, the "substantial facts" of tenements, unemployment, child labor, and open sewers stubbornly persisted. Inside the "serene volcano" of contemporary life burned an urban hell that might soon explode. While Bellamy promised that monopolies and extended suffrage would deliver a utopia of shopping-center socialism, and while Howells shipped off bored aristocrats to a fertile island, other utopians announced that American society was plunging into a fiery catastrophe that could not be wished away by long naps, space travel, or fortuitous shipwrecks. Poverty and political impotence kindled angry predictions of social turmoil.

The apocalyptic utopia, however, was not a call for revolution but a desperate warning against social passivity. Since the time of Engels, critics of utopian visions have pointed to the delusive dangers of conjuring up an ideal society. But from Thomas More to Ernst Bloch, from Edward Bellamy to Melvin Lasky, utopian writers and scholars have assumed that vision and action are wed to one another. Lasky argues that utopias always contain a secret injunction, a tacit exhortation to change, and he reminds us that at the heart of all utopian thinking lies the problem of means and ends.

Certainly, More and Burke, Owen and Lenin asked, "What is to be done?"[2] Some reference to a method whereby social change can be achieved, whether practical or fanciful, legislative or revolutionary, hopeful or terrifying, is implicit in the finest utopian thinking. Alone, neither the dream nor the deed will realize political purpose.

Three distinct narrative stages of activity picture the passage to the future in apocalyptic utopias: first, there is the satire of contemporary power and poverty, often framed in naturalistic detail; second, a tale of urban destruction; and, finally, a story of creation, the birth of a rather frightened, and often anti-industrial, new world. Violent revolution—punitive and redemptive—emerges as the logical consequence of the painful inequalities of the current era, the imagined result of factory labor, slum life, and immigration. But after the smoke settles, America stumbles upon Eden: violent social eruption becomes a redeeming event for the lost nation, bounded as it was, according to utopian writer Arthur

Bird, "on the east by the first chapter of the Book of Genesis and on the west by the day of Judgement."[3]

In the late nineteenth century, to represent the paradoxical function of destruction and deliverance, utopian authors turned to the narrative and imagistic conventions of a genre that traditionally represented annihilation and regeneration: religious apocalypse.[4] Derived from the Greek word *apokalypsis,* meaning uncovering or revelation, the apocalypse unveils the future as the realm of both heaven and hell.[5] It served nineteenth-century utopians as a metaphor for social change, portending the fiery destruction of a degenerate world while promising the millennium. Thus, as an extended image for historical change, it contained the two critical elements of utopian fiction, satire and teleology.

As a consequence of a critical social vision that offers no sustained alternative, violence has often hovered at the edge of satire. But within apocalyptic utopias, social violence is a necessary phase in the literary passage to the millennial future. However, it also represents a warning to a concerned reading public about the possibility of class warfare; often the details of well-known strikes or recent street riots provide the details for satirical comments and fictional revolutions. Yet in the end, violence undermines the utopian faith in human rationality. In 1894 Frank Rosewater anticipated that a revolution would come as early as 1896. In his novel *'96: A Romance of Utopia,* a banker warns:

"It is we who must strike ere conscience sleeps, benumbed under the chilling gaze of this hideous reptile! It is we who must rouse from our lethargy ere the maddened multitude add horror to the horrors already here. Even in our land we have had warnings—at Chicago and Homestead, at Cincinnati and Pittsburgh and Buffalo—The cry has been loud and long—Awake! Awake!" (P. 267)

Naturalistic exposés of tenement life and portraits of a benumbed middle class make the coming violence appear inevitable to the traveler or visitor. In Henry Salisbury's *The Birth of Freedom: A Socialist Novel* (1891) the head of a workers' committee takes a group of wealthy philanthropists and reporters on a tour of Brooklyn tenements where they see child prostitutes, children selling pails of rancid food, and young girls carrying heavy loads of firewood on their backs. Although the visitors are surprised and sympathetic with the plight of the poor, they ask the committee to call off its plans for a general strike; in frustration, the guide refuses, explaining that the slum dwellers are tired of "gunpowder, cold steel and whimpering, psalm singing preachers keeping us down" (p. 59). The working people organize the strike, but they are too ignorant and angry to create a more humane society. Despite the charitable efforts of the philanthropists, the strike explodes in urban warfare in the streets of New York, and Manhattan burns to the ground.

Despite economic explanations for such outbursts, images of violence in *The Birth of Freedom* and other apocalyptic utopias call into question the faith in human nature usually characteristic of the genre. Salisbury suggests that urban workers, in their daily struggle to find food and a place to sleep, have retained "primitive instincts" that reappear in the street battle as they burn their tenements and hang their landlords, while soldiers shoot unarmed immigrants hiding under subway bridges. Although the Darwinian rhetoric of evolution justifies the week-long clash as a struggle for survival, the battle discredits Darwin's claim that change moves toward the amelioration of the species. For Salisbury, even the philanthropists must be exiled or destroyed before a pastoral world can reappear. Thus, while documenting the sources of anger and predicting the violent consequences of social inequality, in utopian fiction revolutions undermine the wish-fulfillment aspect typical of the genre.

Paradoxically, the totality of retribution provides space for a second kind of utopian rhetoric: the tenement has a garden, the countryside endures outside the barricades, promising a sequel to the tale of proletarian insurrection. As Ignatius Donnelly claims in his Populist utopia *The Golden Bottle* (1892), even though an urban plutocracy has fortified its power with futuristic technologies and ingenious controls of the gold market, America remains "the yeoman's republic, founded by fishers and ploughers and hunters, by men in homespun and deerskin" (p. 127).

Explanations linking violence to national rebirth stem from two popular yet contradictory views of America's future course: Jeffersonian and socialist. In the versions of Salisbury and Donnelly, the United States has deviated from its pastoral and democratic path.

115

By destroying New York, Chicago, Boston, and San Francisco with posionous gases and fire bombs, the revolutionaries chasten the nation and give the country a second chance at Jeffersonian democracy. The workers' revolts, framed in imagery taken from the Book of Revelation, represent punishment and purgation; the still youthful nation is allowed to try again.[6]

But for Albert Adams Merrill in *The Great Awakening* (1899), and Morrison Swift in *A League of Justice; or, Is It Right to Rob Robbers?* (1893), social violence is an inevitable consequence of class tensions rather than a metaphor for historical error; revolution is the next stage in the movement from capitalism to socialism. Merrill's utopian hero recalls the "chaotic era":

In looking at the history of those times I do not see how society could have undergone the radical change needed without a terrible slaughter of the upper classes. . . . If these upper classes had been allowed to exist, their inborn tendency to manage and control the lives of other men, coming from the fact that they had become so used to controlling capital that it was second nature to them, would have been a constant menace to a just social organization. Alas, that life must forever feed its growth on death. (P. 215)

Whether a theological or political metaphor for historical tension, the apocalypse represents a call to action. From the time of John's Revelation (written partially in response to the persecutions of the Roman empire),[7] apocalyptic literature has had a purposeful relationship to its historical moment; life and art are linked in a social-literary symbiosis. David Ketterer thus distinguishes apocalyptic from mystic literature: "Unlike the mystic, who attempts to break through material reality, the apocalyptic arrives at his revelation through an understanding of the true significance of events in the historical world."[8] According to Ernest Tuveson, the genre has, in particular, spoken to the terror of retribution for the poverty and persecution of the oppressed. In the 1890s, when state militias, federal troops, and local police were used to repress the growing labor movement, social unrest again fanned the flames of apocalyptic fears.

Apocalyptic utopias, which project a fiery passage to the future, appeared during one of the most violent epochs in the history of the American labor movement. During the Homestead Strike in July 1892, Andrew Carnegie hired 300 Pinkerton guards to block striking members of the Amalgamated Association of Iron and Steel Workers. For twenty-four hours the strikers held the Pinkertons as "prisoners of war" inside the factory. In less than a week ten men were killed and over thirty wounded. Reports of the violence at Homestead encouraged militant actions across the country. Within a few days, fierce strikes in the Coeur d'Alene mines in Idaho, in the coal mines in Tennessee, and in Buffalo's transit system contributed to a cataclysmic view of labor conflict. Two years later, in 1894, when the Pullman strike stopped all railroad traffic between Chicago and the West, President Cleveland sent in the cavalry and field artillery, provoking armed resistance by the railroad employees.[9] In May 1897, the president of the Western Federation of Miners urged every union in Colorado and Idaho to purchase arms, "so that in two years we can hear the inspiring music of the martial tread of 25,000 armed men in the ranks of labor."[10] The volcano was less serene than it once was.

Meanwhile, the country was experiencing the worst depression in its history. By 1894 one-fourth of all railroads fell into receivership while domestic consumption of American-made products declined to three-fourths of industrial capacity. In 1895 alone, over one million workers participated in 394 strikes, and roving bands of unemployed men and women followed Jacob Coxey's march on Washington to demand relief.[11] According to a contemporary editorial in the *Nation*, Coxey's ragged "troops" brought America "dangerously near the conditions of things at the time of the French revolution."[12]

This view was shared by a utopian writer named Frank Rosewater. In his novel entitled *'96: A Romance of Utopia*, the revolution that launches his democratic utopia begins as a rebellion in a prison for the unemployed. Children are raised there until they are old enough to go to the factories, where they wait on their knees outside the gates, praying for jobs. When a revolt arises in the prison, Rosewater comments, "The terrible reign of inhumanity that darkened the city for many days thereafter was but the extension of the rule that had preceded. It was the outgrowth of a society cemented only by force and forced beliefs—a mock realm whose rocks were tinsel and whose truths refused to face scrutiny"

117

(p. 234). To Rosewater, the abuses brought about by industrial capitalism would inevitably lead to violence.

Yet despite the widespread concern for providing shelter, food, and jobs for the poor and unemployed, the urban press in the 1890s spread the alarm that reformers—particularly immigrants and socialists—were bloodthirsty creatures. As Frederick Adams observed in *President John Smith: The Story of a Peaceful Revolution* (1897), although the regular army had shot hundreds of unarmed pickets in the railroad strikes of 1877, the press blamed socialists for the violence:

They were the ones who did it—the terrible socialists and anarchists. Innocent people were almost frightened to death by stories of the plotting of the bloodthirsty socialists. Little children were told that socialists would catch them if they did not behave. So it came to pass that for many years following the riots the word "socialist" was used as a general term to designate a rioter, a revolutionist, a plotter against good government, a worthless vagabond who imagined that the world owed him a living.[13]

For writers of the apocalyptic utopia, the approach of violence is inexorable; according to the apocalyptic vision, the future will unfold in three prescribed stages: criticism, resistance, and renovation.[14] In the first stage, which Albert Merrill—author of *The Great Awakening* (1899)—called the "era of degeneration," the traveler observes and defines the sources of the evil. In this stage, naturalistic details of ghetto life and bad government usually convince a skeptical hero that the present state of affairs is sinful and corrupt. Eventually lumpen and working-class organizations develop, often as paramilitary clubs such as the one described in the title of Morrison Swift's *A League of Justice; or, Is It Right to Rob Robbers?*, the Brotherhood of Destruction in Ignatius Donnelly's *Caesar's Column*, or the Army of Peace in Frank Rosewater's *'96*. Generally, the organizations first strive for reforms and adopt peaceful, if illicit, tactics to improve social conditions. The League of Justice, for example, is financed by bank clerks who have embezzled funds from their "rapacious" employers to start workers' schools, community newspapers, and neighborhood clinics.

But, according to the apocalyptic tradition, conditions get worse before they get better. Soon the traveler witnesses the resistance or "decline" called the "chaotic era" by Merrill and "Sheol" by Donnelly, a painful time of loss and tribulation that precedes the *renovatio mundi*. In Salisbury's tale *(The Birth of Freedom)*, street violence begins when the bank clerks are betrayed and the police arrest 250,000 league members, mainly teachers, nurses, and writers; in Donnelly's *Caesar's Column,* the revolution starts when the army sells bombers to the workers' Brotherhood of Destruction. Often, then, this first moment of violence is sparked by perfidy and deception on the part of the oppressors.

Despite the aerial bombs and poison gases, a small band of the faithful survive the battle. As we have seen, this is traditional in the genre. Usually pictured as the chosen people or the "saving remnant," this group has followed a gospel of justice that guides them in their mission, and alone they form the nucleus of a new era—born again in a georgic community. The redeemers, believing that eternity unfolds in stages, see the present as an era of transition, a providential moment in time. In the end is the beginning; the plutocrats are destroyed and the reign of freedom begins in utopia. Still, the true promise, the glorious consummation, the apotheosis of history, awaits the future.

Although in these novels the representation of secular change is embodied in a religious metaphor, apocalypse is taken as a political paradigm: the image of the future is contained in the destruction of the old order. Utopia in apocalyptic literature represents no mere social projection of one author's fantasy or nightmare but is the logical outcome of the events of history: the dream of the future activates those who had despaired, transforming crisis into climax, revolution into utopia. It initiates at the same time that it completes historical process.

Nevertheless, the idealized society in nineteenth-century apocalyptic visions is still a literary resolution rather than a workable model for the goal of social change: as in pastoral utopias, the promise is made in the garden. While the evil described in the novel refers to contemporary politics and while the resistance suggests a charred memory of the Haymarket riots and the Homestead massacre, the utopia realizes the promise of the pastoral, an unlikely return to the past and an improbable fulfillment through the negation of history. What appears most predictive in these tales are the images of impending violence. Extensively described, often in obsessively gory detail, the social cataclysms themselves become the real telos.

Despite the final moment in the garden, these tales are antiutopian. In *Caesar's Column* (1890) by Ignatius Donnelly, a Populist senator, apocalypse represents the failure of the Populist imagination. Known in the 1890s as the "great apostle of protest," Donnelly held the common Populist view that contemporary American history could be understood as controlled by a sustained conspiracy of an international monied class. Populists dramatized history as a confrontation between oppressors (bankers, railroad executives, and government officials) and the oppressed (debt-ridden farmers). Typical Populist concerns were a loss of faith in the two-party system, anticipation of apocalypse, a focus on the luxuries and vices of the plutocrats, xenophobia, and an appeal to native simplicity and "folk" virtues.

Caesar's Column tells the story of a proletarian revolution that overthrows a cruel plutocracy of Jewish-Italian aristocrats, and then destroys itself in its own lawlessness and hatred.[15] Gabriel Welstein, a wool merchant from a Swiss colony in Uganda, comes to New York in the year 1988, attempting to break an international cartel and to sell his wool directly to American manufacturers and retailers—the shepherd has become the salesman.[16] The story is narrated through a series of letters to his brother at home in Uganda.

At first Gabriel is stunned by the advances in technology he sees in New York. From the windows of his airship he observes the lights of the city from a hundred miles away and learns that they are powered by the energy of the Aurora Borealis. In New York he discovers subways running beneath glass sidewalks. At the plush Hotel Darwin, Gabriel's weight on the dining-room chair activates a televised menu, which offers him birds' nests from China, buffalo hump from the West, and varieties of edible spiders. But while he is feasting, Gabriel notices that hundreds of other hotel guests, with "the same soulless likeness," are also eating alone, silently reading stories of expansion and colonization from their televised newspapers. Soon he has an intimation of coming disaster, recalling that the lights of the airship were reflected in the sky with the "glare of a great conflagration" (p. 19).

Gabriel learns that this industrial paradise is ruled by a secret oligarchy of wealthy immigrant "plutocrats" who threaten even the innocent visitor. Within days of his arrival, Gabriel gets into trouble when he prevents a coach driver from beating an old beggar who had fallen under his wheels. The owner of the carriage is Prince Cabano—a Jewish-Italian industrial count (né Jacob Isaacs) who controls the oligarchy; the beggar is Max Petion,[17] a disguised leader of the Brotherhood of Destruction, an underground organization of impoverished and ruthless urban workers. No longer safe as tourist or merchant, Gabriel goes into hiding in Max's house in the slums; here he discovers the miserable and impoverished underside of New York, which is described in full naturalistic detail. Gabriel eventually joins the cause of the revolutionary proletariat, mainly to plot the escape of a beautiful virgin slave imprisoned in the harem of the Prince Cabano.

This battle between good and evil, the innocent and the damned, fit comfortably with the Populists' two-class view of society. Donnelly believed that history was unfolding in melodramatic ways. In 1892 he wrote most of the official platform for the Populist party which concluded in a warning anticipated in *Caesar's Column:* "A vast conspiracy against mankind has been organized on two continents, and it is rapidly taking possession of the world. If not met and overthrown at once it forbodes terrible social convulsions, the destruction of civilization, or the establishment of an absolute despotism."[18] The origins of this chiliastic vision are to be found both in Donnelly's view of a polarized society in which mighty forces have reached a precarious impasse, and in his melancholic preoccupation with catastrophic events, stemming perhaps from a disappointing series of personal political setbacks.

When Ignatius Donnelly has not been altogether ignored by literary critics, he has enjoyed such sobriquets as the "Prince of Cranks," the "Sage of Ninninger," "Tribune of the People," and the "Apostle of Discontent."[19] At one time or another, the Populist congressman from Minnesota tried his hand at law, land speculation, geology, local politics, and classical studies. Although his political allegiances were erratic—Donnelly argued alternately, but passionately, for Democrats, Republicans, and Populists, for tight and easy money, for high and low tariffs—his rebellious solutions were always visionary, and because he was an outspoken advocate of land reform, his sentiments were always with the farmers.[20] In 1890 the *New York Sun* observed that a reform convention in Minnesota without Donnelly would be "like a catfish without waffles in Philadelphia."[21]

Donnelly believed that the United States was nearing the climax of a historical cycle, following a pattern similar to those described in two novels that preceded *Caesar's Column*. Both *Atlantis: The Antediluvian World* (1882) and *Ragnorak: The Age of Fire and Gravel* (1883) describe the destruction of a corrupt civilization by natural calamaties. In *Atlantis*, the highest of ancient pastoral civilizations perishes under volcanic ash.[22] In *Ragnorak*, Donnelly adds a divine agent of retribution: a fiery Norse god rains dust and ashes on the earth as punishment for degeneracy and "sensual sins": soon an age of icy blackness descends and "the remnants of poor humanity wander . . . stumbling awestruck but filled with an insatiable hunger . . . living upon the bark of the few trees that have escaped, or on the bodies of the animals that have perished and even upon one another."[23]

In *Atlantis: The Antediluvian World*, Donnelly presents his own country as having similarly fallen from a harmonious agrarian condition. "It was the true antediluvian world; the garden of Eden; the gardens of the Hesperides; the mesomphalos; the Loympos; the Asgard of the traditions of the ancient nations; representing a universal memory of a great land, where early mankind dwelt for ages in peace and happiness."[24] The garden civilization recalls the utopias of William Morris and William Dean Howells. Even after the fall—annihilation in a fiery flood—a rural ethic persists as a reminder of history and a promise of a future utopia.

Images of a pastoral world also frame the action in Donnelly's *Caesar's Column*. References to his African homeland intensify the shepherd's critique of the city: "And so," he writes from the Hotel Darwin,

from all this glory and splendour I turn back to the old homestead, amid the high mountain valleys of Africa, to the primitive, simple shepherd life. . . . This gorgeous gilded room fades away and I see the leaning hills, the trickling streams, the deep gorges where our wooly thousands graze; and I hear once more the echoing Swiss horns of our herdsmen reverberating from the snow tipped mountains. But my dream is gone. The roar of the mighty city rises around me like the bellow of cataracts. (Pp. 7–8)

Ignatius Donnelly and the Apocalyptic Utopias

The sounds of the city, marked by both Howells and Bellamy as the defining difference between city and country life, penetrate and destroy memory. The frame of the golden age, the pastoral references at the beginning and the end of the novel, anticipates Donnelly's chiliastic view of time and reinforces the Populist identification of the countryside with the idealized past and future, and the city with the flawed present.

In *Caesar's Column*, however, Donnelly does not pose the tension between the city and the country as a simple choice between materialism and austerity, commercial networks and intimate relationships. As a good Populist, Donnelly sees the colonial dependence of the city on the country. Not only has this network caught Gabriel, who fails to break the wool cartel, but also it has forced a simple peasant, Caesar Lomellini, to become the brutal revolutionary leader of a sinister proletarian brotherhood. His is an archetypal Populist tale: once a "quiet, peaceable industrious" farmer, Caesar married young and settled down to work his land. One night lightning killed his horses and his homespun security was destroyed. Forced to mortgage his farm to buy another team, Caesar found himself trapped in a monopoly of urban bankers who demanded exorbitant interest on his loan. Soon his cattle and machinery were also covered with mortgages and the farm was lost, all for the price of two horses. Driven from his land, Caesar fled to the mountains where he gathered a band of other desperate farmers and together they planned a bloody war against society. Thus the city not only wallows in its own decadence, awaiting catastrophe, but also destroys the country, once the fount of regeneration and purity.

Gabriel's air voyage from Africa to New York signifies the passing of agrarian society and the historical rise of the industrial city. Unlike Uganda and Atlantis, New York in 1988 annihilates desire in the wealthy classes by its facile satiation of all human needs. Where Atlantis honored traditional values of work, family, and commitment, the America Gabriel discovers has bred citizens who lack motivation and identity. On his second day in the city, Gabriel discovers neighborhood suicide chambers where elderly New Yorkers volunteer to die at the city's expense. He thus analyzes the situation: "In this vast, over-crowded city, man is a drug,—a superfluity,—and I think many men and women end

123

their lives out of an overwhelming sense of their own insignificance;—in other words, from a mere weariness of feeling that they are nothing, they become nothing" (p. 18). New York, a crowded setting for collective activity and, potentially, collective consciousness, isolates its citizens by denying the existence of common social needs. "What struck me most," Gabriel observes of urban mill operators on their way to work one morning, "was their incalculable multitude and their silence" (p. 38).

Slumming with Max, his revolutionary guide, Gabriel sees how the city has deformed the workers' capacity to communicate: "See them as they eat their mid-day meal. No delightful pause from pleasant labor: no brightly arrayed table; no laughing and loving faces around a plenteous board, with delicacies from all parts of the world: no agreeable interchange of wisdom and wit and courtesy and merriment" (p. 40). The isolation, similar to the anomie of the Hotel Darwin dining room, portends the death of affection, of manners, indeed, of culture itself. Inhibited in speech and action, the city workers have reverted to animal behavior, becoming brutish creatures of the environment: "Without stopping in their work, under the eyes of sullen taskmasters, they snatch bites out of their hard dark bread, like wild animals, and devour it ravenously" (p. 40). Inevitably, they become objects rather than subjects of their own consciousness.

Through Gabriel, we observe New York and its inhabitants from the outside; the nineteenth-century city is "estranged" through the perspective of the shepherd, who sees in the absence of nature the disappearance of precapitalist social and economic relationships. Unlike Bellamy in *Looking Backward* or Howells in *A Traveller from Altruria*, Donnelly refuses to see the city as a community, an enlarged version of the idealized village. Because of its large population and geographical complexity, Gabriel can comprehend the city only by generalizing from accessible bits of evidence that he presumes typify industrial life: the street outside a factory, a church service, a socialist meeting. Nevertheless, while the city for Bellamy is a setting for utopian gadgets such as umbrellas for buildings, the city for Donnelly becomes a realistic presence in its own right:

Night and day are all one, for the magnetic light increases automatically as the day-light wanes; and the business parts of the city swarm as much at midnight as at high noon. In the old times, I was told, part of the streets was reserved for foot-paths for men and women, while the middle was given up to horses and wheeled vehicles; and one could not pass from side to side without danger of being trampled to death by the horses. But as the city grew it was found that the pavement would not hold the mighty, surging multitudes. (P. 8)

The city has also become an image for Donnelly's conception of the historical moment itself. Gabriel's voyage from Africa to New York reflects the accelerated tempo of life in post–Civil War America; it reenacts the passage from a quiet rural childhood to tumultuous industrial adulthood, the passage from predictability to chance. For Gabriel, the city of New York fuses time and space.

But there is no future within this industrial paradise. When Gabriel attends a meeting of the workers' Brotherhood of Destruction, he discovers that the future holds only death: "It was a solemn silent gloomy assemblage, and the sight of it thrilled through my very flesh and bones. I was not frightened, but appalled, as I saw all those eyes, out of those expressionless dark faces, fixed upon me. I felt as if they were phantoms, or dead men, in whom only the eyes lived" (p. 148). Under capitalism, social evolution moves toward irrationality: "A great injustice, or series of wrongs, working through many generations, had wrought out results that in some sense duplicated each other. Brutality above had produced brutality below; cunning there was answered by cunning here; cruelty in the aristocrat was mirrored by cruelty in the workman. High and low were alike victims—unconscious victims—of a system" (p. 149).

This degeneration is epitomized in the racist caricature of Caesar, the president of the brotherhood, whose

great arms hung down until the monstrous hands almost touched the knees. His skin was quite dark, almost negroid; and a thick, close mat of curly black hair covered his huge head like a thatch. His face was muscular, ligamentous; with great bars, ridges and whelks of flesh, especially about the jaws and on the forehead. But the eyes fascinated me. They were the eyes of a wild beast, deep-set, sullen and glaring; they seemed to shine like those of the cat-tribe, with a luminosity of their own. (P. 149)

This Italian-black alloy illustrates the social Darwinist assumption that social forces can mold physical appearance. The images

surrounding Caesar express a historical reversal, defined throughout the novel as a movement from white to black racial characteristics. Indeed, the black members of the brotherhood serve to
make the prospect of rebellion most terrifying. As John Patterson
has noted, in Donnelly's view, "the blacks of the South are
members of it to a man. Their former masters have kept them in
a state of savagery, instead of elevating them: and the result is
they are as barbarous and bloodthirsty as their ancestors were
when brought from Africa, and fit subjects for such a terrible
organization."[25]

If Caesar and the blacks provide the brute force for the brotherhood, "the brains of the organization" are supplied by a crippled
Russian Jew, whose

face was mean and sinister; two fangs alone remained in his mouth; his
nose was hooked; the eyes were small; sharp, penetrating and restless;
but the expanse of brow above them was grand and noble. It was one of
those heads that look as if they had been packed full, and not an inch of
space wasted. His person was unclean, however, and the hands and the
long finger-nails were black with dirt. (Pp. 149–50)

This unnamed Russian radical is the workers' counterpart to the
Jewish financiers who ruthlessly control New York through a mer-
cantile conspiracy. The demonic and over-ratiocinated Jew is tied
to the city because, as Donnelly observes in *The Golden Bottle*,
Jews are a "trading, not an agricultural people."[26] They cannot
enter the garden because they do not cultivate the soil.[27]

Within the brotherhood Gabriel finds no solution for the crises of
industrial poverty he has discovered in America. At the workingmen's meeting he listens to cynical laborers denounce Marxist
parties, cooperative movements, and universal education alike.
They angrily object to a clergyman's plea for rejoicing in poverty.
Only the speaker who appeals to force stirs the crowd: "There is no
remedy but the utter destruction of the existing order of things" (p.
173). The meeting ends when the police arrive, clubbing members
of the audience and arresting the speakers. This, then, is animated
anarchy: there is no longer a valid plan for an organized future in
New York. All solutions have canceled each other out, permitting
Gabriel to remove himself from the debate and thus from the histori-

cal moment itself. Donnelly the Populist shows his narrator observing events from a distance; like those in the farmers' party, he saw no solution to the nation's problems in urban politics. But the idealized world contained in his pastoral vision was also fast disappearing. The nihilistic images that follow indicate that Donnelly had reached a political and literary impasse—the impossibility inherent in the genre (how can the future be told if it does not yet exist?)—and that he contemplated the impending demise of both the agrarian and industrial worlds.

Shifts in Gabriel's point of view mirror his political frustration. At first he writes to his brother, in admiration of the new civilization, "Who can fix a limit to the intelligence or the achievements of our species?" (p. 7). But later he observes a "joyless, sullen crowd." Soon the tired workers refuse to collaborate in this subject-object relationship: "Many of them scowled at us, as we pass by them in our carriage." There is no hint that in its angry passivity this joyless mass will transform the future. Lacking Julian West's faith in human capacity, Gabriel increasingly sees the workers of New York as victims, hopeless jests of forces they cannot possibly understand: "These vast, streaming, endless swarms were the condemned, marching noiselessly as shades to unavoidable and everlasting misery. . . . It seemed to me that I was witnessing the resurrection of the dead" (pp. 37–38). Eventually Gabriel realizes that the slow and rhythmic march of the living dead who "unroll" before him offers at best stolid resignation, mere endurance, death in life in a world without end. The future belongs to desperate people who fish for rats in the sewers of New York and who, "if not prevented by the police, would consummate their animal-like nuptials in the streets" (p. 41); yet they are "merely automata, in the hands of some ruthless and unrelenting destiny," reduced to the machinery they construct and operate. Donnelly develops both bestial and mechanical images to underscore the workers' inability to design a better society. With sacerdotal resonance, now thoroughly distanced from the mill operators, Gabriel proclaims, "The illusions of the imagination, which beckon us all forward, even in the roughest paths and through the darkest valleys and shadows of life, had departed from the scope of their vision" (p. 38). Gabriel watches as the slum dwellers, marked by "inferior" physique, lacking all intellectual or creative outlets, become the easy prey of Caesar Lomellini's fanaticism, and obey his orders to destroy New York.

In making his Populist critique, Donnelly borrowed a number of devices from the sentimental tradition: a declaration of a high didactic purpose, an emphasis on feeling, and a melodramatic view of human nature as divided between the extremes of good and evil.

Donnelly introduces *Caesar's Column* with these words: "May it, under the providence of God, do good to this generation and posterity." But in apocalyptic utopias, the intention to "do good" was more than a device to free authors to tell lascivious tales of lust, romance, and revolution; this pretense at historical accuracy furthered the prophetic function. In this introduction, Donnelly—a bit immodestly—fuses his didactic and political intention and establishes his prophetic role:

It must not be thought, because I am constrained to describe the overthrow of civilization, that I desire it. The prophet is not responsible for the event he fortells. . . . I seek to preach into the ears of the able and rich and powerful the great truth that neglect of the sufferings of their fellows, indifference to the great bond of brotherhood which lies at the base of Christianity, and blind, brutal and degrading worship of mere wealth, must—given time and pressure enough—eventuate in the overthrow of society and the destruction of civilization. (P. 3)

Two love stories in *Caesar's Column* exploit the sentimental novel's principles of literary construction—linking realism to melodrama, rage to pathos, and satire to romance. But Donnelly's purpose is different from that of the conventional romance. Love increases Gabriel's commitment to the social cause. Donnelly's fusion of sentiment and politics was part of a tradition in later nineteenth-century popular literature.[28] Following the religious revivals of the 1850s, sentimental or "domestic" novelists, such as Maria Cummens and Susannah Warner, attached the experience of religious conversion to commitment to a variety of social causes, keeping the revivalists' emphasis on intense feeling and the visible expression of emotion (a lachrymose tendency probably welcomed by readers of the drier tracts of socialist literature). In addition to adopting the "purgation by tears" motif,

Donnelly and other apocalyptic utopians took another device from the sentimental repertory: domestic novelists traditionally rewarded their characters with marriage and inheritance for social acts of compassion and benevolence.

The author of *Caesar's Column,* like other writers of apocalyptic utopias, tried to avoid the taint of "fiction," despite the fervid melodrama of their novels. Many apocalyptic tales bore such subtitles as "A True History," "Founded on Fact," "Drawn from Incidents in Real Life." Disguised as diaries, journals, letters, and autobiographies, these case histories of virtue rewarded (in utopia) obeyed the contemporary critical injunction to tell the truth, while also avoiding some of the narrative demands of the novel. Thus Donnelly exploits two elements of sentimental fiction: the transcription of "actual" events and the depiction of powerfully dramatic incidents that illustrate the importance of a virtuous life.

At the same time, like other writers, Donnelly adapted the sentimental tradition to the political and aesthetic demands of the utopian novel. As in the sentimental genre, the plot of the apocalyptic utopia follows the young hero and heroine (often orphaned literary progeny of Jane Eyre) as they endure a series of trials—unemployment, foreclosed mortgages—that introduce them to the sordid realities of capitalism (it is a story "founded on fact"), test their wills, and encourage them to seek a safe corner in pastoralism (the story portrays "virtue rewarded").

But in the presentation of the female protagonist, utopians altered the earlier sentimental pattern, popular in the United States since the 1850s, whereby the abandoned heroine, exposed to poverty and loneliness, finds economic security and social status only through marriage.[29] Unlike "the damned mob of scribbling women" who tormented Hawthorne with their maudlin plots and high sales, apocalyptic utopians rejected marriage as a plot resolution and the praise of domesticity as an incentive to female conformity. Rather than rewarding submission to authority—whether to God, society, or a sublunary father figure—they fashioned heroines who rebelled against materialistic and authoritarian norms. In Donnelly's second utopia, *The Golden Bottle,* the Populist mill worker Sophie Hetherington is arrested after she horsewhips the mill owner who has tried to rape her. Finally released from prison, Sophie organizes sewing cooperatives where seamstresses, who have been "ruined" by their employers, share their profits and protect themselves from sexual harassment.

In *Caesar's Column,* although Gabriel and Max abandon the proletariat to its own conflagration, they rescue two of its most genteel virgins from poverty and eventual prostitution, rewarding them not only with marriage but also with life ever after in Uganda.[30] Gabriel has discovered that poor Estella Washington (who can trace her ancestry back to presidential respectability) has been sold into Prince Cabano's harem by a wicked aunt, and he urges her to take up a poisoned dagger to defend her virginity from the assaults of the Jewish-Italian industrialist:

"If [Cabano's servants] break in, . . . use your knife on the first man that touches you. If they send you food or drink, do not use them. If they attempt to chloroform you, stop the pipe with soap. If the worse comes to the worst, use the rope ladder. If you manage to get outside the garden gate, call a hack and drive to that address." Here I gave her your direction on a small piece of tissue paper. "If you are about to be seized, chew up the paper and swallow it. Do not in any event destroy yourself," I added, "until the last desperate extremity is reached; for you have a powerful organization behind you, and even if recaptured, you will be rescued. Good by."[31]

Donnelly exploits a tradition that justified graphic and titillating descriptions of urban vice to "produce the best moral result upon the reader and make his heart better."[32] However, he expands on the political implications of the theme of the impoverished maid pursued by the lascivious aristocrat. In apocalyptic utopias, female melodrama heightens the cataclysmic view of unfolding events and pictures the dangers of capitalism through an exhibition of the perils of yet another kind of abuse: the threat to chastity. Although he borrowed the tradition of abduction from *Pamela* and Pamela's popular literary daughters, Donnelly's concerns with seduction and rape reflect new fears about sexual pressures on girls who leave home to work in the cities, girls who, as Donnelly says, "should have become the mothers of farm boys" instead.[33] Donnelly's Sophie Hetherington in *The Golden Bottle* commands a division of Russian Populists who fight the tsar, while the women in Albert Merrill's *The Great Awakening* operate "aerodrome bombers" in his civil war.[34] But most female characters in apocalyptic utopias

130

eventually settle down. Even Sophie, once the little seamstress, later the "Yankee woman [who] had won Armageddon! the Western girl [who] had achieved the millennium," returns to the midwest to establish women's "liberation" schools that offer diplomas for the finest cooking, cleanest house, and purest butter.

The plight of female characters in *Caesar's Column* not only dramatizes the moral debauchery of the plutocracy and heightens the sense of impending violence, but also introduces the rural alternative to industrial decay. Although technology and human depravity have warped God's kingdom on earth, a small group survives the destruction and prepares for the eternal future. The apocalyptic project traditionally holds utopian moments within it: the millennium occurs before the Day of Judgment, and represents a worldly pause, a recess of a thousand years, during which the devils are bound. In *Caesar's Column*, this intermission is pastoral, marking the spiritual as well as the social wrongs of the Gilded Age, uniting the chosen people and initiating the triumph of agrarian good over urban evil.

The spiritual passage begins when Max falls in love with Christina Jansen, a Scandinavian singer who supports her large family by performing in a music hall. But despite her dubious calling, Christina has maintained her innocence: "There was not the slightest suggestion of art, or craft, or double dealing, or thought within a thought, or even vanity." Hers is a natural female purity of purpose that has a transforming effect on the vulgar crowd. Her songs, "like . . . the gushing music of birds welcoming the red light of dawning day while the dew and silence lie over all nature," transcend the smoke and beer and lurid calls and quiet the crowd "like a revelation, and [she] walked about them like a singing spirit in the halls of light" (p. 200). Prefiguring rebirth, nature imagery surrounds Christina. One night she resists the advances of a wealthy admirer, and he stabs her in the throat. Again the urban danger is posed in a sexual metaphor.

But on the apocalyptic journey, suffering under despotism is transformed into a virtue. To protect Christina's impoverished family from the growing turmoil, Max rents a farm for them in upstate New York. Although this move from the city to the country ignores Donnelly's earlier discussions of agrarian poverty and rural violence, his intention, like Howells's, is to validate the country as a place for safety, regeneration, and emotional healing. Here Max the brooding revolutionary and Gabriel the disenchanted wool merchant climb trees, string garlands of wild flowers for the cows, and write romantic verses, cribbed from Bailey and Shakespeare. True to the pastoral tradition, in the country Gabriel and Max rediscover their ability to be playful and artistically creative, a vision derived from the agrarian myth.[35] Donnelly's vivid language, however, collapses to a cliché version of the convention: "The breezes touched us and dallied with us and delighted us, like ministering angels" (p. 234). His countryside lacks the particularities of detail and geography that mark the urban landscape.

Yet only in the country does Gabriel realize his capacity for aesthetic creativity, hope, and love. Moreover, the pastoral sojourn suggests to him the possibility of eternal life: "My soul rose upon wings and swam in the ether like a swallow; and I thanked God that he had given us this majestic, this beautiful, this surpassing world and had placed within us the delicate sensibility and capability to enjoy it. In the presense of such things death—annihilation—seemed to me impossible" (p. 234). In the garden, the human capacity to perceive beauty revives to confront annihilation. Here too, the characters' social purpose revives, placing the urban destruction of character in a larger framework. At the farm, on the eve of the revolution, Gabriel marries Estella Washington and Max marries Christina Jansen. The two discourses, the religious and the social, are woven together, the first making possible the second. Unlike New York, whose inhabitants are about to destroy themselves in their anger and guilt, the natural world will endure:

The grass covers the graves. The flowers grow in the furrows of the cannon balls; the graceful foliage festoons with blossoms the ruins of the prison and the torture chamber; and the corn springs alike under the boot of the helot or yeoman. And I said to myself that even though civilization should commit suicide, the earth would still remain—and with it some remnant of mankind. (P. 235)

Thus, on the eve of the holocaust, Gabriel discovers the apocalyptic paradox: annihilation is at once destruction and a means of redemption. There is no "useable past" for him in the world of social activity, but the green world will abide, if only to disguise the debased artifacts of human activity. Nature will compensate for our failure in our own time, and a small remnant of humanity will survive to transfer the lessons from the secular past to the eternal future and fulfill the Christian promise of salvation. Nevertheless, the moment in the garden cannot be sustained: "I felt that we were like silly sheep gamboling on the edge of the volcano," says Gabriel (p. 238).

The visit to the farm provides a sharp contrast to the impending destruction, picturing the moral as well as the economic dependence of the city on the country: nature shows how far city life has deviated from human possibility. New Yorkers have ignored the imperatives of the garden that are critical to Donnelly's reading of history, a reading that repudiates the explanations provided by evolutionary theory or the doctrine of rational Christian progress.[36] By framing the urban battle with images of pastoral life, Donnelly indicates the positive charge of revolution—the apocalyptic duality—that places the promise of the Ugandan garden in the inevitable historical cycle. Revelation and apocalypse give history a dramatic structure. Characters become actors who are moved, episodically, toward a conclusion; a series of conflicts leads, teleologically, to a hymn of rejoicing.

After the double wedding, the families return to the city to await the workers' revolt. Donnelly has no other choice: pastoralism, even for a Populist, is only an idea, a literary tradition that offers no functional alternative to urban capitalism. But even the redeemer figures lack options that might satisfy the angry workers. Max and Gabriel are resigned to watching New York burn in a fiery holocaust.

Destruction is total, as it must be. The very streets and buildings of the city bear the marks of the guilt and responsibility of the capitalists and burn as their punishment. Urban warfare, represented as divine retribution, discloses the existence of an angry class which, because of its perverted development, destroys society as a whole, including its own members and their achievements. Like the archangel who failed to convince Christians to awaken the heathen nations, with the self-righteous frustration of the unheeded prophet Gabriel concedes, "Now there is just one cure—the Brotherhood of Destruction." And from a rooftop the

133

shepherd watches the imperial metropolis itself become colonized as a series of angry groups—immigrants, women, farmers, and finally the desperately poor—ravage it in turn.

Thus the battle imaginatively realizes the political abstractions of the earlier naturalistic chapters: it is at once an image of political inevitability and an image of the final polarization of the forces of good and evil. As Tuveson notes, "All the cohorts of the enemy gather at Armageddon."[37] On the day appointed for the battle, the army, unaware that its corrupt commander has sold aerial bombers or "Demons" to the Brotherhood of Destruction, marches into a trap of barricades constructed in the ghetto by the enraged mob. In an image taken from Revelation, the Demon bombers are let loose to rain their poison "vials" from the sky. As Gabriel watches the army unwittingly march to their deaths, he observes "the very efflorescence of the art of war—the culmination of destruction— the perfect flower of ten thousand years of battle and blood" (p. 251). This mockery of evolutionary progress, in its "bravery of banners and uniforms, and shining decorations" forms a powerful contrast "with that gloomy, dark ragged sullen multitude" who will die along with the soldiers in the slums (p. 250). Donnelly's prophecy inverts Bellamy's vision of the army as a glamorous instrument for unity and social organization.

Metropolitan warfare is described in sharply realistic language. Gabriel sees wooden barricades alive with fire while poison bombs rain a "hail of death" on the surprised soldiers. "With my glass," observes Gabriel, "I can almost see the dynamite bullets exploding in the soldiers, tearing them to pieces, like internal volcanoes" (p. 254). The panicked soldiers, pursued by the mob, break into houses where they are garrotted in closets and under beds, or tossed alive and shrieking into the deadly fog of poison below. The volcano has erupted.

Next, the lumpen classes, the "ravenous wretches," seize the streets of the prostrate and smoking city. After them come the women, "or creatures that pass for such—having the bodies of women and the habits of ruffians;—harpies—all claws and teeth and greed—bold—desperate—shameless—incapable of good. They too are here. . . . They dart hither and thither; they swarm— they dance—they howl—they chatter—they quarrel and battle like carrion vultures over the spoils!" (p. 257). Donnelly pictures an angry image of the destructive momentum of uncontained female energy. His representation of social violence thus bridges two kinds of rhetoric: the fantastic and the naturalistic. The descriptions of women and workers derive from Donnelly's naturalistic account of urban brutality which flattens character and exaggerates biological drives. As agents of total social destruction and cosmic retribution, these bestial figures also point to the explosive imagery of the fantastic. Together they construct a powerful prediction of national suicide.

Thus the battle in *Caesar's Column* is, in large part, a literary projection of current middle-class fears: the masses, Gabriel determines, are "omnipotent to destroy; they are powerless to create" (p. 250). Caesar Lomellini, the brutish leader of the workers' cabal, bears out this nihilistic vision when he is distracted from war by Frederika, Prince Cabano's mistress. He pursues her, "crashing through the shrubbery like an enraged mammoth; and soon the cripple [the Jew of the brotherhood] laughed one of his dreadful laughs, for he saw the giant returning, dragging the fair girl after him by the hair of her head, as we have seen, in the pictures, ogres hauling off captured children to destruction" (p. 263). Using bestial images from the fairy tale, Donnelly again resorts to a sexual metaphor to delineate upper-class fears of the poor. Inexplicably, the working-class leader has been transformed into an evil dictator and the society must pay for its faith in false prophets: "Civilization is gone, and all the devils are loose! No more courts, nor judges, nor constables, nor prisons! That which took the world ten thousand years to create has gone in an hour" (p. 257). From the inverted perspective of the battle, Gabriel mourns the institutions he had satirized earlier as the instruments if not the very causes of social inequality.

Human nature itself fuses the images of annihilation and utopia, and it alone determines the course of history. Caesar Lomellini, originally the white pastoral victim, is now "so black with dust and blood that he looked like a Negro. He was hatless and his mat of hair rose like a wild beast's mane. He had been drinking; his eyes were wild and rolling; he roared when he spoke. A king devil, come fresh out of hell, could scarcely have looked more terrible" (p. 272). No longer the hardworking white yeoman deprived of his land, with his children's birthright usurped by railroads and mortgage companies, the revolutionary Caesar is deranged, massive, and threateningly sexual, and portrayed as having stereotypical "Negro" traits.[38] By enraging the betrayed mob, he finally thwarts the possibility for rational social rebirth.

Caesar's own "monument to this day's glorious work" is not a new society wrested from the ashes of the old but Caesar's Column, a giant pyramid built in Union Square from the corpses of the quarter of a million dead, laid to rest in cement by the intellectuals and professionals under the whips of the liberated proletariat. "It was Anarchy personified; the men of intellect were doing the work; the men of muscle were giving the orders" (pp. 277–78). Projecting the dystopian fears of the powerless middle class, Gabriel's shift in allegiance is complete.

But this is a rite of social purification, and the cataclysm must continue to the end. Within the apocalyptic metaphor, history shows the working out of the Christian promise that evil will be destroyed and that destruction will bring about the Day of the Lord. Although Donnelly attached a Populist perspective to his apocalyptic vision, even the peasants, the last group to seize the city, are perverted by the inexorable movement of the revolution. The street battle in New York derives from the biblical genre that prescribes a movement from Sheol (the title of the chapter) to the New Jerusalem, a traditional passage which Donnelly shaped to his observations of industrial capitalism. But this battle differs from traditional apocalyptic visions in its realistic projection of the details of urban warfare; Donnelly does not reverse "the ground rules of the extra-textual world" which traditionally propels a description of apocalypse into the literary world of the fantastic. Although informed by the rhetoric and distorted by the teleology of apocalypse, the images in Donnelly's siege arise organically from his naturalistic pictures of urban life.[39]

By nightfall, crowds of farmers reach New York, but these are "no longer the honest yeomanry who had filled, in the old time, the armies of Washington and Jackson, and Grant and Sherman, with brave patriotic soldiers; but their brutalized descendants— fierce serfs, cruel and bloodthirsty peasants. Every man who owned anything was their enemy and their victim" (p. 280). With humanity now divided into the condemned who must die and the redeemed who must escape, no third force remains to rebuild the nation. Loading an airship with samples of American technology and volumes of its literature, Max and Gabriel flee with their families in a Demon bomber—a modern Noah's ark. Only the idle rich remain to lead, but they have degenerated and fail to pass on their strength to their offspring—Cabano, the Jew, and Caesar die unmarried.

With Babylon fallen, the travelers can turn their swords into plowshares—searching, as Marx wrote in the *Eighteenth Brumaire*, "for salvation behind society's back." The new society to be built in Uganda will thrive as a counterpoise to the world just destroyed. It will neither correct nor resolve the conditions of urban struggle that Gabriel discovered in New York. That story must remain unfinished, because, by tradition, the millennium is a time when the power of evil is bound for one thousand years; it is not vanquished. Uganda is merely the last earthly chance to live well, which in both Populist and apocalyptic assumptions means to live close to nature; it is not an eternal option. Ultimately, pastoralism is the avenging angel and the prince of peace.

In Uganda the ethics of Eden and the politics of Populism will together thrive. Donnelly conceives of history geographically: only in the garden can democracy bloom. Soon after the Demon lands in Africa with its cargo of American literature and political refugees, Gabriel and Max plan for a new Ugandan society to fulfill their Populist prophecies. Recognizing the moral and fiscal determinants of rural life, Gabriel and Max organize the state into autonomous villages whose governments are shared by workers, manufacturers, and intellectuals—but this time the workers hold veto power. Despite these specialized roles, the division of labor is rudimentary, and everyone is somehow self-employed. Uganda enjoys a "natural harmony" of production and consumption—the apotheosis of laissez-faire liberalism. However, to prevent competition and monopolization, the government builds and operates the railroads, telephone lines, and mines—a solution borrowed directly from the farmers' party platform. Because the primacy of money itself was crucial to the Populists' conspiracy theory of history (where a monied Jewish class controlled the spendable wealth), Uganda has abolished gold and silver, as well as all interest on loans. To control the bourgeoisie, the state limits prop-

137

erty holdings and stipulates that merchants may trade only with foreign countries whose wages are as high as Uganda's, an unusual innovation in nineteenth-century utopian fictions written at the early edge of international corporatism. Still, Uganda pursues a high level of technology (the economic implications of this are as invisible as its peasants) which is allowed to flourish only as long as it remains a means to the nation's spiritual concerns. Most important to the Populist society is the law that there shall be only one major town in Arcadia.

In Uganda Max and Gabriel have reconstructed a God-fearing agrarian past built from Donnelly's nostalgic memories of Minnesota in the 1850s. The village itself, with its tempered prosperity, family life, modest houses, and tree-lined streets, brings human conduct into conformity with the idea of right and prepares the yeoman to receive his weekly dose of "morality and religion." Where Bellamy anticipated a natural development from agrarianism to technocracy, Donnelly foresaw reversals within a historical cycle. As the end of secular history, Uganda marks the restoration of the original American society. The embittered but visionary politician allowed Adam's Yankee children to return to Eden. But perhaps Donnelly could not fully repress the image he drew of the Brotherhood of Destruction. Although Uganda is the kingdom of God on earth, it is to be governed by "graceful men": "For good purposes and honest instincts we may trust to the multitude; but for longsighted thoughts of philanthropy, of statesmanship and statecraft, we must look to a few superior intellects" (pp. 301–02).

In Uganda, the naturalist and apocalyptic metaphors which have sustained each other divide, and there are two endings to *Caesar's Column*—the secular and the utopian, the nihilist and the hopeful. After five years in Africa, Max leaves in the flying Demon to explore the outside world where he discovers that

three fourths of the human race, in the civilized lands, have been swept away. In France and Italy and Russia the slaughter has been most appalling. In many places the Demon sailed for hundreds of miles without seeing a human being. The wild beasts—wolves and bears—are reassuming possession of the country. In Scandinavia and in Northern America, where the severity of the climate somewhat mitigated the ferocity of man, some sort of government is springing up again; and the peasants have formed themselves into troops to defend their cattle and their homes against the marauders. (P. 310)

In the apocalyptic metaphor, the siege in New York and the passage to Uganda signify preparation for eternal destiny, but in the naturalist vision—postlapsarian and premillenarian—the cataclysm marks the end of modern history.

Ultimately the coexistence of the two endings, derived from two literary modes, constitutes a critique of utopianism itself. Utopia, Donnelly has shown, can moderate human nature but it cannot abolish death—indeed, the apocalyptic utopian awaits death. When utopia is anything less than worldwide, it cannot be truly "utopian" for it perforce ignores all the unfortunate people who live outside the "good place," an exclusion which Gabriel justifies by reminding us that Uganda is the land of the chosen people. As the Ugandans barricade the passes to their mountain colony, guilt sneaks under the garden fence.

Utopian fiction is a genre built on a hypothesis; it rests on an imaginative answer to an implied rhetorical question: "What if?" Apocalyptic utopia is the only species of utopian fiction that fills in the temporal space between the question and the answer. Only the apocalyptic utopia represents a transition from the present to the future, an imaginary historical passage that is neither fantastic nor extraneous to the imperatives of satire. Indeed, social cataclysms within utopian fiction bravely develop the consequences of satire by picturing its latent warning: the danger of impending labor violence. In *A Connecticut Yankee in King Arthur's Court,* just before the Battle of the Sandbelt—when Camelot, unified by telephones and sanitized by toothpaste, is about to blow itself up fighting the Catholic church—Hank Morgan observes,

From being the best electric-lighted town in the kingdom and the most like a recumbent son of anything you ever saw, it was becoming simply a blot—a blot upon darkness—that is to say, it was darker and solider than the rest of the darkness, and so you could see it a little better; it made me feel as if the Church was going to keep the upper hand, now, and snuff out all my beautiful civilization just like that.[40]

Satire in apocalyptic utopias intensifies the darkness so we too can "see it a little better" and so we too can be stopped.

139

Paradoxically, in his exaggerated condition, the "recumbent son" is particularly vulnerable to annihilation. Within the rhetoric of apocalypse, darkness is finite, but within the rhetoric of naturalism, darkness is infinite. From his perch in Uganda, Gabriel wonders, "Why, where are the wolves, that used to prowl through the towns and cities of the world that has passed away? The slinking, sullen, bloody-mouthed miscreants, who, under one crafty device or another, would spring upon, and tear and destroy the poor, shrieking, innocent people—where are they?" (p. 313). In his flying Demon, Max discovers they are everywhere but in Uganda, where "mankind moves with linked hands through happy lives to deaths." Inside utopia, the apprehension of a liberating death does not betoken ending itself. With the secularization of the apocalyptic telos, utopia resists the fatalism of literary naturalism and insists on the possibility of hope.

SEVEN

A State of Her Own;
or, What Did Women Want?

*I*n the late 1890s a small group of utopians attempted to answer the Woman Question—a social condition repeatedly posed as a query. These feminist fantasies of social reform and moral regeneration add yet another structural paradox to the utopian novel which, as a genre, reflects real conditions at the same time that it opposes them. Pictures of all-female societies and portraits of female citizens of utopia create an extra twist in this literary paradigm of inversion and exaggeration. Feminist thinkers long before Simone de Beauvoir have shown the multiple ways in which women are regarded, even regard themselves, as "the negative imprint of domination."[1] But in feminist utopias, that internalized designation as the "other" of man expresses itself as a positive proposition: the various expressions of feminine otherness are posed as an alternative to the Gilded Age. Yet in postulating the female "other" as a negation of the male-dominated nineteenth-century world, feminist utopias reproduce many of the real conditions of women's work, as well as patterns of belief about femininity, in the society they seek to transcend.

Utopian novels clearly reflect the social dislocation and dissatisfaction stimulated by women's new economic and social roles after the Civil War. From 1865 on, a "domestic revolution" was under way which freed many women for pursuits other than housework. The development of gas lighting, municipal water systems, domestic plumbing, canning, the commercial production of ice, the improvement of furnaces, stoves, and washtubs, and the popularization of the sewing machine helped growing numbers of women step off the domestic treadmill.[2] Yet except for such northeastern cities as Philadelphia, where 28 percent of working women were employed in factories during the decade following the Civil War, traditional kinds of female activity prevailed. Women worked as dressmakers, seamstresses, hatmakers, and servants, and many did piece-work in their homes. By 1880 these patterns were beginning to change. A few women became doctors. Significant numbers worked as cigar makers, shopkeepers, typesetters, common laborers, and even as fortunetellers, while over one-third of working women—mainly widows and married women—ran boarding houses.[3] As the corporation became the dominant form of business organization, the number of working women increased further; clerical jobs such as typing and operating a telephone switchboard joined traditional female occupations such as sewing, teaching, and domestic service. (By 1910 in cities with populations of 100,000 or more, nearly one-third of all adult women worked outside the home.)[4] However, women generally received wages that were only half to two-thirds of those of men in jobs requiring comparable training and effort. And because women's employment was largely confined to service work or the production of nondurable goods, it appeared to have less economic value or long-term consequence. Following the decline of the Knights of Labor, which had welcomed women, the new American Federation of Labor organized only skilled workers, thus excluding most women by definition. This loss of a large national labor organization hindered women's opportunities to fight for higher wages, the eight-hour day, and the abolition of child labor; at the same time it furthered the sense of the invisibility of women's work.

Meanwhile, many middle-class women who were freed from the constraints of housework, who at first felt "all dressed up with no place to go," soon used their new time in a variety of reform organizations that tried to improve the situation of women and children. The Young Women's Christian Association, for example, concerned itself with the moral and religious life of young girls working away from home. The W.C.T.U. was founded in 1874, at a time when most states placed a married woman's income at the disposal of her husband; thus heavy drinkers were literally consuming their wives' and children's incomes as well as their own. In responding to widespread alcoholism, the Women's Christian Temperance Union expressed concerns that were economic as well as moral.

Many women believed that they could not protect their homes and families without a legal voice in public affairs. The history of the suffrage movement from the 1870s through the difficult final passage of the Nineteenth Amendment in 1920 reflects the many contradictions of feminism.[5] Those who saw women as inherently more virtuous than men believed that women's suffrage would stimulate temperance and antiprostitution legislation; the women's vote would contribute to the moral growth of the nation. Because women were in the forefront of religious and evangelical movements, it seemed to them that they had a moral right to political participation. Others, such as Susan B. Anthony and Florence Kelley, believed that women needed the vote to institutionalize solutions to the economic and urban problems of the industrial revolution. Sarah Moore Grimké and Charlotte Perkins Gilman viewed the vote as a small but symbolic part of a larger struggle for women's equality. Others, such as Mother Jones of the United Mine Workers, believed that the campaign for the vote diverted women from other important issues, while keeping them busy with "suffrage, prohibition, and charity," and announced, "You don't need the vote to raise hell."

What did woman want? Writers of both progressive and feminist utopias believed that she wanted political equality and fundamental rearrangements at home. Acknowledging the lonely and monotonous nature of housework, they replaced it with either collective or mechanical alternatives. From Bellamy on, we find public arrangements for childrearing, for buying and preparing food, and for laundering clothes. Utopian scientists invent sewing machines, electric stoves, refrigerators, washing machines, dishwashers, prepared goods, and ready-made garments—although a glance through the advertisements in later nineteenth-century women's magazines reveals that versions of nearly all these inventions were already available to those who could pay for them. But utopians added the important corollary that domestic technology should be available to all women, not just the rich.

Yet despite the diversity of women's new activities and goals, by the late 1890s there were only two common literary stereotypes of women models available, which Caroline Ticknor portrayed in a fictional interview, "The Steel Engraving Lady and the Gibson

143

Girl," that appeared in the *Atlantic Monthly* in 1901. We discover the Steel Engraving Lady, the woman most often portrayed in magazine and book illustrations, characteristically seated at her window, absorbed with thoughts of her lover. She is modest, idle, and self-contained, for the province of the Steel Engraving Lady, the True Woman, is the home; her world is well defined and enclosed. While she may be curious about life outside, she is an observer only.[6]

By comparison, the Gibson Girl, who has come to interview the lady for a paper on "extinct types," is arrogant and self-sufficient. Not only is she involved in her career, but also she is interested in pleasing no one but herself. The Gibson Girl immediately announces that the keynote of modern thought is not "What does man like?" but "What does woman prefer?" She adds, "You see, I've had a liberal education. I can do everything my brothers do, and do it rather better, I fancy. I am an athlete and a college graduate, with a wide universal outlook. My point of view is free from narrow influences and quite outside of the home boundaries."[7] Although Ticknor clearly sides with the Steel Engraving Lady, she acknowledges that the Gibson Girl is the woman of the future.

Most nineteenth-century utopians made no such concession; despite the True Woman's citizenship in a utopian society of social equals, she still preserves the values of fragility and domesticity, like Edith Leete in *Looking Backward*. With one exception, male authors of utopian fiction projected the conventional dichotomy between the public and the personal sphere onto the future. Only one nineteenth-century writer, William H. Bishop, in *The Garden of Eden, USA* (1895), created female characters who might logically inhabit an egalitarian society.[8] Stella Vernon and Alice Hathaway are outspoken feminists who quite resemble the Gibson Girl. The fable follows two men, Wayne and Stanley, on their bumbling quest for ideal women to join their planned community. In particular, Wayne seeks a Cinderella to elevate as queen of utopia, which he plans to purchase for "moral miners" and "genteel paupers"—his criteria for women seems to parallel his patronizing attitude toward the working class. But he believes that only a woman will bring him into closer sympathy with the "toiling millions of men."[9] Although Wayne and Stanley first search for a woman with "a step like that of a conqueror," Wayne chooses Stella the moment he sees her, sensing that she "has a yielding disposition." As he admits, "I could mold her to my purposes quickly enough" (p. 20), and he persuades her to enter the Garden of Eden.

Like other progressive utopians, the planners of the Garden of Eden make fundamental changes in the political and economic roles of their female members. A guaranteed wage ensures that women do not have to marry to enjoy a household of their own; centralized cooking and mechanical cleaning devices not only free women from housework, but also they ensure that men do not have to marry to obtain a cheap housekeeper. But Bishop's unique contribution to the genre of the feminist utopia lies in the relations he develops between politics and character. Unlike other heroines of utopian fiction of the time, Stella Vernon and Alice Hathaway have internalized the egalitarian politics of their community, giving them a perspective that changes their attitudes toward men and toward their own labor. Alice rejects the notion that women are "butterflies" or "dollbabies" and describes instead her own (somewhat erotic) fascination with machinery: "I delight in the manifestation of power. I could stand and watch a drop hammer all day long, I believe" (p. 170). Their new status in the community is also related to their ability to defend themselves from male violence. *The Garden of Eden, USA* is the first utopia to mention rape as a social problem and to hint at resistance to it. Like every other Edenic woman, Stella has learned to box because "in this age of the world, the power of self-defense or of indignant protest is more necessary to women than to men" (p. 148). And in their love affairs with utopian men, Stella and Alice presume their sexual equality. With a self-confidence born of her power to act in the world, Stella surprises Stanley by frankly expressing her admiration for him. A true Gibson Girl, she takes the initiative by inviting him on a hike. Yet, even despite this break from the model of the True Woman who observes the world of challenge and activity outside her window, Stella feels it necessary to conform to Stanley's expectations by abandoning her trousered gym suit for a skirt. Maddened by her constricted female dress, she complains, "I must consent to be dragged and lifted upward like a New York belle in the Adirondacks, piloted by New York dudes who are only a little less weak than herself" (p. 21). Ultimately Stanley surrenders, thereby renouncing the cult of the True Woman, "I did not want a toy wife. . . . I honored her for the bold aggressive stand which she was taking" (p. 22). In reply, Stella takes off her skirt and flings it over the side of the mountain.

The representation of female freedom in *The Garden of Eden, USA* is, however, still bound by the tensions between sex and class that have haunted the women's movement since the early suffragists. Like the stereotyped Gibson Girl, the flapper, and the swinging single, Stella and Alice simply volunteer for liberation. Although Bishop clearly inverted significant assumptions about femininity, he ignored the underpinnings of those ideas: the facts of reproduction, the economic and social role of the family, the value of a reserve of cheap labor, and woman's role as consumer. Thus the complex functions of patriarchy which retarded social change and reinforced the image of the Steel Engraving Lady remain unexamined. The Garden of Eden simply abolishes patriarchy along with capitalism, just as Bishop launches the utopia itself by neither evolution nor revolution but by the gift of a generous millionaire. In fact, Bishop seems uncomfortable with the characters he has created. Eventually Wayne admits that the women box "only with one another as a rule, more in bravado of conventional prejudices than anything else" (p. 198). And after her day's work in the laundry, Stella leads classes in the social graces.

This sort of paradoxical and yet ultimately reductive portrait of women was attacked by Mary Ford in a review of *Looking Backward* in 1889 in which she criticized the sentimental portrait of the utopian woman. Instead, Ford sought a world that would not treat women as "females" but as "human beings, capable of participating with men on an equal basis in the affairs of the world."[10] A novel published in the same year, *Mizora: A Prophecy* (1889) by Mary H. Lane, would at first seem to fulfill Ford's criteria for utopian feminism. The first fictional creation of an all-female utopian society in American literature, it anticipated the imaginary worlds of Charlotte Perkins Gilman and Joanna Russ. *Mizora* is the journal of a Russian princess whose boat is caught in a storm in the northern seas, is sucked into an ocean in the interior of the earth, where it finally lands on a world inhabited only by women.

The society she finds in Mizora has resolved the problem of female inequality by simply eliminating men.

The princess learns that 3,000 years ago, when men ruled Mizora, "Plots, intrigues, murders, and wars were their active employments." Woman, meanwhile, "was a beast of burden. She was regarded as inferior to man, mentally as well as physically." Although man held woman in "chivalrous regard," her work was more arduous than his, while her wages were lower. But it was not until the inland world faced a civil war around the issue of slavery that Mizoran women recognized their own inequality. At first they organized clubs for their safety and protection, but soon the clubs developed into an active women's army which eventually seized control of the state, and established a new law-and-order government of college-educated females. The first act of the new government was to exclude men from all official affairs, and after a hundred years, "not a representative of the sex was in existence." As in almost all female utopias, the process whereby men become extinct is unexplained.[11]

Paradoxically, the assumptions that support this separatist yet cosmic plan for social regeneration stem directly from the repressive ideology surrounding middle-class women in the nineteenth century. The much-vaunted moral superiority of women, who are seen as instinctively peaceful and pure, is responsible for the achievement of a prosperous and serene society in Mizora. As the princess's storm-tossed ship enters the calm Mizoran sea, she hears soft music coming from a bejeweled boat, shaped like a fish:

Its scales glittered like gems as it moved gracefully and noiselessly through the water. Its occupants were all young girls of the highest type of blonde beauty. It was their soft voices, accompanied by some peculiar stringed instruments they carried, that had produced the music I heard. . . . No animals were visible, nor sound of any. No hum of life. All nature lay asleep on voluptuous beauty, veiled in a glorious atmosphere. . . . Upon the lawn directly before us, a number of most beautiful girls had disposed themselves at various occupations. Some were reading, some sketching, and some at various kinds of needlework. I noticed they were all blondes. (Pp. 25–28)

The Mizoran woman is the True Woman, the "angel of the house"[12] carried to her logical extreme, still contentedly submissive, but strong in her inner purity and religiosity, queen of her own contained realm, which is really the extension of her home. Pious, intellectual, apparently indifferent to the material world she has apparently designed and built, she is the feminized ideal of Anglo-Saxon racial superiority.

Yet it is not simply the visual imagery of this passage which recalls the repressive stereotypes of women. The quietness that characterizes this scene seems to project upon this utopia the shadow of a significant aspect of the actual condition of women. Silence is an ambiguous image for a feminist utopia. In Mizora it is associated with passivity, indeed, with death: "No hum of life. All nature lay asleep on voluptuous beauty." The result of institutional suppression of women's activity and language is ironically presented as positive. Although Mizora is a mechanized society designed by female scientists, built by female carpenters, and governed by female politicians, all the women are represented as virtually asleep. Like Ticknor's Steel Engraving Lady, they embroider, play stringed instruments, and speak in hushed voices. Their beauty is indistinguishable from their Christian grace. Lane's serene images unwittingly point to one of the dilemmas of characterization in utopian fiction; utopian citizens often reproduce the very patterns that the utopian state claims to repudiate. Although Mizora purports to transcend Victorian limitations on women's activity, it nonetheless reflects one of the deepest structures of patriarchy. As Xavière Gauthier has observed,

Women are, in fact, caught in a very real contradiction. Throughout the course of history, they have been mute, and it is doubtless by virtue of this mutism that men have been able to speak and write. As long as women remain silent, they will be outside the historical process. But, if they begin to speak and write as men do, they will enter history subdued and alienated; it is a history that, logically speaking, their speech should disrupt.[13]

Yet in this Mizoran "aristocracy of intellectuals" that thrives without apparent activity, it is hard to picture any role for women's speech—creative or disruptive.

Lane accounts for the matriarchal but not for the androgynous order. The princess learns that female rule originated 3,000 years ago when women formed clubs for their mutual protection. Eventually these organizations grew into a unified military force that "discreetly" took over the state. Over thousands of years, elaborate patterns of conformity have eliminated the need for female originality—indeed, for thought itself. Because the telos of Mizora embodies stasis as a female value, the energizing forces of personality—passion, competition, ambition, love—are irrelevant. In fact, it is impossible to distinguish among Mizoran women because they all partake of an ideal model, a conception of character which contributes to a generalized or stereotypical, as opposed to particularized, portrait of female personality. Thus, despite her new vocation, the Mizoran woman fulfills the same function as her American sister: to uphold and defend the moral values of society.

In Lane's androgynous society, then, sexual roles disappear, but sexual identity remains. The princess contrasts this womblike world hidden in the interior of the earth to the world outside:

In my world man was regarded, or he had made himself regarded, as a superior being. He had constituted himself the Government, the Law, Judge, Jury and Executioner. He doled out reward or punishment as his conscience or judgement dictated. He was active and belligerent always in obtaining and keeping every good thing for himself. He was indispensible. Yet here was a nation of fair, exceeding fair women doing without him, and practicing the arts and sciences far beyond the imagined pale of human science and skill. (P. 4)

The college preceptress informs the princess that after the women's military groups gained power, they "excluded men from all affairs and privileges for a period of one hundred years. . . . At the end of that time, not a representative of the sex was in existence." Ironically, women rendered men extinct simply by depriving them of activity. When the visitor asks a Mizoran girl about men, she receives this reply: "Perhaps it is some extinct animal. . . . We have so many new things to study and investigate, that we pay little attention to ancient history" (p. 55). Lane has projected onto men the "invisibility" that is traditional for females. But even without men, Mizoran women conform to the standards of the cult of True Womanhood—they are pious and pure. Only here women can resolve that embarrassing Victorian contradiction between esteem for motherhood and the eleva-

149

tion of chastity: "We have got rid of the offspring of Lust. Our children come to us as welcome guests through portals of holiest and purest affection" (p. 275).

Thus, although Mizoran women occupy all the positions in the world of politics, science, and economics, much to the princess's surprise (she at first thought it "impossible . . . for a country or government to survive without [man's] assistance and advice" [p. 39]), Lane makes these careers acceptable for women by idealizing them. The preceptress announces that life's "ultimate perfection will be the mind, where all happiness shall dwell, where pleasure shall find fruition, and desire its ecstacy [sic]."[14] Sexual images project pleasure as a form of cerebral fulfillment. In fact, Mary Lane never shows women acting in unladylike ways, regardless of their political role. By telling us that the change from capitalism occured 3,000 years ago—that is, offstage—she avoids showing us a women's army actually seizing the government. Similarly, although ostensibly all Mizoran women may become doctors, machinists, or cooks, we see only teachers at work. Unidentified machines perform the menial labor, but Lane provides no pictures of factories nor of women making or running these labor-saving machines; science is also idealized.

Is Mizora, then, a strategic retreat, a radical alternative, or an image of internalized oppression? Freedom for the Mizoran woman certainly does not present the choices that it does to Hawthorne's Hester Prynne or Howells's Annie Kilburn: it merely promises economic predictability and a slightly relaxed etiquette. Through vegetarianism, equal education, and sexual repression, Mizora programs its citizens to exemplify the ideal, a telos that certainly inhibits an exciting plot. Nothing uncontained will ever happen in Mizora; conflict comes from the outside world, in the form of the visiting princess. But she is soon bored. Although she admits that the world at the center of the earth is productive and serene, she misses men, and sails away from Mizora in her little boat. Caroline Ticknor ended her interview with the True Woman complaining, "Hail the new woman—behold she comes apace! Woman, once man's superior, now his equal!" Mary Lane also begrudged women's "demotion" to equality and designed a utopian society to reclaim her superiority, restricted and repressed though it may have been.

A State of Her Own

In 1915 Charlotte Perkins Gilman, a well-known social scientist and organizer of the California Women's Congress, also wrote an all-female utopian novel, *Herland,* which she serialized in her own journal, *The Forerunner.*[15] *Herland* is a witty story of three American men exploring far-off jungles where they discover a hidden valley of white women beyond a river of sweet red water. Thus Gilman produces the "other" world of women, here literally removed and separate by the very structure of discovery of the utopian alternative. At first the explorers are charmed by the sight of three lithe young women climbing trees, apparently teasing them in a game of hide and seek. But soon the Americans realize that in pursuing these graceful hunters and gatherers they have been led into a mysterious electric net, and they enter Herland as the women's prisoners. The men are locked in an upstairs chamber until they agree to conform to the society's standards of behavior—a nice parodic touch echoing the plight of countless literary females. It is from this perspective of repression and containment that the travelers learn about the outside world.

After months of re-education, during which time they learn the Herland language, the men are released into the feminist society. Here they discover that without men, the women of Herland ably work at all sorts of jobs, from road construction to forestry to child care. In the American era of bustle and bodice, these women wear comfortable trousers and tunics with useful pockets; they play noncompetitive sports; and, of greatest curiosity to the travelers, they somehow reproduce asexually. Biology no longer creates a division of labor. With her own room, her own vocation, and her own name, the woman of Herland is no longer a commodity; ownership is no longer a metaphor for love. By eliminating men from the society, Gilman promises the fulfillment of true human essence, according to her a female trait carried by women's reproductive capacities but retarded by civilization's history of patriarchy and misogyny.

The three visitors learn that Herland was originally a polygamous and slaveholding society.[16] One fateful day 2,000 years before, the male citizens were defending a nearby mountain pass when a volcano erupted, killing the soldiers and sealing in the women and slaves. A violent slave revolt soon threatened the children but this time the young women, "instead of submitting, rose in sheer desperation, and slew their brutal conquerors" (p. 55). With the death of all the men, the women had to teach themselves many skills. Slowly the women learned to work with tools, designed new social institutions, and rebuilt their community. Nonetheless, they still faced extinction until a virgin woman mysteriously bore a daughter. Soon, other women immaculately reproduced, and the female tribe was saved. Without men, the women experience neither fear nor danger; wars have become extinct. In fact, all behavioral traits and activities that Gilman takes to be sex-linked have withered and Herland now recognizes neither masculine nor feminine characteristics. In particular, the "feminine charms," the character structure of a people without power, a people who are taught to honor, please, serve, and submit, have disappeared.

Instead of a misogynistic culture organized around profit, Gilman pictures a society organized around motherhood. She thus centers her asexual utopia on the distinguishing biological feature of women. Surely this is a paradoxical model for the abolition of patriarchy, since bearing children is a neutral, biological fact of reproduction and is in and of itself neither oppression nor liberation. In one sense, making motherhood the central image for a humanitarian vision undermines the utopian goals it represents.

Gilman adapts her ideas about motherhood from a Social Darwinist model, for clearly women's genetic capacity to reproduce and nurture offspring has ensured the survival of this female band. For Gilman, biological principles best explain the social processes of change. In *Women and Economics* (1898) she argued that change must occur in the United States, because the current sexual and economic systems were "unadaptive," according to the laws of evolution.[17] Along with Herbert Spencer, Gilman saw social process as a movement from the homogeneous to the heterogeneous, from the simple to the differentiated. But atavistic social structures, such as the nineteenth-century organization of housework, froze evolution at a simple level. However, Gilman observed that in nature, aggregates or groups that work harmoniously survive while unorganized units perish—an analysis that challenged individualistic readings of Darwin. Thus, Gilman found, because women of her time did not participate in the organized public world, they were "primitive" and they actually retarded social growth.

But this backward stage was not necessarily permanent. A true utopian, Gilman believed in the plasticity of human nature. Initially, she believed, technology would free women from the drudgery that in her time arrested their emotional and economic development. Released by machinery from the undifferentiated and repetitive tasks of housework, women could learn to generalize, classify, and collate information, rather than perpetually observe and describe the simple forms of thinking and speaking encouraged by the condition of housewife. This new woman, freed from social constraints, would recognize her genetic instincts and develop the race, just like the women of Herland. Gilman's utopian program stems from an analysis of patriarchy, rather than class or economic status, as the determining agent of women's oppression.

The travelers to Herland learn that the religious, political, and educational system is "maternal pantheism." The first virgin mother founded a new race of Aryan women capable of mysteriously reproducing themselves (bearing female children) when they enter an estrus-like condition. Over the years all masculine traits have decayed until, "Here was Mother Earth, bearing fruit. All that they ate was fruit of motherhood, from seed or egg or their product. By motherhood they were born and by motherhood they lived" (p. 59). Work is play, cooking is collective, and nurturing the young is of supreme importance. In the words of a Herland citizen: "The children in this country are the one center and focus of all our thoughts. Every step of our advance is always considered in its effect on them—on the race. You see, we are *mothers*" (p. 60). The needs of the children determine what work needs to be done. The number of children which the environment can support determines the size of the valley's population; eugenics determines which women may have children. Not surprisingly, abortion is the unspeakable crime. Thus the adult community is self-sacrificing as a whole.

Like Lane and a few other feminist utopians, Gilman eliminates oppression by simply eliminating men. Like them, she too largely ignores the factors of economic exploitation which coexisted with and stimulated patriarchy. With increasing embarrassment, the American explorers describe the United States as a place of overwork, poverty, and child labor, but Gilman fails to show how

153

women's rule would eliminate these problems, because the model of motherhood she adopts derives from the model of motherhood found in industrial societies. Mothers literally provide the industrial world with workers, whom they socialize, feed, clothe, and often heal. Also mothers are consumers (the necessary concomitant of producers) who select, prepare, and maintain supplies for the family. Because this work is unpaid, both mother and motherhood, laborer and labor are devalued. And since this work does not visibly contribute to profit, its political implications are hidden. Thus capital uses the biological fact of female reproduction to maintain itself.

How does Gilman transform all this in her utopia? By eliminating men, she ipso facto abolishes that division of labor whereby men work outside the home and women work inside it. Nancy Chodorow has observed: "The public sphere is non-familial and extra-domestic. . . . [However,] the public sphere forms 'society' and culture—those intended, constructed forms and ideas that take humanity beyond nature and biology. And the public sphere, therefore 'society' itself, is masculine."[18] And by eliminating the family, Gilman ends the split between public and private life, between masculine activity and feminine activity.

Gilman criticizes the United States precisely along those lines. When a visitor to Herland describes his American homeland, he explains complacently,

"When we say men, man, manly, manhood, and all the other masculine derivatives, we have in the background of our minds a huge vague crowded picture of the world and all its activities. . . . That vast background is full of marching columns of men, . . . of men steering their ships into new seas, exploring unknown mountains, breaking horses, herding cattle, ploughing and sowing and reaping, . . . digging in the mine, building roads and bridges and high cathedrals, . . . managing great business, teaching in all the colleges . . . of men everywhere, doing everything—'the world.' When we say women, we think female—the sex." (P. 137)

Through the voice of her misogynistic narrator, Gilman ironically reveals how housework seems demeaning while mining seems important. In Herland, by contrast, "the world" and "the sex" converge, just as they had long ago in hunting-and-gathering tribes. In her motherly utopia, the public sphere is itself familial. But this synthesis works only because Gilman has collapsed the categories of mental and manual labor, abolishing by utopian fiat the class distinctions separating different sorts of work.

In the end, the three visitors from America want to marry three virgins from utopia. Deciding to give heterosexuality another chance, the elders of Herland allow the weddings to take place, but problems soon arise. The men have already discovered that in this genderless world the girls of Herland never flirt and never wear anything more revealing than loose tunics and knee breeches. Now they find that their brides are indifferent to sexual feeling and will have intercourse only for procreation. Again the travelers are trounced by the ideology of idealized motherhood.

Nevertheless, the narrator eventually discovers that his chaste marriage meets all his needs for attention and affection, and to his surprise he realizes that his sexual desire is decreasing. The sexual response he had been accustomed to proves to have been an artificially stimulated appetite. Public respect and familial peace have somehow diminished his need—here seen as an exclusively masculine need—for sex, and in his friendship with his "good comrade" the visitor finds "a pleasant rested calm feeling, which [he] had imagined could only be attained in one way" (p. 127). Instead, he realizes he has a physical relation (of sorts) with his wife, expressed through nurturing touches: "She was stroking my hair . . . in a gentle motherly way" (p. 127). As he adapts to Herland, this new kind of sexual communion seems a return to latency, when women are seen as sexless and maternal. Another of the explorers also describes his marriage as a return to child-hood: "It gave me a queer feeling, way down deep, as of the stirring of some ancient dim prehistoric consciousness, a feeling that they were right somehow—that this was the way to feel. It was like—coming home to mother" (pp. 147–48).

Regarded historically, the image of utopian chastity presented in *Herland* is not surprising. Charlotte Perkins Gilman wrote *Herland* in the era when Margaret Sanger was sent to jail for distributing birth control devices and information, and she explicitly contrasts the beloved little citizens of Herland with the numbers of unwanted children born in the United States. Gilman's representation of sexuality may well be colored by her personal history as well. In the late 1880s she suffered an acute depression after the birth of her daughter; her husband sent her to the famous clinic of S. Weir Mitchell, who treated Gilman by forbidding all activity, including writing and stimulating conversation.[19] Further, a treatment prescribed by doctors surrounding Mitchell's clinic was clitorectomy, a common type of surgery in the late nineteenth century, and as a patient at the clinic, Gilman may well have been aware of this procedure. In Herland, in any case, women are sexless and chastity is utopian.

Conversely, sexuality is masculine, aggressive, and American in Herland. The story concludes with the women deporting the visitors because one of them has tried to rape his wife—an act which was, as he put it, "within his rights." Frustrated with matriarchal values, "he sought that supreme conquest" over the "neuters, epicenes, bloodless creatures" of utopia (pp. 132–33). Sexuality, then, is Gilman's final image for patriarchy. In *Women and Economics* she argued that although "sex-attraction is an essential factor in the fulfillment of our process of reproduction," our race has developed "a morbid excess in the exercise of this function . . . which tends to pervert and exhaust desire as well as to injure reproduction."[20] The American obsession with sex, she finds, is based on exaggerated distinctions between men and women: "The more widely the sexes are differentiated, the more forcibly they are attracted to each other." This hypersexuality interferes with useful activity, retarding "our progress as individuals and as a race."[21] Thus, in abolishing gender distinctions in Herland, Gilman perpetuates a highly repressive view of sex, and claims that tamed sexuality has freed the women of Herland to design and build their state.

In *Women and Economics* Gilman also traced contemporary views of sexuality to the economic dominance of men:

By the economic dependence of the human female upon the male, the balance of forces [natural selection] is altered. . . . Where both sexes obtain their food through the same exertions, from the same sources, under the same conditions, both sexes are acted upon alike, and developed alike by their environment. Where the two sexes obtain the food under different conditions, and where that difference consists in one of them being fed by the other, then the feeding sex becomes the environment of the fed. . . . In her position of economic dependence in the sex-relation, sex-distinction is with her not only a means of attracting a mate, as with all creatures, but a means of getting her livelihood, as is the case with no other creature under heaven.[22]

Man, then, becomes woman's very world; woman, by definition, is "other" than the environment by the fact of her material dependence, a role that heightens her "femininity." Gilman was thus the first American social theorist to analyze the origins of patriarchy by tying larger economic patterns to domestic production, evolution, and sexuality.[23]

In *Herland,* Gilman abolishes sexual dependence, freeing women from the biological pattern that reinforces it. In its place arises a sprightly world of communal responsibility and material plenty. Not only do the American males discover women botanists and physicists, women gardeners and theologians, but also, in exploring what is "masculine" and what is "feminine," the travelers discover what is irrational in their own society: why some people change their names when they marry, why some healthy people do not work, why some people work for other people, why pets feast and children starve—all these explanations of American life being ironically filtered through the ingenuous instruction of a somewhat utilitarian and slightly male-chauvinist narrator. Yet it is Herland's presumption of women's collective social responsibility that daunts the romantic traveler, who complains, " 'We' and 'we' and 'we'—it was so hard to get her to be personal. And, as I thought that, I suddenly remembered how we were always criticizing our women for being so personal" (p. 126).

Nevertheless, Gilman reifies gender. The most significant developments in Herland—the productive discoveries in forestry, the improved domestication of animals, the scientific arrangements for successful child rearing—all stem from women's nurturing instincts. Motherhood is a sacrificial female instinct rather than a social creation. Gilman suggests that an egalitarian future is simply inherent in the nurturing, home-creating capacity of women, ignoring the historical function of the home which she defines elsewhere as a place of work and only an illusion of refuge. Despite the mechanical skills and the political responsibility of Herland's citizens, home, as an extended metaphor for an ideal state, is the domain that best suits a woman's nature. When men invade utopia, they retain their traditional distance, physical and psychological, from its domestic values. Like Howells, Gilman magically solved contemporary problems in *Herland* by returning to a precapitalist stage of social evolution, in this case the hunting-and-gathering epoch that she thought preceded sexual division and hierarchy.

The representation of woman's space thus derives from this paradoxical image of the home—woman's space: *eutopia*, the good place; woman's space, *outopia*, the nonplace or the unreal place. Feminist utopias reveal a deep tension in the genre—the necessary but still invisible tie between history and belief. Indeed, most utopians still conceive love, sympathy, and motherhood to be woman's natural instincts, and they call upon her to be the moral warden of the new culture, not recognizing the growing disparity between the feminine stereotype and the course of social change for women in industrializing America. Utopia is still at one with ideology. In this period of militant agitation against political and economic inequalities, utopian writers like Bellamy and Howells, as well as Lane, Bishop, and Gilman, designed utopias that unwittingly ratified the ideologies if not the economic structures of the status quo. They projected onto the socialist future nineteenth-century patterns of belief that justified the economic and political inferiority of women while at the same time preserving an image of their moral superiority. Thus, in the long run, utopians supported the claim that gender roles are natural, having developed before and outside of history.

Is Herland then, or Mizora, or Altruria or Boston in the year 2000 *outopia*? *No*-where? Despite their contradictions, Herland and Mizora and Altruria and Boston in the year 2000 are *eutopia*, the good place. None of these imaginary societies contains anything significant that did not already exist somewhere in reality. Utopia is "nowhere" not because it is not real, but because it contains more truth, more information—hence more political possibility—than does everyday reality, in which truth, information, and political possibility are often tucked away, hidden in institutions, personal relations, and cultural traditions. As utopia permits a glimpse at what life can be, we notice, critically or hopefully, what life is. In utopia's inversion of nineteenth-century reality, the Gilded Age rather than utopia appears to be, at least for a moment, unnecessary and untrue. The significance of utopian fiction lies in its moment of confrontation between idealized appearance and historical essence. Of course, the realm of freedom lies beyond the realm of history. Utopian fiction merely identifies the similarities.

NOTES

BIBLIOGRAPHY

INDEX

Notes

Chapter 1. Time Yet to Come: Notions of History and Narrative Forms

1. The major bibliographies of American utopian fiction of the late nineteenth century are in Kenneth Roemer, *The Obsolete Necessity, 1888–1900* (Kent, Ohio: Kent State University Press, 1976); Glenn Negley, *Utopian Literature: A Bibliography* (Lawrence: Regents Press of Kansas, 1977); and Lyman T. Sargent, *British and American Utopian Literature 1516–1975: An Annotated Bibliography* (Boston: G. K. Hall, 1977).

2. As Kenneth Roemer observes, "Defining utopia is itself a utopian venture" ("Defining America as Utopia," in *America as Utopia*, ed. Kenneth Roemer [New York: Burt Franklin, 1981]). His definition of a literary utopia fully satisfies my own criteria: "A literary utopia is a fairly detailed description of an imaginary community, society, or world—a 'fiction' that encourages readers to experience vicariously a culture that represents a prescriptive, normative alternative to their own culture" (p. 3). In defining "utopianism" I am inclined toward the "latitudinarian and ecumenical" standards of Frank Manuel and Fritzie Manuel in *Utopian Thought in the Western World* (Cambridge, Mass: Harvard University Press, 1979) who settled on the "utopian propensity" and then declined to define the term further because their purpose was to endow the idea of utopia with historical meaning, not to formulate a dictionary label or a pat phrase (p. 5). However, such refusal to participate in the terminological babel of the field is possible only because others have performed this task with great care. See Darko Suvin, "Defining the Literary Genre of Utopia: Some Historical Semantics, Some Genealogy, a Proposal and a Plea," *Studies in the Literary Imagination* 6, no. 2 (Fall 1973), 121–45; Lyman T. Sargent, "Utopia: The Problem of Definition," *Extrapolation* 16 (May 1975), 137–48; Glenn Negley, introduction to *Utopian Literature*, pp. xi–xiv; Robert Plank, "Remarks on the Nomenclature We Use," *Alternative Futures* 1 (Spring 1978), 95–96; Raymond Williams, "Utopia and Science Fiction," *Science Fiction Studies* 5 (November 1978), 203–14; Joanna Russ, "Speculations: The Subjunctivity of Science Fiction," *Extrapolation* 15 (December 1973), 51–59; W. Warren Wagar, "Utopian Studies and Utopian Thought: Definitions and Horizons," *Extrapolation* 19 (December 1977), 4–12; Gorman Beauchamp, "Utopia and Its Discontents," *Mid-West Quarterly* 16 (Winter 1975), 161–74.

3. Friedrich Engels, *Socialism: Utopian and Scientific* (Moscow: Progress Pub-

lishers, 1970), p. 56. Elsewhere Engels explains, "The solution of the social problems, which as yet lay hidden in undeveloped economic conditions, the Utopians attempted to evolve out of the human brain. Society presented nothing but wrongs; to remove these was the task of reason. It was necessary then, to discover a new and more perfect system of social order and to impose this upon society from without by propaganda, and, wherever it was possible, by the example of model experiments. These new social systems were foredoomed as Utopian; the more completely they were worked out in detail, the more they could not avoid drifting off into pure phantasies" (p. 40).

4. Ibid., p. 56.

5. Ibid., p. 37.

6. Ernst Bloch, *A Philosophy of the Future* (New York: Herder and Herder, 1970), pp. 84–141.

7. Fredric Jameson, *The Political Unconscious: Narrative as a Socially Symbolic Act* (Ithaca, N.Y.: Cornell University Press, 1981), p. 287.

8. Bloch, *A Philosophy of the Future*, p. 87.

9. Karl Marx, Preface to *A Contribution to the Critique of Political Economy*, in *The Marx-Engels Reader*, ed. Robert C. Tucker (New York: Norton, 1972), p. 5.

10. Terry Eagleton, *Criticism and Ideology* (Trowbridge, Wiltshire: Verso, 1976), p. 88.

11. Northrop Frye, *The Anatomy of Criticism* (Princeton, N.J.: Princeton University Press, 1957), p. 202.

12. Melvyn Dubofsky, *Industrialism and the American Worker 1865–1920* (New York: Thomas Y. Crowell, 1975), p. 16.

13. Robert Wiebe, *The Search for Order, 1877–1920* (New York: Hill and Wang, 1967), pp. 14–15.

14. Leo Huberman, *We the People* (New York: Monthly Review, 1970), p. 222.

15. William Appleman Williams, *The Contours of American History* (Cleveland: World Publishing, 1961), p. 284.

16. Anthony M. Platt, *The Child Savers: The Invention of Delinquency*, 2d ed. (Chicago: University of Chicago Press, 1977), p. 28.

17. Ibid., pp. 20–21.

18. Henry M. Boies, *Prisoners and Paupers: A Study of the Abnormal Increase of Criminals, and the Public Burden of Pauperism in the United States: The Causes and Remedies* (1893; rpt. Freeport, N.Y.: Books for Libraries, 1972), p. 206.

19. Unemployment rose markedly as the decade progressed. In 1890, 4 percent of the civilian labor force age fourteen years and older were unemployed, or 333,800 people; in 1891: 5.4 percent, or 1,000,000 people; by 1893, 11.7 percent, or 2,860,000 were unemployed; the number peaks in 1894 at the height of the depression with 18.4 percent, or 4,612,000 people unemployed. Then the numbers level off, with 14.4 percent, for example, or 3,782,000 in 1896 (*Historical Statistics of the United States* [Washington, D.C.: Government Printing Office, 1975], p. 135).

20. Richard Hofstadter, *Social Darwinism in American Thought* (Boston: Beacon, 1955), p. 61.

21. Two classic discussions of American trade union history that describe the

progress from utopian, antiwage beliefs in the labor organizations of the Jacksonian and post–Civil War periods to the practical "bread and butter" unions of the late nineteenth century are John R. Commons et al., *History of Labor in the United States* (New York: Macmillan, 1918), vols. 2–4; and Philip S. Foner, *History of the Labor Movement in the United States* (New York: International Publishers, 1947).

22. The "agrarian myth" and the issue of land reform run through American utopian fiction of this period. See chapters 3 and 6.

23. Darko Suvin, *Metamorphoses of Science Fiction* (New Haven, Conn.: Yale University Press, 1979), pp. 63–84.

24. Robert Galbreath, "Introduction to the Ketterer Forum," *Science Fiction Studies* 3 (March 1976), 61.

25. W. R. Irvin, *The Game of the Impossible: A Rhetoric of Fantasy* (Champaign, Ill.: University of Illinois Press, 1976), p. 4.

26. Eric Rabkin, *The Fantastic in Literature* (Princeton, N.J.: Princeton University Press, 1976), p. 41.

27. Tzvetan Todorov, *The Fantastic: A Structural Approach to a Literary Genre,* trans. Richard Howard (Ithaca, N.Y.: Cornell University Press, 1973), p. 25.

28. Suvin, *Metamorphoses,* p. 63.

29. Ursula LeGuin, *The Dispossessed* (New York: Avon, 1974).

30. George Lukács, *Realism in Our Time: Literature and Class Struggle,* trans. John Mander and Necke Mander (New York: Harper and Row, 1964), p. 120.

31. Suvin defines science fiction as "a literary genre whose necessary and sufficient conditions are presence and interaction of estrangement and cognition, and whose main formal device is an imaginative framework alternative to the author's empirical environment"(*Metamorphoses,* p. 8).

32. I am indebted to Sheldon Sachs, *Fiction and the Shape of Belief* (Berkeley and Los Angeles: University of California Press, 1966), for the concept of *apologue.*

33. Occasionally the pattern is reversed and the visitor comes to the United States. See William Simpson, *The Man from Mars* (San Francisco: Bacon, 1891), or William Dean Howells, *A Traveller from Altruria* (1894; rpt. Bloomington: Indiana University Press, 1968).

34. Robert C. Elliott, *The Shape of Utopia: Studies in a Literary Genre* (Chicago: University of Chicago Press, 1972), p. 22; see also Northrop Frye, "Varieties of Literary Utopias," in *Utopias and Utopian Thought,* ed. Frank E. Manuel (Boston: Beacon, 1966), p. 27.

35. Hayden White, *Metahistory: The Historical Imagination in Nineteenth Century Europe* (Baltimore: Johns Hopkins University Press, 1973), p. 15.

36. Ibid., p. 7.

37. David E. Noble, *America by Design: Science, Technology, and the Rise of Corporate Capitalism* (New York: Knopf, 1977), p. 6.

38. H. Bruce Franklin, *Future Perfect: American Science Fiction of the Nineteenth Century* (New York: Oxford University Press, 1966); Robert Scholes and Eric Rabkin, *Science Fiction: History—Science—Vision* (New York: Oxford University Press, 1977).

39. Franklin, *Future Perfect,* p. ix.

40. White, *Metahistory,* p. 9.

163

41. George Kateb, *Utopia and Its Enemies* (New York: Schocken, 1972), p. 140.

42. Christopher Caudwell, *Studies and Further Studies in a Dying Culture* (New York: Monthly Review, 1971), p. 75; see also Allyn B. Forbes, "Literary Quest for Utopia, 1880–1890," *Social Forces* 6 (1927), 179–88.

43. Louis Marin, "Theses on Ideology and Utopia," *Minnesota Review* 6 (Spring 1976), 71.

44. Bloch, *A Philosophy of the Future*, p. 87.

45. Ibid.

46. Elliot, *The Shape of Utopia*, p. 7.

47. Ibid., p. 9.

48. The play between past tense and future tense is also symptomatic of the era's fascination with time itself. This was the era in which geological time confronted biblical time. New discoveries in geology, biology, and anthropology were totally revising older notions of the past, introducing concepts of primeval and even prehistoric life forms that permanently altered theories of change. When Thomas More, Francis Bacon, and Tomasso Campanella set their utopias on remote islands in uncharted seas, their new societies shared the map with France, Britain, and Italy. In the late eighteenth century, when Sebastian Mercier first cast utopia into the future in *L'an 2440*, he supplied an important indication of the emerging idea of progress.

49. Karl Mannheim, *Ideology and Utopia* (New York: Harcourt Brace, 1952), p. 188.

50. Frye, "Varieties of Literary Utopias," p. 25.

51. Frederik Polak, *The Image of the Future* (New York: Oceana, 1961), p. 287.

52. Bloch, *A Philosophy of the Future*, p. 92.

53. Herbert Marcuse, *The Aesthetic Dimension* (Boston: Beacon, 1978), p. 9.

Chapter 2. Edward Bellamy and the Progressive Utopia

1. Edward Bellamy, *Looking Backward: 2000–1887* (Boston: Ticknor, 1888), p. 8. All future references to *Looking Backward* are from this edition.

2. See John R. Commons, *History of Labor in the United States.* (New York: Macmillan, 1918), vols. 2–4; Philip S. Foner, *History of the Labor Movement in the United States* (New York: International Publishing, 1947); Melvyn Dubofsky, *Industrialism and the American Worker, 1865–1920* (New York: Thomas Y. Crowell, 1975); and Robert O. Boyer and Herbert M. Morais, *Labor's Untold Story* (New York: United Electrical, Radio and Machine Workers of America, 1955). August Meier and Elliott Rudwick, *Attitudes of Negro Leaders Toward the American Labor Movement from the Civil War to World War I* (New York: Anchor, 1968) describes the different role for black people in the Knights of Labor and the American Federation of Labor, and documents the class perspective of black leadership after the Civil War. See also Robert H. Wiebe, *The Search for Order, 1877–1920* (New York: Hill and Wang, 1967); and Ray Ginger, *Altgeld's America, 1890–1905* (Chicago: Quadrangle, 1958). William Appleman Williams, *The Roots of the Modern American Empire* (New York: Vintage, 1969), analyzes laissez-faire economic theory in terms of changes in American industrialism and American foreign policy.

More general studies are Richard Hofstadter, *The Age of Reform* (New York: Vintage, 1959); Gabriel Kolko, *The Triumph of Conservatism* (Chicago: Quadrangle, 1963); and Daniel Aaron, *Men of Good Hope* (New York: Oxford University Press, 1951).

3. Edward Bellamy, "How I Came to Write *Looking Backward*," *Ladies' Home Journal* 11 (April 1894), in *Edward Bellamy Speaks Again: Articles, Public Addresses, Letters* (Kansas City, Mo.: Peerage, 1957), p. 224.

4. Lewis Mumford, *The Story of Utopias* (Gloucester, Mass.: P. Smith, 1959).

5. Harry Levin, "Some Paradoxes of Utopia," in *Edward Bellamy, Novelist and Reformer* (Schenectady, N.Y.: Union College Press 1968), p. 18.

6. Edward Bellamy was always attracted to the military. He grew up during the Civil War and avidly read the biographies of Nelson and Napoleon. In 1867 he tried to enter West Point but failed to pass the physical. See Arthur E. Morgan, *Edward Bellamy* (New York: Columbia University Press, 1944); and Sylvia Bowman, *The Year 2000* (New York: Bookman, 1958).

7. Edward Bellamy, "Why I Wrote *Looking Backward*," *Nationalist* 2 (May 1890), reprinted in *Edward Bellamy Speaks Again*, p. 202.

8. David Bleich, "Eros and Bellamy," *American Quarterly* 16 (Fall 1964), 457–58.

9. Georg Lukács, *Realism in Our Time: Literature and the Class Struggle*, trans. John Mander and Necke Mander (New York: Harper and Row, 1964), p. 24.

10. In 1890 the leading ten occupational groups for women workers, in order of size (as reported in the census), were: (1) servants, (2) agricultural laborers, (3) dressmakers, (4) teachers, (5) farmers, planters and overseers, (6) laundresses, (7) seamstresses, (8) cotton mill operatives, (9) housekeepers and stewards, (10) clerks and copyists (Rosalyn Baxandall, Linda Gordon, and Susan Riverby, eds., *America's Working Women: A Documentary History—1690 to the Present* [New York: Vintage, 1976], pp. 406–07).

11. In Bowman, *The Year 2000*, p. 120. While Bowman presents tantalizing evidence from Bellamy's correspondence, her quotations are not individually footnoted and are often impossible to pursue.

12. See Barbara Welter, "The Cult of True Womanhood: 1820–1860," *American Quarterly* 18 (1966), 151–74.

13. Edwin Fussell, "The Theme of Sympathy in *Looking Backward*," unpublished, Dept. of English, University of California, San Diego, 1980.

14. By the 1880s feminist demands had already been extended to include revisions of the male-dominated family structures. Sylvia Bowman suggests that in order to popularize *Looking Backward*, Bellamy deliberately avoided the sexual-social innovations proposed by such reformers as John Humphrey Noyes, founder of the Oneida community, or the socialist Victoria Woodhull. "Without doubt Bellamy wished to escape the odium and the adverse criticism which would certainly attend the introduction of iconoclastic ideas relative to love, marriage, and domestic life. . . . Bellamy was implying changes which he did not wish to state openly" (p. 269). Bowman suggests that Bellamy wrote a chapter on women for *Equality*, his second utopia, in which he demanded easy divorce, the removal of sexual proprietorship, and the rearing of children by the state, but later omitted it

"because the world was not ready for its contents" ("Bellamy's Missing Chapter," *New England Quarterly* 31 [March 1958], 47); however, there seems to be insufficient evidence for this supposition. Daniel Aaron simply blames Bellamy's "distaste for intense emotions" as the reason for the lack of new sexual and social roles in his utopia ("Bellamy—Utopian Conservative," in *Edward Bellamy, Novelist and Reformer* [Schnectady, N.Y.: Union College Press, 1968], p. 13).

15. Edward Bellamy, "The Religion of Solidarity" (1873), in *Edward Bellamy Speaks Again: Articles, Public Addresses, Letters* (Kansas City, Mo.: Peerage, 1957).

16. All short stories referred to here are collected in Edward Bellamy, *The Blindman's World and Other Stories* (Boston: Houghton Mifflin, 1898). See in particular "Two Days Solitary Imprisonment" and "Pott's Painless Cure" for stories about this theme. The main figure nearly drowns in "Six to One," nearly dies in "Deserted" and nearly freezes in "The Cold Snap," but the crises allow the impersonal to surface and balance the personal. In "A Positive Romance," which Bellamy wrote after reading Auguste Compte, the hero observes impersonal love between two strangers. He sees the woman, a humanist, free the man, an individualist, through tender concern. In "Hooking Watermelons," a light story of a watermelon theft, the aristocratic heroine recognizes commonality through joining in the adventure. She discovers that humanity transcends class, although even here Bellamy suggests that social transcendence does not undermine the rights of private property, and the theft is appropriately punished.

17. Fredric Jameson, "Magical Narratives: Romance as Genre," *New Literary History* 7 (1975), 139.

18. Ibid., p. 140.

19. Northrop Frye, *Anatomy of Criticism* (Princeton, N.J.: Princeton University press, 1957), pp. 186–93.

20. Frank Kermode, introduction to *The Tempest*, Arden Shakespeare (New York: Methuen, 1962), p. lvi.

21. James D. Hart, *The Popular Book: A History of America's Literary Taste* (New York: Oxford University Press, 1950), pp. 168–69.

The progressive utopias of that era are:

1889 Charles Joseph Bellamy, *An Experiment in Marriage*
      Crawford S. Griffin, *Nationalism*
1888 Edward Bellamy, *Looking Backward*
1890 Henry Salisbury, *The Birth of Freedom*
1891 Henry Francis Allen, *A Strange Voyage: A Revision of the Key of Industrial Cooperative Government, an Interesting and Instructive Description of Life on Planet Venus. By Pruning Knife*
      Ludwig A. Geissler, *Looking Beyond: A Sequel to "Looking Backward" by Edward Bellamy and an Answer to "Looking Forward" by Richard Michaelis*
      Thomas Lake Harris, *The New Republic: A Discourse of the Prospects, Dangers, Duties, and Safeties of the Times*
1892 M. Louise Moore, *Al-Modad; or, Life Scenes Beyond the Polar Circumflex, a Religio-Scientific Solution of the Problem of Present and Future Life. By an Untrammeled Free Thinker*

Archibald McCowan, *Philip Meyer's Scheme*

Albert Chavannes, *The Future Commonwealth; or, What Samuel Balcom Saw in Socioland*

Samuel Crocker, *That Island: A Political Romance by Theodore Oceanic Islet*

1893 Anon., *The Beginning: A Romance of Chicago as It Might Be*

Henry Olerich, *A Cityless and Countryless World: An Outline of Practical and Co-operative Individualism*

1894 Fayette Stratton Giles, *Shadows Before; or, A Century Onward*

Solomon Schindler, *Young West: A Sequel to Edward Bellamy's Celebrated Novel "Looking Backward"*

1896 Stephen H. Emmens, *The Sixteenth Amendment: A Plain Citizen*

1897 Charles W. Caryl, *A New Era: Presenting the Plans for the New Era Union to Help Develop and Utilize the Best Skill There Is Available to Realize the Highest Degree of Prosperity That Is Possible for All Who Will Help to Attain It—Based on Practical and Successful Business Methods*

Benjamin O. Flower, *Equality and Brotherhood*

George Harris, *Inequality and Progress*

1898 Zebina Forbush, *The Co-opolitan: A Story of the Cooperative Commonwealth of Idaho*

22. Bellamy, "How I Came to Write *Looking Backward*," p. 220.

23. From Edward Bellamy to William Dean Howells, 17 June 1888, in Joseph Schiffman, "Mutual Indebtedness: Unpublished Letters of Edward Bellamy to William Dean Howells," *Harvard Library Bulletin* 12 (1958), 370.

24. In Bowman, *The Year 2000*, pp. 126–30.

25. In a letter to William Dean Howells dated 17 June 1888, Bellamy claims not to have read Gronlund before writing *Looking Backward* (Schiffman, "Mutual Indebtedness," p. 364).

26. Ibid., p. 370.

27. Noticeably absent from any journals, diaries, articles, and reviews of utopian fiction of this era is a reference to the American communitarian movement, or to early utopian socialists such as Saint-Simon, Fourier, or Owen.

28. Bellamy, "Why I Wrote *Looking Backward*," p. 202.

29. Friedrich Engels, *Socialism, Utopian and Scientific* (New York: International Publishers, 1935), p. 56.

30. Bellamy, "How I Came to Write *Looking Backward*," pp. 217, 223.

31. Ibid., p. 224.

32. James D. Hart, *The Popular Book: A History of America's Literary Taste* (Berkeley and Los Angeles: University of California Press, 1963), p. 109.

33. Granville Hicks, *The Great Tradition* (New York: Macmillan, 1935), p. 140.

34. William Dean Howells, "Editor's Study," *Harper's New Monthly Magazine* 77 (1888), 154.

35. Edward Bellamy, "The Progress of Nationalism in the United States," *North American Review* 154 (June 1892), 742–52.

36. In Bowman, *The Year 2000*, p. 74.

37. In ibid., p. 115.

38. In Morgan, *Edward Bellamy*, p. 246.

39. William Dean Howells, "Edward Bellamy," *Atlantic Monthly* 82 (1898), 254.

40. Hart, *The Popular Book*, pp. 170–71; see also Bowman, *The Year 2000*, p. 121, who cites somewhat lower figures.

41. In Morgan, *Edward Bellamy*, p. 246.

42. In ibid., p. 577.

43. Lynn Boyd Porter, *Speaking of Ellen* (New York: G. W. Dillingham, 1890), preface.

44. Bowman, *The Year 2000*, p. 124.

45. Ibid.

46. William Higgs, "Some Objections to Mr. Bellamy's Utopia," *New Englander and Yale Review* 52 (March 1890), 231–39.

47. W. T. Harris, "Edward Bellamy's Vision," *Forum* 8 (October 1889).

48. Schiffman, "Edward Bellamy's Altruistic Man," *American Quarterly* 6 (1954), 203.

49. Ibid.

50. "*Looking Backward*," *Los Angeles Times*, 18 March 1894.

51. Albert Levi, "Edward Bellamy: Utopian," *Ethics* 55 (1945), 133.

Chapter 3. William Dean Howells and the Pastoral Utopia

1. William Dean Howells, *The Altrurian Romances*, ed. Clara Kirk and Rudolf Kirk (Bloomington: Indiana University Press, 1968), p. 187. All future references to the trilogy, which includes *A Traveller from Altruria, Letters of an Altrurian Traveller,* and *Through the Eye of the Needle,* are taken from this edition.

2. In the late 1880s and early 1890s Howells was deeply concerned with industrial violence, as well as the legal injustices it spawned. Howells was the only prominent literary intellectual to take a public stand on the proceedings against the Chicago anarchists who were unjustly tried for the infamous bombings in Haymarket Square. Although in 1888 Howells wrote to their judge, Roger Pryor, that he believed that the anarchists were innocent and had been unjustly convicted, he refused to call for financial or legal support on their behalf. However, when the Supreme Court upheld the guilty verdicts, Howells decided to protest publicly. After John Greenleaf Whittier and George William Curtis refused to join him, Howells alone wrote to Governor Altgeld of Illinois demanding clemency for the anarchists and he alone paid for a *New York Herald Tribune* advertisement describing the injustice. The ad brought criticism from his friends and strong denunciations in the press. "Some of the papers abused me as heartily as if I had proclaimed myself a dynamiter," he wrote to Thomas S. Perry on 14 April 1888. On 15 Jaunary 1888 he had written to Hamlin Garland, "You'll easily believe that I did not bring myself to the point of openly befriending those men who were murdered in Chicago without thinking and feeling much, and my horizons have been infinitely widened by the process."

3. See Richard Hofstadter, *The Age of Reform* (New York: Vintage, 1955), pp. 60–93.

4. Raymond Williams, *The Country and the City* (New York: Oxford University Press, 1973), p. 120. Three other studies of postindustrial pastoralism are Henry Nash Smith, *Virgin Land* (Cambridge, Mass.: Harvard University Press, 1950); William Empson, *Some Versions of Pastoral* (New York: New Directions, 1960); Leo Marx, *The Machine in the Garden* (New York: Oxford University Press, 1967). Bernard Rosenthal, *City of Nature* (Newark: University of Delaware Press, 1980) discusses the relationships between the city and descriptions of nature in the romantic era in America. See also Walter R. Davis, *A Map of Arcadia: Sidney's Romance in Its Tradition* (New Haven, Conn.: Yale University Press, 1965); Peter Marinelli, *Pastoral* (London: Methuen, 1971); and Harold Toliver, *Pastoral Forms and Attitudes* (Berkeley and Los Angeles: University of California Press, 1971).

5. William Dean Howells, "Equality as the Basis of Good Society," *Century Magazine* 29 (November 1895), 63–67.

6. Ibid.

7. To Sylvester Baxter, 27 July 1896, in *Life in Letters of William Dean Howells,* ed. Mildred Howells (Garden City, N.Y.: Doubleday, Doran, 1928).

8. To Hamlin Garland, 15 January 1888, in ibid.

9. William Dean Howells, "Are We a Plutocracy?" *North American Review* 158 (1894), 185–96.

10. Howells, *Life in Letters* 2:25.

11. Fredric Jameson, unpublished manuscript, Dept. of English, University of California, San Diego, 1975. Howells criticism has been much concerned with his attitude toward the city, and the entire debate assumes that Howells used the pastoral utopia normatively rather than satirically. I would agree. Kenneth Eble, Benjamin Sokoloff, and Edwin Cady have tied the Altrurian patterns of socialism to Howell's Ohio childhood (Kenneth Eble, "The Western Ideals of William Dean Howells," *Western Humanities Review* 2 [1957], 331–38; Benjamin Sokoloff, "William Dean Howells and the Ohio Village: A Study in Environment and Art," *American Quarterly* 11 [1959], 58–75; Edwin Cady, *The Realist at War: The Mature Years of William Dean Howells, 1885–1920* [Syracuse, N.Y.: Syracuse University Press, 1958]). Jan Dietrichson, Morton White, and Lucia White read the Altrurian romances as Howells's revolt against the city (Jan W. Dietrichson, *The Image of Money in the American Novel in the Gilded Age* [New York: Humanities Press, 1969]; Morton White and Lucia White, *The Intellectual versus the City* [Cambridge, Mass.: Harvard University Press, 1962], pp. 102–22). However, for Gregory Crider, Howells believed that the cities' problems could be remedied and that cities best organized human life (Gregory Crider, "Howells' Altruria: The Ambivalent Utopia," *Old Northwest* 1 [1975], 405–18).

12. To Henry James, 10 October 1888.

13. Howells, "Equality," p. 64.

14. William Dean Howells, *My Literary Passions* (New York: Harper, 1895), p. 252.

15. The major pastoral utopias of this period are:

1880 Henry A. Gaston, *Mars Revisited, or Seven Days in the Spirit World*
1885 James Casey, *A New Moral World and a New State of Society*

1892 Mary Agnes Tinckner, *San Salvador*
1893 Joaquin Miller, *The Building of the City Beautiful*
1894 William Dean Howells, *A Traveller from Altruria*
1898 Alexander Craig, *Ionia: Land of Wise Men and Fair Women*
1907 William Dean Howells, *Through the Eye of the Needle*

16. Howells, *My Literary Passions,* p. 252.

17. In Morton White and Lucia White, *The Intellectual versus the City* (Cambridge, Mass.: Harvard University Press, 1962), pp. 114–15.

18. Robert L. Hough, *The Quiet Rebel: William Dean Howells as Social Commentator* (Lincoln: University of Nebraska Press, 1959), p. 63.

19. William Dean Howells, preface to Edward Bellamy, *The Blindman's World and Other Stories* (Boston: Houghton Mifflin, 1898), p. xiii.

20. Howells, "Equality," p. 17.

21. William Dean Howells, "Editor's Study," *Harper's New Monthly Magazine* 80 (January 1890), 323.

22. To William Cooper Howells, 27 April 1890.

23. William Dean Howells, "Edward Bellamy," *Atlantic Monthly* 82 (1898), 254.

24. S. Kirk, "America, Altruria and the Coast of Bohemia," *Atlantic Monthly* 74 (1894), 703.

25. Review of *A Traveller from Altruria, Nation* 59 (1894), 107.

26. Review of *A Traveller from Altruria, Critic* 21 (1894), 434.

27. In Harry Walsh, "Tolstoy and the Economic Novels of William Dean Howells," *Comparative Literature Studies* 14 (June 1977), 147.

28. Review of *A Traveller from Altruria, Dial* 12 (1894), 154.

29. Ibid.

30. Newton Arvin, "The Usableness of Howells," *New Republic,* 30 June 1937, p. 227.

31. In C. Hartley Grattan, "Howells: Ten Years After," *American Mercury* 20 (May 1930), 77.

32. Mary Agnes Tinckner, *San Salvador* (Boston: Houghton Mifflin, 1892).

33. Joaquin Miller, *The Building of the City Beautiful* (Chicago: Stone and Kimball, 1893).

Chapter 4. Dystopias: Parody and Satire

1. I have classified the following texts as dystopias of this period:

1884 Alfred Denton Cridge, *Utopia; or, The History of an Extinct Planet*
1887 Anna Bowman Dodd, *The Republic of the Future: or, Socialism a Reality*
1888 James DeMille, *A Strange Manuscript Found in a Copper Cylinder*
1890 Richard Michaelis, *Looking Further Forward: An Answer to "Looking Backward" by Edward Bellamy*
      W. W. Satterlee, *Looking Backward and What I Saw*
      Arthur Dudley Vinton, *Looking Further Backward*

1893   Charles Elliot Niswonger, *The Isle of Feminine*

       J. W. Roberts, *Looking Within: The Misleading Tendencies of "Looking Backward" Made Manifest*

1894   William Harben, *The Land of the Changing Sun*

       Solomon Schindler, *Young West: A Sequel to Edward Bellamy's Celebrated Novel "Looking Backward"*

1895   Paul Haedicke, *The Equalities of Para-Para: Written from the Dictation of George Rambler, M.D., F.R.G.S.*

1896   Julius Chambers, *"In Sargasso." Missing: A Romance*

       Ingersoll Lockwood, *1900; or, The Last President*

1900   Charles J. Bayne, *The Fall of Utopia*

2. Louis Marin, "Theses on Ideology and Utopia," *Minnesota Review* 6 (1976), 71.

3. Useful discussions of the definition of dystopia are: David Ketterer, *New Worlds for Old The Apocalyptic Imagination, Science Fiction, and American Literature* (Garden City, N.Y.: Anchor, 1974), pp. 96–122; Darko Suvin, "The Riverside Trees, or SF and Utopia: Degrees of Kinship," *Minnesota Review* 3 (1974), 108–15; Fredric Jameson, "Of Islands and Trenches: Neutralization and the Production of Utopian Discourse," *Diacritics* 7, no. 2 (1977), 2–21; Lyman T. Sargent, "Utopia: The Problem of Definition," *Extrapolation* 16 (1975), 137–48; Darko Suvin, "Defining the Literary Genre of Utopia," in *Metamorphoses of Science Fiction* (New Haven Conn.: Yale University Press, 1979).

4. Eric Rabkin, *The Fantastic in Literature* (Princeton, N.J.: Princeton University Press, 1977), p. 140.

5. Suvin, "The Riverside Trees," pp. 110–11. Suvin also argues that perfection "just does not exist as a requirement of the genre. Even in More there is slavery, strict control of movement, death penalty for atheism. . . . A radical change from the author's situation is clearly implicit in utopias, but it is not necessarily a final one that cannot be improved upon" (p. 111).

6. Claudio Guillén, *Literature as System* (Princeton, N.J.: Princeton University Press, 1971).

7. Tzvetan Todorov argues, "As a rule . . . a genre is always defined in relation to the genres adjacent to it" (*The Fantastic* [Ithaca, N.Y.: Cornell University Press, 1975], p. 27).

8. Anna Bowman Dodd, *The Republic of the Future* (New York: Cassell, 1887), p. 12.

9. Todorov establishes the following distinctions, "The fantastic, we have seen, lasts only as long as a certain hesitation: a hesitation common to reader and character, who must decide whether or not what they perceive derives from 'reality' as it exists in the common opinion. At the story's end, the reader makes a decision even if the character does not; he opts for one solution or the other, and thereby emerges from the fantastic. If he decides that the laws of reality remain intact and permit an explanation of the phenomena described, we say that the work belongs to another genre: the uncanny. If, on the contrary, he decides that new laws of nature must be entertained to account for the phenomenon, we enter the genre of the marvelous," (*The Fantastic*, p. 41).

10. Dodd, *The Republic of the Future*, p. 19.

11. Ibid.

12. Ibid., pp. 19, 21.

13. Ibid., p. 23.

14. Ibid., p..62.

15. Ibid., p. 59.

16. David F. Noble, *America by Design: Science, Technology, and the Rise of Corporate Capitalism* (New York: Oxford University Press, 1977), p. 6.

17. Dodd, *The Republic of the Future*, p. 20.

18. Ibid., p. 23.

19. Ibid., p. 48.

20. Jameson, "Of Islands and Trenches," pp. 3, 7.

21. Eleanor Flexner, *Century of Struggle: The Women's Rights Movement in the United States* (New York: Athenaeum, 1974), p. 191.

22. Quoted in Henry Nash Smith, *Popular Culture and Industrialism*, 1965–1890 (Garden City, N.Y.; Anchor, 1967), p. 248.

23. Arthur Dudley Vinton, *Looking Further Backward, Being a Series of Lectures Delivered to the Freshman Class at Shawmut College by Professor Wong Lung Li* (Albany, N.Y.: Albany Book Co., 1890), p. 9.

24. The nineteenth-century dystopian hero differs markedly from the "cultural primitives" of the twentieth-century dystopias, described by Gorman Beauchamp, "Cultural Primitivism as Norm in the Dystopian Novel," *Extrapolation* 19 (1975), 88–89. Julian is not the "instictive," "spontaneous," "proto-hippie" Beauchamp finds in the dystopias of Wells and Forster.

25. Vinton, *Looking Further Backward*, p. 76.

26. Ibid., p. 80.

27. See Simone de Beauvoir, *The Second Sex*, trans. H. M. Parshley (New York: Knopf, 1953): "Thus humanity is male and man defines woman not in herself but as relative to him; she is not regarded as an autonomous being; . . . she is simply what man decrees; thus she is called 'the sex,' by which is meant that she appears essentially to the male as a sexual being. For him she is sex—absolute sex, no less. She is defined and differentiated with reference to man and not he with reference to her; she is the incidental, the inessential as opposed to the essential. He is the Subject, he is the Absolute—she is the Other" (p. xix).

28. For a discussion of a parallel phenomenon in popular fiction in England of the same period, see Elaine Showalter, *A Literature of Their Own: British Women Novelists from Brontë to Lessing* (Princeton, N.J.: Princeton University Press, 1977), esp. pp. 153–81.

29. Rosalyn Baxandall, Linda Gordon, and Susan Riverby, eds., *America's Working Women: A Documentary History—1690 to the Present* (New York: Vintage, 1976), pp. 406–07.

30. Dodd, *The Republic of the Future*, p. 40.

31. Ibid., p. 31.

32. Vinton, *Looking Further Backward*, p. 180.

33. Charles Elliot Niswonger, *The Isle of Feminine* (Little Rock, Ark.: Brown, 1893), p. 54.

34. Ibid., p. 61.
35. Ibid., p. 156.

Chapter 5. Conservative Utopias: The Future Moves Toward the Present in Righteous Dominion

1. David H. Wheeler, *Our Industrial Utopia and Its Unhappy Citizens* (Chicago: A. C. McClurg, 1895), p. 10.

2. The category of conservative utopias includes:

1883 John Macnie, *The Diothas; or, A Far Look Ahead,* by Ismar Thiusen
1890 Alvardo M. Fuller, *A.D. 2000*
1891 Amos K. Fiske, *Beyond the Bourne: Reports of a Traveller Returned from the Undiscovered Country, Submitted to the World*
     Walter H. McDougall, *The Hidden City*
     Chauncey M. Thomas, *The Crystal Button; or, Adventures of Paul Prognosis in the Forty-Ninth Century*
     William Simpson, *The Man from Mars, His Morals, Politics and Religion,* by Thomas Blot
1893 John Bachelder, *A.D. 2050: Electrical Development at Atlantis,* by a Former Resident of the Hub
     Addison Peale Russell, *Sub-Coelum: A Sky-Built Human World*
1894 John Jacob Astor, *A Journey in Other Worlds: A Romance of the Future*
1899 Arthur Bird, *Looking Forward: A Dream of the United States of the Americas in 1999*

3. See Walter LaFeber, *The New Empire An Interpretation of American Expansions* (Ithaca, N.Y.: Cornell University Press, 1967); William Appleman Williams, *The Contours of American History* (Chicago: Quadrangle, 1966) and *The Roots of Modern American Empire* (New York: Random, 1969); Richard Hofstadter, "Manifest Destiny and the Philippines," in *America in Crisis: Fourteen Crucial Episodes,* ed. Daniel Aaron (Hamden, Conn.: Archon, 1971); Frederick Merk, *Manifest Destiny and Mission in American History* (New York: Knopf, 1963); Albert K. Weinbery, *Manifest Destiny* (Chicago: Quadrangle, 1963); Norman A. Graebner, *Empire on the Pacific: A Study in American Continental Expansion* (New York: Ronald, 1955).

4. Many scholars agree that business leaders saw a choice between either a permanent situation of surplus, unemployment, and strikes, or government intervention in establishing and maintaining markets. They uniformly contradict Richard Hofstadter's analysis that the colonial ventures of the 1890s were unpremeditated and ad hoc reactions to events initiated by other nations. See John D. Hicks, *The American Nation: 1865 to the Present* (Boston: Houghton Mifflin, 1941); Robert Wiebe, *The Search for Order 1977–1920* (New York: Hill and Wang, 1967); Gabriel Kolko, *The Triumph of Conservatism* (Chicago: Quadrangle, 1963); Richard Hofstadter, *The Age of Reform: From Bryan to F.D.R.* (New York: Vintage, 1955).

5. Ernest Lee Tuveson, *Redeemer Nation: The Idea of America's Millennial Role* (Chicago: University of Chicago Press, 1968), p. 95.

6. Ibid., p. 105.

7. Ibid., p. 131.

8. Kolko, *The Triumph of Conservatism*, pp. 2–3, 58–59.

9. Arthur Bird, *Looking Forward: A Dream of the United States of the Americas in 1999* (Utica, N.Y.: L. C. Childs, 1899; rpt. New York: Arno, 1973), p. 4.

10. Henry Everett, *The People's Program: The Twentieth Century Is Theirs* (New York: Workman's Publishing Co., 1892), p. 192.

11. In Wiebe, *The Search for Order*, p. 234.

12. In Williams, *The Contours of American History*, p. 364.

13. Bird, *Looking Forward*, p. 4.

14. Amos K. Fiske, *Beyond the Bourne: Reports of a Traveller Returned from the Undiscovered Country, Submitted to the World* (New York: Howard and Hulbert, 1891), p. 77.

15. Alvarado M. Fuller, *A.D. 2000* (Chicago: Laird and Lee, 1890), p. 262.

16. John Bachelder, *A.D. 2050: Electrical Development at Atlanta, by a Former Resident of the Hub* (San Francisco: Bancroft, 1893), p. 7.

17. Walter H. McDougall, *The Hidden City* (New York: Cassell, 1891), p. 131.

18. Leslie Fiedler and Richard Slotkin have suggested that Americans required a rationalization for the extermination of over one million original inhabitants and that this need was in part satisfied by the literary stereotypes of the Indian. See Leslie Fiedler, *The Return of the Vanishing American* (London: Jonathan Cape, 1968),• p. 22; Richard Slotkin, *Regeneration Through Violence: The Mythology of the American* (Middletown, Conn.: Wesleyan University Press, 1973). See also Richard Ellis, ed., *The Western American Indian: Case Studies in Tribal History* (Lincoln: University of Nebraska Press, 1972).

19. Edwin Fussell, *Frontier: American Literature and the American West* (Princeton, N.J.: Princeton University Press, 1965), p. 330.

20. Roy Harvey Pearce, *Savagism and Civilization: A Study of the Indian and the American Mind* (Baltimore: Johns Hopkins Press, 1965), pp. 199–200.

21. Ibid., p. 212.

22. John Jacob Astor, *A Journey in Other Worlds: A Romance of the Future* (New York: Appleton, 1894), pp. 29–41.

23. Kenneth Roemer, *The Obsolete Necessity: America in Utopian Writings, 1888–1900* (Kent, Ohio: Kent State University Press, 1976), pp. xii–xiii, 6.

24. Henry Nash Smith, *Virgin Land: The American West as Symbol and Myth* (Cambridge, Mass.: Harvard University Press, 1950), pp. 84–85.

25. Northrop Frye, *The Anatomy of Criticism* (Princeton, N.J.: Princeton University Press, 1957).

Chapter 6. Ignatius Donnelly and the Apocalyptic Utopias

1. Utopian novels of this period that contain extended representations of apocalyptic passages or social cataclysms which propel history into a utopian future include:

1890 Ignatius Donnelly, *Caesar's Column*, by Edmond Boisgilbert

Henry Barnard Salisbury, *The Birth of Freedom: A Socialist Novel* (also published as *Miss Worden's Hero; or, The Birth of Freedom*)

Mrs. C. H. Stone, *One of "Berrian's" Novels*

1892 Ignatius Donnelly, *The Golden Bottle; or the, The Story of Ephraim Benezet of Kansas*

1893 Morrison I. Swift, *A League of Justice; or, Is It Right to Rob Robbers?*

1894 Frank Rosewater, *'96: A Romance of Utopia*

1897 Frederick Upham Adams, *President John Smith: The Story of a Peaceful Revolution*

1899 Albert Adams Merrill, *The Great Awakening: The Story of the Twenty-Second Century*

2. Melvin Lasky, *Utopia and Revolution: On the Origins of a Metaphor, or Some Illustrations of the Problem of Political Temperament and Intellectual Climate and How Ideas, Ideals, and Ideologies Have Been Historically Related* (Chicago: University of Chicago Press, 1976), p. 17.

3. Arthur Bird, *Looking Forward: A Dream of the United States of the Americas in 1999* (Utica, N.Y.: L.C. Childs, 1899; rpt. New York: Arno, 1973), p. 8.

4. Ernest Lee Tuveson, *Redeemer Nation: The Idea of America's Millennial Role* (Chicago: University of Chicago Press, 1968), p. 30.

5. David Ketterer, *New Worlds for Old: The Apocalyptic Imagination, Science Fiction, and American Literature* (Garden City, N.Y.: Anchor, 1974), p. 5.

6. Tuveson writes: "The millennium is not to be confused with the true heavenly order. Nor is the first 'binding of Satan' the end of his strength; the whole millennialist hypothesis depends on the point that evil men will be repressed, not annihilated. For this reason the millennium is utopia, not heaven" (*Redeemer Nation*, p. 43).

7. Ketterer, *New Worlds for Old*, p. 7.

8. Ibid., p. 12.

9. See Frederic Cople Jaher, *Doubters and Dissenters: Cataclysmic Thought in America, 1885–1918* (London: Collier Macmillan, 1964), for a finely documented history of apocalyptic ideology in American politics.

10. In John D. Hicks, *The American Nation, 1865 to the Present* (New York: Houghton Mifflin, 1955), p. 184.

11. Jaher, *Doubters and Dissenters*, p. 42.

12. "The New Lawlessness," *Nation* 58 (May 10, 1894), 340.

13. Frederick Upham Adams, *President John Smith: The Story of a Peaceful Revolution* (Chicago: Charles H. Kerr, 1897), pp. 65–66.

14. Lasky, *Utopia and Revolution*, p. 22; see also Tuveson, *Redeemer Nation*, p. 30.

15. Despite fears that the book would incite people to revolution, *Caesar's Column* found a publisher who decided that it was a warning against rather than an incentive to revolution. A best-seller, it sold 2,000 copies within weeks, and a total of 60,000 copies were sold in the United States in 1891. Three English editions were issued and translations appeared in Sweden, Germany, and Norway.

16. Gabriel, literally "man of God," is the herald of good tidings; he declares

Notes to Pages 121–130

the coming of the Messiah. Alexander Saxton points out that Gabriel's last name in translation is "world stone," a reference to Peter the Rock ("Caesar's Column: The dialogue of Utopia and Catastrophe," *American Quarterly* 19 [1967], 233). This translation helps us to read Gabriel as Peter in his role as founder of the true church and head of the·apostolic band.

17. Walter Rideout suggests that Donnelly possibly derived Max's last name from an associate and later a Girondist opponent of Robespierre. Rideout also suggests that in the novel's later chapters describing the revolt of the Brotherhood of Destruction, a number of details appear to have been inspired by accounts of the French Revolution (Walter Rideout, introduction to Ignatius Donnelly, *Caesar's Column*, by Edmond Boisgilbert [Chicago: F.J. Schute, 1890; rpt. Cambridge, Mass.: Harvard University Press, 1960], p. 26).

18. Ignatius Donnelly, "Preamble to the Platform Acclaimed by the First National Convention of the People's Party," Omaha, Nebraska, July 4, 1892.

19. Donnelly criticism reflects the debate as to whether Populism was the seedbed of "proto-fascism" or a progressive movement. See Allan Axelrad, "Ideology and Utopia in the Works of Ignatius Donnelly," *American Studies* 12 (Fall 1971), 47; John D. Hicks, *The Populist Revolt: A History of the Farmers' Alliance and the People's Party* (Lincoln: University of Nebraska Press, 1961); Richard Hofstadter, *The Age of Reform: From Bryan to F.D.R.* (New York: Vintage, 1955); Walter Nugent, *The Tolerant Populists* (Chicago: University of Chicago Press, 1968); and Norman Pollack, *The Populist Response to Industrial America* (Cambridge, Mass.: Harvard University Press, 1976).

20. Ignatius Donnelly, *Congressional Globe*, 40th Congress, 2d sess., pt. 2 (7 May 1868), 2385. See also Jaher, *Doubters and Dissenters*, p. 98.

21. In Hicks, *The Populist Revolt*, p. 163.

22. Ignatius Donnelly, *Atlantis: The Antediluvian World* (New York: Harper, 1882).

23. Ignatius Donnelly, *Ragnarak: The Age of Fire and Gravel* (New York: D. Appelton, 1883), pp. 406–07, 438–39.

24. Donnelly, *Atlantis*, pp. 1–2.

25. John Patterson, "From Yeoman to Beast: Images of Blackness in *Caesar's Column*," *American Studies* 12, no. 2 (Fall 1971),

26. Donnelly, *The Golden Bottle*, p. 280.

27. Axelrad, "Ideology and Utopia," p. 61.

28. Barbara Carolyn Quissell, "The Sentimental and Utopian Novels of Nineteenth-Century America: Romance and Social Issues," Ph. D. diss., University of Utah, 1973, p. 58.

29. Henry Nash Smith, "The Scribbling Women and the Cosmic Success Story," *Critical Inquiry* 1 (September 1974), 49.

30. Larzer Ziff describes how Gabriel's melodramatic rescue of Estella Washington "provides an awesome glimpse into the way the artifacts of civilization, unknown on the farm, were equated with viciousness"; the art objects in Cabano's house are equated with Estella's concubinage; their absence in the humble home results from the poor man's virtue, not his poverty. *Caesar's Column* reveals the Populists' "dark suspicion that there was a connection between riches, art, and

sexuality" (*The American 1890s: Life and Times of a Lost Generation* [New York: Viking, 1966], pp. 83–84).

31. *Caesar's Column*, p. 81. Ziff has observed that the political rhetoric of Populism recalls the sentimental language of the contemporary culture. "The familiar high flown changes in Biblical rhetoric . . . reassert the glory of patriotism in the romantic lyrics of the cardboard motto, written to be sung to the accompaniment of the melodeon" (ibid., pp. 81–82).

32. Quissell, "The Sentimental and Utopian Novels," p. 58.

33. Donnelly, *The Golden Bottle*, p. 98.

34. In the middle to late nineteenth century, there are few references to women warriors or to women dressed as men. Most notable in America was Mark Twain's *Personal Recollections of Joan of Arc;* (1896); most notable in England was *Glorianna, or the Revolution of 1900* (1890), by Lady Florence Dixie.

35. Hofstadter writes, in *The Age of Reform* (pp. 62–63): "According to the agrarian myth, the health of the state was proportionate to the degree to which it was dominated by the agricultural class, and this assumption pointed to the superiority of an earlier age. . . . Nature, as the agrarian tradition had it, was beneficent. The United States was abundantly endowed with rich land and rich resources, and the 'natural' consequences of such an endowment should be the prosperity of the people. If the people failed to enjoy prosperity, it must be because of a harsh and arbitrary intrusion of human greed and error."

36. Axelrad, "Ideology and Utopia," p. 52.

37. Tuveson, *Redeemer Nation*, pp. 6–7.

38. Patterson, "From Yeoman to Beast," p. 26.

39. Thus these images exclude what Eric Rabkin terms the "non-normal" occurrence, the unexpected and irrelevant which mark the boundaries of the fantastic (*The Fantastic in Literature* [Princeton, N.J.: Princeton University Press, 1976], pp. 8, 42).

40. Mark Twain, *A Connecticut Yankee in King Arthur's Court (New York: Charles L. Webster, 1889).*

Chapter 7. A State of Her Own; or, What Did Women Want?

1. Simone de Beauvoir, *The Second Sex*, trans. H. M. Parshley (New York: Knopf, 1953), p. xvii.

2. Eleanor Flexner, *Century of Struggle: The Women's Rights Movement in the United States* (New York: Atheneum, 1974), p. 179; see also Elizabeth M. Bacon, "The Growth of Household Conveniences in the United States from 1865 to 1900," Ph.D. diss., Radcliffe College, 1942.

3. Mary Lou Locke, "Working Women of the Urban Far West: San Francisco, Portland, and Los Angeles, 1870 to 1910." Ph.D. diss, University of California, San Diego, 1982, p. 26.

4. Ibid., p. 1.

5. Ellen C. Du Bois, *Feminism and Suffrage: The Emergence of an Independent Women's Movement in America 1848–1869* (Ithaca, N.Y.: Cornell University Press, 1978).

6. Barbara Welter, "The Cult of True Womanhood: 1820–1860," *American Quarterly* 18 (1966), 151–74.

7. Caroline Ticknor, "The Steel Engraving Lady and the Gibson Girl," *Atlantic Monthly* 81 (1901), p. 106.

8. The utopias of this period that include major reevaluations of the situation of women include:

1889   Mary E. Lane, *Mizora: A Prophecy. A Manuscript Found Among the Private Papers of the Princess Vera Faravitch: Being a True and Faithful Account of Her Journey to the Interior of the Earth with a Careful Description of the Country and Its Inhabitants, Their Customs, Manners, and Government*
       Charles Bellamy, *An Experiment in Marriage: A Romance*
1890   Linn Boyd Porter, *Speaking of Ellen, by Albert Ross*
1892   Ignatius Donnelly, *The Golden Bottle; or the Story of Ephraim Benezet of Kansas*
1893   Alice Ilgenfritz Jones and Ella Merchant, *Unveiling a Parallel: A Romance by Two Women of the West*
       Henry Olerich, *A Cityless and Countryless World: An Outline of Practical Co-operative Individualism*
1895   William H. Bishop, *The Garden of Eden, USA: A Very Possible Story*
       Albert Chavannes, *In Brighter Climes; or, Life in Socioland: A Realistic Novel*
1900   Alcanoan O. Grigsby and Mary P. Lowe, *Nequa; or, The Problem of the Ages, by Jack Adams*

9. William H. Bishop, *The Garden of Eden, USA: A Very Possible Story* (Chicago: Charles Kerr, 1895), p. 8.

10. Mary H. Ford, review of *Looking Backward*, *Nationalist* 1 (1889), 352–57.

11. Mary E. Lane, *Mizora: A Prophecy. A Manuscript Found Among the Private Papers of the Princess Vera Faravitch: Being a True and Fathful Account of Her Journey to the Interior of the Earth with a Care-Description of the Country and Its Inhabitants, Their Customs, Manners, and Government* (New York: G. W. Dillingham, 1889), p. 199–214.

12. Elaine Showalter, *A Literature of Their Own: British Women Novelists from Brontë to Lessing* (Princeton, N.J.: Princeton University Press, 1977), p. 14.

13. Xavière Gauthier, "Existe-t-il une ecriture de femme?" in *New French Feminisms*, ed. Elaine Marks and Isabelle de Courtivron (New York: Schocken, Books, 1981), pp. 161–64.

14. P. 220. Mizora synthesizes the spiritual domain of ideality with the phenomenal world of science, providing a religious justification for material improvements:

That wonderful civilization I met with in Mizora, I may not be able to more than faintly shadow forth here, yet from it, the present age may form some idea of that grand, that ideal life, that is possible for our remote posterity. Again and again, has religious enthusiasm pictured a life to be eliminated from the grossness and imperfections of our material existence. The Spirit—the Mind—that mental gift, by or through which we think, reason, and suffer is by one tragic and awful struggle to free itself from temporal blemishes and difficulties and become spiritual and perfect. Yet who, sweeping the limitless fields of space with a telescope, glancing at myriads of worlds that a lifetime could not count, or gazing through a microscope at a tiny world in a drop of water, has dreamed that patient Science, and practise could evolve for the living human race, the ideal life of exalted knowledge: the life I found in Mizora: that Science had made real and practicable. (P. 9)

Thus, through science, heaven, the world of ideality, is available here on earth. Science becomes a glib alternative to death and blurs the boundary between heavenly and earthly possibility as it becomes endowed with spiritual significance. By defining its benefits in terms of material satisfaction and earthly success, the religious experience is degraded. *Mizora* thus resides in the genteel tradition, which George Santayana defined as an ideology of success, civilization, and progress, rationalized by a fusion of evangelical Christianity and transcendentalism. Whatever is "becomes the will of God" because whatever is, is God (see George Santayana, "The Genteel Tradition in American Philosophy," in *The Genteel Tradition* (Cambridge, Mass.: Harvard University Press, 1967), pp. 38–64.

15. Although *Herland* is outside the general chronological boundaries of this study, I include it because its narrative devices and sociosexual solutions harken back to progressive utopias and develop the form in significant ways (Charlotte Perkins Gilman, *Herland* [1915; rpt. New York: Pantheon, 1979]).

16. In Charlotte Perkins Gilman, *Women and Economics: A Study in the Economic Relation Between Men and Women as a Factor in Social Evolution* (1898; rpt. New York: Harper and Row, 1966), slavery and polygamy are shown to be contemporaneous and mutually dependent structures (p. 214).

17. This paragraph is based on ibid., pp. 1, 102, 164. See also Lois N. Magner, "Women and the Scientific Idiom: Textual Episodes from Wollstonecraft, Fuller, Gilman, and Firestone," *Signs* 4 (1978), esp. 68–77.

18. Nancy Chodorow, "Mothering, Male Dominance, and Capitalism," *Capitalist Patriarchy and the Case for Socialist Feminism,* ed. Zillah R. Eisenstein (New York: Monthly Review, 1979), p. 88.

19. This episode forms the basis of Gilman's powerful short story of madness and confinement, *The Yellow Wallpaper* (Old Westbury, N.Y.: Feminist Press, 1973).

20. Gilman, *Women and Economics,* p. 31.

21. Ibid.

22. Ibid., p. 38.

23. See Friedrich Engels, *The Origins of the Family, Private Property and the State* (1884; rpt. Laurence and Wishart: London, 1972), and August Bebel, *Woman Under Socialism* (1883; rpt. New York: Schocken, 1971). See also Zillah R. Eisenstein, "Developing a Theory of Capitalist Patriarchy and Socialist Feminism," in *Capitalist Patriarchy and the Case for Socialist Feminism,* ed. Zillah R. Eisenstein (New York: Monthly Review, 1979), pp. 5–40; and "Relations of Capitalist Patriarchy," *Feminism and Materialism: Women and Modes of Production,* ed. Annette Kuhn and Ann Marie Wolpe (London: Routledge and Kegan Paul, 1978), pp. 41–55.

Bibliography

Utopian Fiction in America, 1880–1900

Adams, Frederick Upham. *President John Smith: The Story of a Peaceful Revolution.* Chicago: Charles H. Kerr, 1897.

Aikin, Charles. *Forty Years with the Damned; or, Life Inside the Earth.* Evanston, Ill.: Regan Printing House, 1895.

Allen, Henry Francis. *The Key of Industrial Cooperative Government, by Pruning Knife.* St. Louis: Author, 1886.

———. *A Strange Voyage: A Revision of the Key of Industrial Government, an Interesting and Instructive Description of Life on Planet Venus, by Pruning Knife.* St. Louis: Monitor, 1891.

Anon. *The Beginning: A Romance of Chicago as It Might Be.* Chicago: Charles H. Kerr, 1893.

Anon. *Man Abroad: A Yarn of Some Other Century.* New York: G. W. Dillingham, 1887. Reprint. Boston: Greg Press, 1976.

Anon. *Man or Dollar, Which? A Novel, by a Newspaper Man.* Chicago: Charles H. Kerr, 1896.

Anon. *The Rise and Fall of the United States; A Leaf from History, A.D. 2060, by a Diplomat.* New York: F. Tennyson Neely, 1898.

Astor, John Jacob. *A Journey in Other Worlds: A Romance of the Future.* New York: D. Appleton, 1894.

Bachelder, John. *A.D. 2050: Electrical Development at Atlantis, by a Former Resident of the Hub.* San Francisco: Bancroft, 1893.

Badger, Joseph E., Jr. *The Lost City.* Boston: Dana, Estes, 1898.

Baker, William Elliott Smith. *The Battle of Coney Island: or, Free Trade Overthrown.* Philadelphia: J. A. Wagenseller, 1883.

Ballou, William Hosea. *The Bachelor Girl: A Novel of 1400.* New York: Lovell, 1890.

Bartlett, J. W. B. *A New Aristocracy, by Birch Arnold.* Detroit: Bartlett, 1891.

Batchelor, John M. *A Strange People.* New York: J. Ogilvie, 1888.

Bayne, Charles J. *The Face of Utopia.* Boston: Eastern Publishing Co., n.d.

———. *The Fall of Utopia.* Boston: Eastern Publishing Co., [1900].

Bellamy, Charles Joseph. *An Experiment in Marriage.* Albany, N.Y.: Albany Book Co., 1889.

181

Bibliography

Bellamy, Edward. *See* pp. 202–05.

Berwick, Edward. "Farming in the Year 2000, A.D." *Overland*, 2d ser. 15 (June 1890), 263–73.

Bird, Arthur. *Looking Forward: A Dream of the United States of the Americas in 1999.* Utica, N.Y.: L. C. Childs, 1899. Reprint. New York: Arno, 1973.

Bishop, William H. *The Garden of Eden, USA: A Very Possible Story.* Chicago: Charles H. Kerr, 1895.

Bond, Daniel. *Uncle Sam in Business.* Chicago: Charles H. Kerr, 1899.

Bouve, Edward T. *Centuries Apart.* Boston: Little, Brown, 1894.

Bradshaw, William R. *The Goddess of Atvatabar.* New York: J. F. Douthitt, 1892.

Brady, Adhemer. *The Mathematics of Labor.* Chicago: Charles H. Kerr, 1899.

Braine, Robert D. *Messages from Mars, by Aid of the Telescope Planet.* New York: J. S. Ogilvie, 1892.

Bridge, James Howard. *A Fortnight in Heaven: An Unconventional Romance.* New York: Henry Holt, 1886.

Brooks, Bryon A. *Earth Revisited.* Boston: Arena, 1894.

Brown, John Macmillan. *Riallaro, The Archepelago of Exiles, by Godfrey Sweven.* New York: Putnam's, 1901.

Browne, Walter. *2894; or, The Fossil Man: A Midwinter's Night Dream.* New York: G. W. Dillingham, 1894.

Bunce, Oliver Bell. "The Story of Happinolande." In *The Story of Happinolande and Other Legends.* New York: D. Appleton, 1889.

Call, Henry L. *The Coming Revolution.* Boston: Arena, 1895.

Caryl, Charles W. *A New Era: Presenting the Plans for the New Era Union to Help Develop and Utilize the Best Skill There Is Available to Realize the Highest Degree of Prosperity That Is Possible for All Who Will Help to Attain It—Based on Practical and Successful Business Methods.* Denver: New Era Union, 1897.

Casey, James. *A New Moral World, and a New State of Society.* Providence, R. I.: Author, 1885.

Caswell, Edward A. *Toil and Self, by Myself and Another.* Chicago: Rand, Mcnally, 1900.

Centennius, Ralph. *The Dominion in 1983.* Peterborough, Ont.: Tober, 1883.

Chamberlain, Henry R. *6,000 Tons of Gold.* Meadville, Pa.: Flood and Vincent, 1894.

Chambers, Julius. *"In Sargasso." Missing: A Romance.* New York: Transatlantic, 1896.

Chambers, Robert W. *The Maker of Moons.* New York: Putnam's, 1896.

Chavannes, Albert. *The Future Commonwealth: or, What Samuel Balcom Saw in Socioland.* New York: True Nationalist, 1892.

———. *In Brighter Climes; or, Life in Socioland: A Realistic Novel.* Knoxville, Tenn.: Chavannes, 1895.

Child, William Stanley. *The Legal Revolution of 1902.* Chicago: Charles H. Kerr, 1898. Reprint. New York: Arno, 1973.

Clark, Francis E. *The Mossback Correspondence Together with Mr. Mossback's Views on Certain Practical Subjects, with a Short Account of His Visit to Utopia.* Boston: D. Lothrop, 1889.

Bibliography

Colburn, Frona E. W. *Yermah, the Dorado: The Story of a Lost Race.* San Francisco: W. Doxey, 1897.

Cole, Cyprus. *The Aurorophone.* Chicago: Charles H. Kerr, 1890.

Coste, F. H. P. *Towards Utopia.* Frank Hill Perry, 1894.

Coverdale, Henry Standish. *The Fall of the Great Republic.* Boston: Roberts Brothers, 1895.

Cowan, Frank. *Revi-Lona: A Romance of Love in a Marvelous Land.* Greensburg, Pa.: Tribune Press, 188–?

Cowan, James. *Daybreak: A Romance of An Old World.* New York: George H. Richmond, 1896.

Craig, Alexander. *Ionia: Land of Wise Men and Fair Women.* Chicago: E. A. Weeks, 1898.

Crawford, T. C. *A Man and His Soul: An Occult Romance of Washington Life.* New York: Charles B. Reed, 1894.

Cridge, Alfred Denton. *Utopia; or, The History of an Extinct Planet.* Oakland, Calif.: Winchester and Pew, 1884.

Crocker, Samuel. *That Island: A Political Romance by Theodore Oceanic Islet.* Oklahoma City: C. E. Streeter, 1892.

Dail, C. C. *Willmoth, The Wanderer; or, The Man from Saturn.* Atchison, Kans.: Haskill, 1890.

Dake, Charles Romyn. *A Strange Discovery.* New York: H. Ingalls Kimball, 1899.

Daniel, Charles. *Ai: A Social Vision.* Philadelphia: Miller, 1892.

Davenport, Benjamin Rush. *Uncle Sam's Cabins: A Story of American Life Looking Forward a Century.* New York: Mascot, 1895.

De Medici, Charles. *Two Lunatics: A Remarkable Story.* New York: Oxford, 1889.

DeMille, James. *A Strange Manuscript Found in a Copper Cylinder.* New York: Harper, 1888.

Dodd, Anna Bowman. *The Republic of the Future; or, Socialism a Reality.* New York: Cassell, 1887.

Donnelly, Ignatius. *Atlantis: The Antediluvian World.* New York: Harper, 1882.

———. *Caesar's Column, by Edmund Boisgilbert.* Chicago: F. J. Schulte, 1890. Reprint. Cambridge, Mass.: Harvard University Press, 1960.

———. *The Golden Bottle; or, The Story of Ephraim Benezet of Kansas.* New York: D. D. Merrill, 1892.

———. *Ragnarok: The Age of Fire and Gravel.* New York: D. Appleton, 1883.

Dooner, Pierton W. *The Last Days of the Republic.* San Francisco: Alta California, 1880.

Doughty, Francis W. *Mirrikh; or, a Woman from Mars.* New York: Burleigh and Johnston, 1892.

Drayton, Henry S. *In Oudemon: Reminiscences of an Unknown People by an Occasional Traveller.* New York: Grafton, 1900.

Edson, Milan C. *Solaris Farm: A Story of the Twentieth Century.* Washington, D.C.: Author, 1900.

Emmens, Stephen H. *The Sixteenth Amendment: A Plain Citizen.* New York: 1896.

Everett, Henry L. *The People's Program: The Twentieth Century Is Theirs. A Romance of the Expectations of the Present Generations.* New York: Workmen's, 1892.

183

Bibliography

Farnell, George. *Rev. Josiah Hilton, The Apostle of the New Age.* Providence, R.I.: Journal of Commerce, n.d.

Fayette, John B. *Voices from Many Hill Tops, Echoes from Many Valleys; or, The Experiences of Spirits Eon and Eona, in Earth Life and Spirit Spheres, in Ages Past, in the Long, Long Ago, and Their Many Incarnations in Earth Life, and on Other Worlds, Given Through the Sun Angels' Order of Light.* Springfield, Mass.: Press Springfield Company, 1886.

Fiske, Amos K. *Beyond the Bourne: Reports of a Traveller Returned from the Undiscovered Country, Submitted to the World.* New York: Fords, Howard and Hulbert, 1891.

Fitch, Thomas, and Anna M. Fitch. *Better Days; or, A Millionaire of To-morrow.* Rev. ed. Chicago: F. J. Schulte, 1892.

Fitzpatrick, Ernest Hugh. *The Marshall Duke of Denver; or, The Labor Revolution of 1920. A Novel, by Hugo Barnaby.* Chicago: Donohue and Henneberry, 1895.

Flower, Benjamin O. *Equality and Brotherhood.* Boston: Arena, 1897.

Forbush, Zebina. *The Co-opolitan: A Story of the Cooperative Commonwealth of Idaho.* Chicago: Charles H. Kerr, 1898.

Franklin, Abraham Benjamin. *The Light of Reason: Showing the First Step the Nation Should Take Toward a Social Order Based on Justice.* Chicago: Charles H. Kerr, 1899.

Fuller, Alvarado M. *A.D. 2000.* Chicago: Laird and Lee, 1890.

Galloway, James M. *John Harvey: A Tale of the Twentieth Century by Anon Moore.* Chicago: Charles H. Kerr, 1897.

Gaston, Henry A. *Mars Revealed; or, Seven Days in the Spirit World.* San Francisco: A. L. Bancroft, 1880.

Geissler, Ludwig A. *Looking Beyond: A Sequel to "Looking Backward" by Edward Bellamy and an Answer to "Looking Forward" by Richard Michaelis.* New Orleans: L. Graham and Sons, 1891.

Giles, Fayette Stratton. *Shadows Before; or, A Century Onward.* Humboldt, 1894.

Gillette, King Camp. *Human Dritt.* Boston: New Era, 1894.

Griffin, Crawford S. *Nationalism.* Boston: Author, 1889.

Griggs, Sutton Elbert. *Imperium in Imperio.* Cincinnati: Editor Publishing, 1899. Reprint. New York: Arno, 1969.

Grigsby, Alcanoan Q., and Mary Lowe. *Nequa; or, The Problem of the Ages, by Jack Adams.* Topeka, Kans.: Equity, 1900.

Grimshaw, Robert. *Fifty Years Hence; or, What May Be in 1943; A Prophecy Supposed to Be Based on Scientific Deductions by an Improved Graphical Method.* New York: Practical Publishing, 1892.

Haedicke, Paul. *The Equalities of Para-Para: Written from Dictation of George Rambler, M.D., F.R.G.S.* Chicago: Schuldt-Gathmann, 1895.

Hale, Edward Everett. *How They Lived in Hampton: A Study of Practical Christianity Applied in the Manufacture of Woolens.* Boston: J. S. Smith, 1888.

Harben, William N. "In the Year Ten Thousand," *Arena* 6 (November 1892), 743–49.

———. *The Land of the Changing Sun.* New York: Merriam, 1894.

Harney, Gilbert Lane. *Philoland.* New York: F. Tennyson Neely, 1900.

Bibliography

Harris, George. *Inequality and Progress*. Boston: Houghton Mifflin, 1897.

Harris, Thomas Lake. *The New Republic: A Discourse of the Prospects, Dangers, Duties, and Safeties of the Times*. Santa Rosa, Calif.: Fountaingrove, 1891.

Hartshorne, Henry. *1931: A Glance at the Twentieth Century*. Philadelphia: E. Claxton: 1881.

Hawthorne, Julian. "June, 1993." *Cosmopolitan* 14 (1893), 450–58.

Hertzka, Theodor. *Freeland: A Social Anticipation*. Trans. Arthur Ransom. New York: D. Appleton, 1891.

Heywood, D. Herbert. *The Twentieth Century: A Prophecy of the Coming Age*. Boston: n.p., 1890.

Holford, Castello N. *Aristopia*. Boston: Arena, 1895.

Howard, Albert W. *The Milltillionaire, by M. Auburre Hovorre*. Boston: n.p., 1895.

Howells, William D. *See* pp. 203–05.

James, Henry. "The Great Good Place," *Scribner's Magazine* 27 (January 1900), 99–112.

Jones, Alice Ilgenfritz, and Ella Merchant. *Unveiling a Parallel: A Romance, by Two Women of the West*. Boston: Arena, 1893.

Lane, Mary E. *Mizora: A Prophecy. A Manuscript Found Among the Private Papers of the Princess Vera Faravitch: Being a True and Faithful Account of Her Journey to the Interior of the Earth with a Care-Description of the Country and Its Inhabitants, Their Customs, Manners, and Government*. New York: G. W. Dillingham, 1889.

Leggett, M. D. *A Dream of a Modest Prophet*. Philadelphia: J. B. Lippincott, 1890.

Leland, Samuel Philps. *Peculiar People*. Cleveland: Aust and Clark, 1891.

Leonhart, Rudolph. *Either, Or*. Canton, Ohio: Roller, 1893.

———. *The Treasure of Montezuma*. Canton, Ohio: Cassidy, 1888.

Lloyd, John Uri. *Editorpha*. 2d ed. Cincinnati: Robert Clarke, 1896.

Lockwood, Ingersoll. *1900; or, The Last President*. New York: American News, 1896.

Lockwood, John. *Hi-Li, the Moon Man*. Brooklyn, N.Y.: n.p., 1896.

Macnie, John. *The Diothas; or, A Far Look Ahead, by Ismar Thiusen*. New York: Putnam's, 1883.

McCowan, Archibald. *Philip Meyer's Scheme: A Story of Trader Unionism, by Luke A. Hedd*. New York: J.S. Ogilvie, 1892.

McCoy, John. *A Prophetic Romance: Mars to Earth, by the Lord Commissioner*. Boston: Arena, 1895.

McDougall, Walter H. *The Hidden City*. New York: Cassell, 1891.

McMartin, Donald. *A Leap into the Future; or, How Things Will Be. A Romance of the Year 2000*. Albany, N.Y.: Weed, Parsons, 1900.

Mendes, H. Pereira. *Looking Ahead: Twentieth Century Happenings*. 1899. Reprint. New York: Arno, 1973.

Merrill, Albert Adams. *The Great Awakening: The Story of the Twenty-Second Century*. Boston: George, 1899.

Michaelis, Richard. *Looking Further Forward: An Answer to "Looking Backward" by Edward Bellamy*. Chicago: Rand McNally, 1890.

Miller, Joaquin. *The Building of the City Beautiful*. Chicago: Stone and Kimball, 1893.

185

Bibliography

Mitchell, John Ames. *The Last American.* N.p., n.d., 1889.

Mitchell, Willis. *The Inhabitants of Mars, Their Manners and Advancement in Civilization and Their Opinion of Us.* Malden, Mass.: C. E. Spofford, 1895.

Moore, M. Louise. *Al-Modad; or, Life Scenes Beyond the Polar Circumflex, a Religio-Scientific Solution of the Problem of Present and Future Life, by an Untrammelled Free-Thinker.* Cameron Parish, La.: Author, 1892.

Mundo, Oto. *The Recovered Continent: A Tale of the Chinese Invasion.* Columbus, Ohio: Harper-Osgood, 1898.

Niswonger, Charles E. *The Isle of Feminine.* Little Rock, Ark.: Brown, 1893.

Oberholtzer, Ellis Paxson. *The New Man.* Philadelphia: Levytype, 1897.

Olerich, Henry. *A Cityless and Countryless World: An Outline of Practical Co-operative Individualism.* Holstein, Iowa: Gilmore and Olerich, 1893.

Peck, Bradford. *The World a Department Store: A Story of Life Under the Cooperative System.* Lewiston, Me.: Author, 1900.

Persinger, Clark Edmund. *Letters from New America; or, An Attempt at Practical Socialism.* Chicago: Charles H. Kerr, 1900.

Petersilea, Carlyle. *The Discovered Country, by Ernst von Himmel.* Boston: Ernst von Himmel, 1899.

Phelps, Corwin. *An Ideal Republic: or, The One Way out of the Fog.* Chicago: n.p., 1896.

Phelps, E. S. *Beyond the Gates.* Boston: Houghton Mifflin, 1883.

Pittock, M. A. *The God of Civilization: A Romance.* Chicago: Eureka, 1890.

Pomeroy, William C. *The Lords of Misrule: A Tale of Gods and of Men.* Chicago: Laird and Lee, 1894.

Pope, Gustavus W. *Journey to Mars. The Wonderful World: Its Beauty and Splendor; Its Mighty Races and Kingdoms; Its Final Doom. Romances of The Planets,* no. 1. New York: G. W. Dillingham, 1894. Reprint. Westport, Conn.: Hyperion, 1974.

Porter, Linn Boyd. *Speaking of Ellen, by Albert Ross.* New York: G. W. Dillingham, 1890.

Pratt, Parley Parker. *The Angel of the Prairies: A Dream of Future.* Salt Lake City: Deseret News, 1880.

Ramsey, Milton W. *Six Thousand Years Hence.* Minneapolis: Alfred Roper, 1891.

Rehm, Warren S. *The Practical City: A Future City Romance; or, A Study in Environment, by Owen Nemo.* Lancaster, Pa.: Lancaster County Magazine, 1898.

Reynolds, Thomas. *Prefaces and Notes Illustrative, Explanatory, Demonstrative, Argumentative and Expostulatory to Edward Bellamy's Book "Looking Backward."* London: Thomas Reynolds, 1890.

Reynolds, Walter Doty. *Mr. Jonnemacher's Machine: The Port to Which We Drifted, by Lord Prime, Esq.* Philadelphia: Knickerbocker, 1898.

Roberts, J. W. *Looking Within: The Misleading Tendencies of "Looking Backward" Made Manifest.* New York: A. S. Barnes, 1893.

Rogers, John Rankin. *The Graftons; or, Looking Forward. A Story of Pioneer Life, by S. L. Rogers.* Chicago: Milton George, 1893.

Rosewater, Frank. *'96: A Romance of Utopia.* Omaha, Nebr.: Utopia, 1894.

Bibliography

Russell, Addison Peale. *Sub-Coelum: A Sky-Built Human World.* Boston: Houghton Mifflin, 1893.

Salisbury, Henry Barnard. *The Birth of Freedom: A Socialist Novel.* New York: Humboldt, 1890. (Also published as *Miss Worden's Hero: A Novel.* New York, G. W. Dillingham, 1890.)

Sanders, George A. *Reality, or Law and Order vs. Anarchy and Socialism: A Reply to Edward Bellamy's "Looking Backward" and "Equality," A Collection of Indignant Essays.* N.p., 1887.

Satterlee, W. W. *Looking Backward and What I Saw, 1890–2101.* Minneapolis: Harrison and Smith, ca. 1890. Reprint. New York: Arno, 1973.

Schindler, Solomon. *Young West: A Sequel to Edward Bellamy's Celebrated Novel "Looking Backward."* Boston: Arena, 1894.

Schwahn, John George. *The Tableau; or, Heaven as a Republic.* Los Angeles: Franklin, 1892.

Sears, Alfred. *The Lost Inca; A Tale of Discovery in the Vale of Inti-Mayu, by the Inca-Pancho-Ozollo.* New York: Cassell, 1889.

Sheldon, Charles M. *In His Steps: "What Would Jesus Do?"* Chicago: Advance, 1896.

Shelhamer, M. T. *Life and Labor in the Spirit World.* Boston: Colby and Rich, 1885.

Simpson, William. *The Man from Mars, His Morals, Politics and Religion, by Thomas Blot.* San Francisco: Bacon, 1891.

Smith, Titus K. *Altruria.* New York: Altruria, 1895. Reprint. New York: Arno, 1973.

Smythe, Alfred. *Van Hoff; or, The New Planet.* New York: American Publishers, 1897.

Southwick, E. B. *The Better World.* New York: Truth Seeker, 1895.

Stone, Mrs. C. H. *One of "Berrian's" Novels.* New York: Welch, Fracker, 1890.

Stump, D. L. *From World to World: A Novel.* Asbury, Mo.: World to World, 1896.

Swan, Herbert E. *It Might Be: A Story of the Future Progress of the Sciences, the Wonderful Advancement in the Methods of Government and the Happy State of the People.* Stafford, Kans.: H. E. Swan, 1896.

Swift, Morrison I. *A League of Justice; or, Is It Right to Rob Robbers?* Boston: Commonwealth Society, 1893.

Thomas, Chauncey M. *The Crystal Button; or, The Adventure of Paul Prognosis in the Forty-Ninth Century.* Boston: Houghton Mifflin, 1891.

Thorne, Gerald. *Heaven on Earth.* New York: Lovell, 1896.

Tibbles, T. H., and Elia M. Peattie. *The American Peasants: A Timely Allegory, By T. H. Tibbles and Another.* Indianapolis: Vincent, 1892.

Tincker, Mary Agnes. *San Salvador.* Boston: Houghton Mifflin, 1892.

Truman, O. H. *The Conquest: A Story of the Past, Present, and Future, Real and Ideal.* Monticello, Iowa: O. H. Truman, 1884.

Twain, Mark. *A Connecticut Yankee in King Arthur's Court.* New York: Charles L. Webster, 1889.

———. "The Curious Republic of Gondour." *Atlantic Monthly* 36 (October 1875), 461–63.

Bibliography

Van Deusen, Alonzo. *Rational Communism: The Present and the Future Republic of North America.* New York: Social Science, 1885.

Vinton, Arthur Dudley. *Looking Further Backward, Being a Series of Lectures Delivered to the Freshman Class at Shawmut College by Professor Wong Lung Li.* Albany, N.Y.: Albany Book Co., 1890.

Walker, Samuel. *The Reign of Selfishness: A Story of Concentrated Wealth.* New York: M. K. Pelletrean, 1891.

Waterloo, Stanley. *Armageddon: A Tale of Love, War, and Invention.* Chicago: Rand, McNally, 1898.

Welcome, S. Byron. *From Earth's Center: A Polar Gateway Message.* Chicago: Charles H. Kerr, 1894.

Wellman, B. J. *The Legal Revolution of 1902, by a Law-Abiding Revolutionist.* Chicago: Charles H. Kerr, 1898.

Wheeler, David H. *Our Industrial Utopia and Its Unhappy Citizens.* Chicago: A. C. McClurg, 1895.

Wilbrandt, Conrad. *Mr. East's Experiences in Mr. Bellamy's World. Records of the Years 2001–2002.* Trans. Mary Joanna Safford. New York: Harpers, 1891.

Wilkes, A. B. *The Great Social Boycott; or, Society Readjusted and the Causes Leading to Its Establishment. This Is a Small Picture Gallery and Your Portrait Hangs in It.* Brownwood, Tex: Author, 1895.

Williams, Frederic Conde, ed. *"Utopia": The Story of a Strange Experience.* Cambridge, Mass.: Metcalfe, 1895.

Windsor, William. *Loma: A Citizen of Venus.* St. Paul, Minn.: Windsor and Lewis, 1897.

Wood, Mrs. J. *Pantaletta: A Romance of Shekeland.* New York: American News, 1882.

Worley, Frederick U. *Three Thousand Dollars a Year: Moving Forward or How We Got There, by Benefice.* Washington, D.C.: J. P. Wright, 1890.

Utopian Theory and American Utopian Fiction: Books

Aaron, Daniel. *Men of Good Hope: A Story of American Progressives.* London: Oxford University Press, 1951.

———. *Writers on the Left: Episodes in American Literary Communism.* New York: Harcourt, Brace and World, 1961.

Adams, Frederick B., Jr. *Radical Literature in America.* Stamford, Conn.: Overbrook, 1939.

Aldiss, Brian W. *Billion Year Spree.* London: Weinfeld and Nicholson, 1973.

Amis, Kingsley. *New Maps of Hell.* New York: Ballantine, 1960.

Armytage, W. H. G. *Yesterday's Tomorrows: A Historical Survey of Future Societies.* Toronto: University of Toronto Press, 1968.

Bailey, J. O. *Pilgrims Through Space and Time: Trends and Patterns in Science and Utopian Fiction.* New York: Argus, 1947.

Barkun, Michael. *Disaster and the Millennium.* New Haven, Conn.: Yale University Press, 1974.

Bibliography

Barr, Marlene. *Future Females: A Critical Anthology.* Bowling Green, Ohio: Bowling Green State University Popular Press, 1981.

Bebel, August. *Woman Under Socialism.* Trans. Daniel de Leon. New York: Schocken, 1971.

Berneri, Marie Louise. *1918–1949. Journey through Utopia.* Boston: Beacon, 1950.

Bloch, Ernst. *A Philosophy of the Future.* Trans. John Cumming. New York: Herder and Herder, 1970.

———. *Freiheit and Ordnung; Abrisse der Sozial-Utopien.* New York: Aurora Verlag, 1946.

———. *Geist der Utopie.* Munich: Duncker and Humblot, 1918.

———. *Das Prinzip Hoffnung.* 3 vols. Berlin: Aufbau-Verlag. 1955–1959.

Bloomfield, Paul. *Imaginary Worlds, or the Evolution of Utopia.* London: Hamilton, 1932.

Brisbane, Albert. *Social Destiny of Man, or Association and Re-organization of Industry.* Philadelphia: C. F. Stollmeyer, 1840.

Buber, Martin. *Paths in Utopia.* Trans. R. F. C. Hull. Boston: Beacon, 1958.

Calverton, Victor. *Where Angels Dared to Tread.* New York: n.p., 1941.

Chianese, Robert L., ed. *Peaceable Kingdoms: An Anthology of Utopian Writings.* New York: Harcourt Brace Jovanovich, 1971.

Clarke, Ignatius Frederick. *Tale of the Future, from the Beginning to the Present Day; a Check-List of Those Satires, Ideal states, Political Warnings, and Forecasts, Interplanetary Voyages and Scientific Romances . . . That Have Been Published in the United Kingdom Between 1664 and 1960.* London: Library Association, 1961.

Cohn, Norman. *The Pursuit of the Millennium: Revolutionary Messianism in Medieval and Reformation Europe.* New York: Harper and Row, 1961.

Davenport, Basil. *Inquiry Into Science Fiction.* New York: Longmans Green, 1955.

Davenport, Basil, et al. *The Science Fiction Novel: Imagination and Social Criticism.* Chicago: Advent, 1959.

De Camp, L. Sprague. *Science Fiction Handbook: The Writing of Imaginative Fiction.* New York: Hermitage House, 1953.

De Camp, L. Sprague, and Willy Ley. *Lost Continents: The Atlantis Theme in History, Science, and Literature.* New York: Gnome, 1954.

Doig, Ivan, ed. *Utopian America: Dreams and Realities.* Rochelle Park, N.J.: Hayden, 1976.

Dombrowski, James. *The Early Days of Christian Socialism in America.* New York: Columbia Press, 1936.

Dubos, René. *The Dreams of Reason; Science and Utopias.* New York: Columbia University Press, 1961.

Elliott, Robert C. *The Power of Satire, Magic, Ritual, Art.* Princeton, N.J.: Princeton University Press, 1960.

———. *The Shape of Utopia: Studies in a Literary Genre.* Chicago: University of Chicago Press, 1970.

Engels, Friedrich. *Socialism: Utopian and Scientific.* Moscow: Progress Publishers, 1970.

Bibliography

Eurich, Nell. *Science in Utopia.* Cambridge, Mass.: Harvard University Press, 1967.

Flower, B. O. *Progressive Men, Women and Movements of the Past Twenty-Five Years.* Boston: New Arena, 1914.

Franklin, H. Bruce. *American Science Fiction of the Nineteenth Century.* New York: Oxford University Press, 1966.

Garrett, John Charles. *Utopias in Literature Since the Romantic Period.* Christchurch, New Zealand: University of Canterbury Press, 1968.

George, Henry. *Progress and Poverty: An Inquiry into the Causes of Industrial Depressions and of Increase of Want with Increase of Wealth—The Remedy.* San Francisco: William Hinton, 1879.

Gerber, Richard. *Utopian Fantasy: A Study of English Utopian Fiction since the End of the Nineteenth Century.* London: Routledge and Kegan Paul, 1955.

Goodman, Paul. *Utopian Essays and Critical Proposals.* New York: Vintage, 1964.

Goodman, Paul, and Percival Goodman. *Communitas.* New York: Vintage, 1960.

Gronlund, Laurence. *The Cooperative Commonwealth.* London: LeBas and Lowry, 1886.

Hart, James D. *The Popular Book: A History of America's Literary Taste.* Berkeley and Los Angeles: University of California Press, 1963.

Hayden, Dolores. *Seven American Utopias: The Architecture of Communitarian Socialism 1790–1975.* Cambridge, Mass: MIT Press, 1976.

Hertzler, Joyce O. *The History of Utopian Thought.* New York: Cooper Square, 1965.

Hicks, Granville. *The Great Tradition: An Interpretation of American Literature Since the Civil War.* New York: Macmillan, 1935.

Hillegas, Mark R. *The Future as Nightmare: H. G. Wells and the Anti-Utopians.* New York: Oxford University Press, 1967.

Infield, Henrik F. *Utopia and Experiment: Essays in the Sociology of Cooperation.* New York: Praeger, 1955.

Jaher, Frederic Cople. *Doubters and Dissenters: Cataclysmic Thought in America, 1885–1918.* London: Collier-Macmillan, 1964.

Kateb, George. *Utopia and Its Enemies.* New York: Schocken, 1963.

Kaul, A. N. *The American Vision: Actual and Ideal Society in Nineteenth Century Fiction.* New Haven, Conn.: Yale University Press, 1963.

Kerr, Charles H. *The Story of a Socialist Publishing House.* Chicago: Charles H. Kerr, 1912.

————. *What Socialism Is.* Chicago: Charles H. Kerr, n.d.

Ketterer, David. *New Worlds for Old: The Apocalyptic Imagination, Science Fiction, and American Literature.* Garden City, N.Y.: Anchor, 1974.

Knight, Damon. *In Search of Wonder: Essays on Modern Science Fiction.* Chicago: Advent, 1956.

Laidler, Harry W. *History of Socialism.* New York: Thomas Y. Crowell, 1934.

————. *Social-Economic Movements: An Historical and Comparative Survey of Socialism, Communism, Cooperation, Utopianism, and Other Systems of Reform and Reconstruction.* London: Routledge and Kegan Paul, 1949.

190

Bibliography

Lasky, Melvin J. *Utopia and Revolution*. Chicago: University of Chicago Press, 1976.

Levin, Harry. *The Myth of the Golden Age in the Renaissance*. Bloomington: Indiana University Press, 1969.

Lewis, Arthur O., ed. *American Utopias: Selected Short Fiction*. New York: Arno, 1971.

Loubere, Leo A. *Utopian Socialism: Its History Since 1800*. Cambridge, Mass.: Schenkman, 1974.

Lowenthal, Leo, and Norbert Guterman. *Prophets of Deceit: A Study of the Techniques of the American Agitator*. New York: Harper, 1949.

Mannheim, Karl. *Ideology and Utopia: An Introduction to the Sociology of Knowledge*. New York: Harcourt, Brace, 1952.

Mannin, Ethel. *Bread and Roses: A Utopian Survey and Blueprint*. London: MacDonald, 1944.

Manuel, Frank E., ed. *Utopias and Utopian Thought: A Timely Appraisal*. Boston: Beacon, 1966.

Manuel, Frank, and Fritzie P. Manuel. *Utopian Thought in the Western World*. Cambridge, Mass.: Harvard University Press, 1979.

Marbury, M. M. *Splendid Poseur: The Story of a Fabulous Humbug*. London: Frederick Miller, 1954.

Marcuse, Herbert. *An Essay on Liberation*. Boston: Beacon, 1969.

———. *Das Ende der Utopie*. Berlin: Verlag Peter von Maikowski, 1967.

———. *Eros and Civilization: A Philosophical Inquiry Into Freud*. London: Sphere. 1969.

———. *The Aesthetic Dimension*. Boston: Beacon, 1977.

Marin, Louis. *Utopiques: Jeux d'espaces*. Paris: Minuit, 1973.

Martin, Jay. *Harvests of Change: American Literature 1865–1914*. Englewood Cliffs, N.J.: Prentice-Hall, 1967.

Masso, Gildo. *Education in Utopias*. New York: Columbia University Press, 1927.

Molnar, Thomas. *Utopia: The Perennial Heresy*. New York: Sheed and Ward, 1967.

Morton, Arthur Leslie. *The English Utopia*. London: Laurence and Wishart, 1952.

Moskowitz, Samuel. *Explorers of the Infinite: Shapers of Science Fiction*. Cleveland: World, 1963.

———. *Science Fiction by Gaslight: A History and Anthology of Science Fiction in the Popular Magazines, 1891–1911*. Cleveland: World, 1968.

Mott, Frank Luther. *A History of American Magazines*. Vol. 4, *1885–1905*. Cambridge, Mass.: Harvard University Press, 1938.

Mullen, R. D., and Darko Suvin, eds. *Science Fiction Studies: Selected Articles on Science Fiction 1973–1975*. Boston: G. K. Hall, 1976.

Mumford, Lewis. *The Story of Utopias*. New York: Boni and Liveright, 1922.

Negley, Glenn R., and J. Max Patrick. *The Quest for Utopia: An Anthology of Imaginary Societies*. New York: Schuman, 1952.

Nelson, William, ed. *Twentieth-Century Interpretations of Utopia*. Englewood Cliffs, N.J.: Prentice-Hall, 1968.

Nisbet, Robert. *The Quest for Community: A Study in the Ethics of Order and Freedom*. New York: Oxford University Press, 1953.

Bibliography

Noyes, John Humphrey. *History of American Socialism*. 1870. Reprint. New York: Hilary House, 1901.

Parrington, Vernon L., Jr. *American Dreams: A Study of American Utopias*. New York: Russell and Russell, 1964.

Passmore, John. *The Perfectibility of Man*. New York: Scribner, 1970.

Plattel, Martin G. *Utopian and Critical Thinking*. Pittsburgh, Pa.: Duquesne University Press, 1972.

Polak, Frederik L. *The Image of the Future*. Trans. E. Boulding. New York: Oceana, 1961.

Rabkin, Eric J. *The Fantastic in Literature*. Princeton, N.J.: Princeton University Press, 1976.

Rhodes, Harold V. *Utopia in American Political Thought*. Tucson: University of Arizona Press, 1967.

Riley, Dick. *Critical Encounters: Writers and Themes in Science Fiction*. New York: Frederick Ungar, 1978.

Roemer, Kenneth. *America As Utopia*. New York: Burt Franklin, 1961.

———. *Build Your Own Utopia: Instructions and Feedbacks*. Washington, D.C.: University Press of America, 1981.

———. *Build Your Own Utopia: Study Guide*. Arlington: University of Texas Press, 1978.

———. *The Obsolete Necessity: America in Utopian Writings, 1888–1900*. Kent, Ohio: Kent State University Press, 1976.

Rose, Lois, and Stephen Rose. *The Shattered Ring: Science Fiction and the Quest for Meaning*. Richmond, Va.: John Knox, 1970.

Ross, Harry. *Utopias Old and New*. London: Ivor Nicholson and Watson, 1938.

Russell, Frances Theresa. *Touring Utopia, the Realm of Constructive Humanism*. New York: Dial, 1932.

Scholes, Robert. *Structural Fabulation: An Essay on Fiction of the Future*. Notre Dame, Ind.: University of Notre Dame Press, 1975.

Scholes, Robert, and Eric Rabkin. *Science Fiction: History—Science—Vision*. New York: Oxford University Press, 1977.

Sheehan, Donald. *This Was Publishing: A Chronicle of the Book Trade in the Gilded Age*. Bloomington: Indiana University Press, 1952.

Shklar, Judith M. *After Utopia: The Decline of Political Faith*. Princeton, N.J.: Princeton University Press, 1957.

Stern, Madeline. *Imprints on History: Book Publishers and American Frontiers*. Bloomington: Indiana University Press, 1956.

Suvin, Darko. *Metamorphoses of Science Fiction*. New Haven, Conn.: Yale University Press, 1979.

Taylor, Walter Fuller. *The Economic Novel in America*. Chapel Hill: University of North Carolina Press, 1942.

Todorov, Tzvetan. *The Fantastic: A Structural Approach to a Literary Genre*. Trans. Richard Howard. Ithaca, N.Y.: Cornell University Press, 1973.

Tuveson, Ernest Lee. *Millennium and Utopia: A Study in the Background of the Idea of Progress*. New York: Harper, 1964.

Bibliography

————. *Redeemer Nation: The Idea of America's Millennial Role.* Chicago: University of Chicago Press, 1968.

Wagenknecht. Edward. *Utopia Americana.* Seattle: University of Washington Bookstore, 1929.

Walsh, Chad. *From Utopia to Nightmare.* New York: Harper and Row, 1962.

Ziff, Larzer. *The American 1890s: Life and Times of a Lost Generation.* New York, Viking, 1966.

Utopian Theory and American Utopian Fiction: Articles

Anon. "William Harben." In vol. 5 of *Library of Southern Literature,* ed. Edwin A. Alderman and Joel Chandler Harris. Atlanta: Martin and Hoyt, 1907.

Axelrad, Allen M. "Ideology and Utopia in The Works of Ignatius Donnelly." *American Studies* 12 (Fall 1971), 47–65.

Beauchamp, Gorman. "Cultural Primitivism as Norm in the Dystopian Novel." *Extrapolation* 19 (December 1977), 88–96.

————. "Future Words: Language and the Dystopian Novel." *Style* 8 (Fall 1974). 462–76.

————. "Utopia and Its Discontents," *Midwest Quarterly* 16 (Winter 1975), 161–74.

Borgese, Elizabeth Mann. "Women in Neverland." In *Ascent of Woman.* New York: George Braziller, 1963, pp. 111–32.

Bowman, Sylvia E. "Utopian Views of Man and the Machine," *Studies in the Literary Imagination* 6 (Fall 1973), 105–20.

Brinton, Crane. "Century of Utopian Dreams and Catholic Realism." *Social Justice Review* 48 (August 1955), 116–19.

Carlson, W. A. "Professor Macnie as a Novelist." *Alumni Review of the University of North Dakota,* December 1934, 4.

Cary, Francine C. "The World a Department Store: Bradford Peck and the Utopian Endeavor." *American Quarterly* 29 (1977), 370–84.

Clareson, Thomas D. "An Annotated Checklist of American Science Fiction: 1880–1915." *Extrapolation* 1 (December 1959), 5–20.

————. "Major Trends in American Science Fiction: 1880–1915." *Extrapolation* 1 (December 1959), 2–4.

————. "The Scientist as Hero in American Science Fiction 1880–1920." *Extrapolation* 7 (December 1965), 18–28.

————, and Edward S. Lauterback, "A Checklist of Articles Dealing with Science Fiction." *Extrapolation* 1 (May 1960), 29–34.

Clarke, I. F. "The Nineteenth Century Utopia," *Quarterly Review* 9 (January 1958), 80.

Dodge, David. "The Utopian Pointer." *Century Magazine* 41 (March 1891), 730–32.

Eliade, Mircea. "Paradise and Utopia: Mythical Geography and Eschatology." In *Utopias and Utopian Thought,* ed. Frank E. Manuel. Boston: Beacon, 1967, pp. 260–80.

193

Bibliography

Elliott, Robert C. "Literature and the Good Life: A Dilemma." *Yale Review* 65 (Autumn 1975), 24–37.

Finley, M. I. "Utopianism Ancient and Modern." In *Critical Spirit: Essays in Honor of Herbert Marcuse,* ed. Kurt H. Wolff and Barrington Moore. Boston: Beacon, 1967, pp. 3–20.

Flower, Benjamin O. "The Latest Social Vision." *Arena,* 18 October 1897, pp. 517–34.

Forbes, Allyn B. "The Literary Quest for Utopia." *Social Forces* 6 (December 1927), 179–88.

Franklin, H. Bruce. "Fictions of the Future." *Stanford Today,* no. 17 (Summer 1966), 6–11.

Frazer, Ray. "Looking Backward: Books in the '80s." *Claremont Quarterly 1* (Spring 1963), 29–33.

Friend, Beverly. "Virgin Territory: The Bonds and Boundaries of Women in Science Fiction." In *Many Futures, Many Worlds: Theme and Form in Science Fiction,* ed. Thomas D. Clareson. Kent, Ohio: Kent State University Press, 1977, pp. 140–63.

Frye, Northrop. "Varieties of Literary Utopias." In *Utopias and Utopian Thought,* ed. Frank E. Manuel. Boston: Beacon, 1967, pp. 25–49.

Galbreath, Robert. "Introduction to the Ketterer Forum." *Science Fiction Studies* 3 (March 1976), 60–63.

Gemorah, Solomon. "Laurence Gronlund—Utopian or Reformer?" *Science and Society* 33 (Fall 1969), 446–58.

Gilman, Nicholas P. "The Way to Utopia." *Unitarian Review* 34 (July 1890), 48–66.

Gronlund, Laurence. "Our Destiny." *Nationalist,* March–September 1890.

Hamilton, John B. "Notes Toward a Definition of Science Fiction." *Extrapolation* 4 (1962).

Hawthorne, Julian. "A Popular Topic." *Lippincott's Magazine* 45 (1890), 883–88.

Hicks, John D. "The Political Career of Ignatius Donnelly." *Mississippi Valley Historical Review* 8 (June–September 1921), 80–132.

Hillegas, Mark R. "Dystopian Science Fiction: New Index to the Human Situation." *New Mexico Quarterly* 31 (Autumn 1961), 238–49.

Howe, Irving. "The Fiction of Anti-Utopia." In *A World More Attractive: A View of Modern Literature and Politics.* New York: Horizon, 1963, pp. 227–50.

Jakiel, S. James, and Rosandia Levinthal. "The Laws of Time Travel." *Extrapolation* 21 (Summer 1980), 130–38.

Jameson, Fredric. "Of Islands and Trenches: Neutralization and the Production of Utopian Discourse." *Diacritics* 7 (June 1977), 2–21.

———. "To Reconsider the Relationship of Marxism to Utopian Thought." *Minnesota Review* 6 (Spring 1976), 53–58.

Kerr, Charles H. "Publisher's Department." *International Socialist Review* 5 (1904–05), 62–63, 317–318, 761; 9 (1908), 79.

Lasky, Melvin J. "The Birth of Metaphor: On the Origins of Utopia and Revolution." *Encounter* 34 (February 1970), 35–45; 34 (March 1970), 30–42.

194

Bibliography

Laveleye, Emile. "Two New Utopias." *Contemporary Review* 57 (January 1890), 1–19.

Levin, Harry. "Some Paradoxes of Utopia." In *Edward Bellamy, Novelist and Reformer*. Schenectedy, N.Y.: Union College Press, 1968, p. 18.

Lewis, Arthur O. "The Anti-Utopian Novel: Preliminary Notes and Checklist." *Extrapolation* 2 (May 1961), 27–32.

———. "The Utopian Dream." In *Directions in Literary Criticism*, ed. Stanley Weintraub and Philip Young. University Park: Pennsylvania State University Press, 1973, pp. 192–200.

Lokke, Virgil. "The American Utopian Anti-Novel." In *Frontiers of American Culture*, ed. Ray B. Brown et al. Purdue, Ind.: Purdue University Press, 1968, pp. 123–53.

Maher, P. E. "Laurence Gronlund: Contributions to American Socialism." *Western Political Quarterly* 15 (December 1962), 618–24.

Marin, Louis. "Theses on Ideology and Utopia," *Minnesota Review* 6 (Spring 1976).

Mott, Frank Luther. "The Magazine Revolution and Popular Ideas in the 90s." *Proceedings of the American Antiquarian Society* 64, pp. 195–214.

Mullen, R. D. "The Arno Reprints." *Science Fiction Studies* 2 (July 1975), 179–94.

Mumford, Lewis. "Fashions Change in Utopia." *New Republic* 48 (June 1926), 114–15.

———. "Utopia, The City and the Machine." In *Utopias and Utopian Thought*, ed. Frank E. Manuel (Boston: Beacon, 1967), pp. 3–24.

Nationalist (Boston) 1 (May 1889)–3 (May 1891), entire issues.

Negley, Glenn. "Utopia and Dystopia: A Look Backward." In *Utopia/Dystopia?*, ed. Peyton E. Richter. Cambridge, Mass.: Schenkman, 1975, pp. 21–27.

Nation (Boston) 1 (January 1891); 2 (December 1892), entire issues.

Patrick, J. Max. "Iconoclasm, The Complement of Utopianism," *Science Fiction Studies* 3 (July 1976), 157–60.

Patterson, John. "From Yeoman to Beast: Images of Blackness in *Caesar's Column*," *American Studies* 12, no. 2 (1977), 21–31.

Penny News. Ed. and publ. by Edward Bellamy and Charles Bellamy, beginning 24 February 1880. (No copies available 20 March 1880–24 September 1880. Edward Bellamy's connection with the paper extended from the first issue to about the end of 1880.)

Pfaelzer, Jean. "American Utopian Fiction 1888–1896: The Political Origins of Form." *Minnesota Review* 6 (Spring 1976), 114–17.

———. "Parody and Satire in American Dystopian Fiction of the Nineteenth Century." *Science Fiction Studies* 7 (March 1980), 61–72.

———. "A State of One's Own: Feminism as Ideology in American Utopias 1880–1915." *Extrapolation* 24 (Winter 1983), 311–28.

Plank, Robert. "Remarks on the Nomenclature We Use." *Alternative Futures* 1 (Spring 1978), 95–96.

Polak, Frederik L. "Utopia and Cultural Renewal." In *Utopias and Utopian Thought*. ed. Frank E. Manuel. Boston: Beacon, 1967, pp. 281–95.

Bibliography

Pollack, Norman. "Ignatius Donnelly on Human Rights: A Study of Two Novels." *Mid America, an Historical Review* 47 (April 1965), 99–112.

Reynolds, Mack, Franz Rottensteiner, and Fredric Jameson. "Change, SF, and Marxism: Open or Closed Universes?" *Science Fiction Studies* 1 (Fall 1974), 269–75.

Ridge, Martin. "The Humor of Ignatius Donnelly." *Minnesota Historian* 33 (1953), 326–30.

Riesman, David. "Observations on Community Plans." *Yale Law Journal* 57 (1947).

Roemer, Kenneth M. "The Heavenly City of the Late Nineteenth-Century Utopians." *Journal of the American Studies Association of Texas* 4 (1973), 5–13.

———. "1984 in 1894: Harken's Land of the Changing Sun." *Mississippi Quarterly* 26 (Winter 1972–73), 29–42.

———. "Sex Roles, Utopias and Change: The Family in Late Nineteenth-Century Utopian Literature." *American Studies* 13 (Fall 1972), 33–47.

———. " 'Utopia Made Practical': Compulsive Realism." *American Literary Realism* 7 (Summer 1974), 273–76.

Russ, Joanna. "*Amor Vincit Feminam:* The Battle of the Sexes in SF." *Science Fiction Studies* 7 (March 1980), 2–15.

———. "The Image of Women in Science Fiction." In *Images of Women in Fiction: Feminist Perspectives,* ed. Susan Koppelman Cornillon. Bowling Green, Ohio: Bowling Green University Popular Press, 1972, pp. 79–94.

———. "Speculations: The Subjunctivity of Science Fiction," *Extrapolation* 15 (December 1973), 51–59.

Sanford, Charles. "Classics of American Reform Literature," *American Quarterly* 10 (1958), 295–31.

Sargent, Lyman T. "An Ambiguous Legacy: The Role and Position of Women in the English Utopia." *Extrapolation* 19 (December 1977), 39–49.

———. "English and American Utopians, Similarities and Differences." *Journal of General Education* 28 (Spring 1976), 16–22.

———. "A Note on the Other Side of Human Nature in the Utopian Novel." *Political Theory* 3 (February 1975), 88–97.

———. "Opportunities for Research on Utopian Literature to 1900." *Extrapolation* 19 (December 1977), 16–26.

———. "Utopia: The Problem of Definition." *Extrapolation* 16 (1975), 137–48.

———. "Women in Utopia," *Comparative Literature Studies* 10 (December 1973), 302–16.

Sargent, Pamela. "Women in Science Fiction," *Futures* 7 (October 1975), 433–41.

Saxton, Alexander. " 'Caesar's Column': The Dialogue of Utopia and Catastrophe." *American Quarterly* 19 (1967), 224–38.

Schäfer, Martin. "The Rise and Fall of Anti-Utopia." *Science Fiction Studies* 6 (November 1979), 287–95.

Segal, Howard P. "Technological Utopianism and American Culture, 1830–1940." Ph.D. diss., Princeton University, 1975.

———. "Young West: The Psyche of Technological Utopianism." *Extrapolation* 19 (December 1977), 50–58.

Bibliography

Sempers, C. T. "Utopian Dreams of Literary Men." *Harvard Monthly* 3 (December 1886), 95–104.

Shklar, Judith. "The Political Theory of Utopia: From Melancholy to Nostalgia." In *Utopias and Utopian Thought,* ed. Frank E. Manuel. Boston: Beacon, 1967, pp. 101–15.

Sinclair, Upton. "A Utopian Bookshelf." *Saturday Review of Literature,* 7 December 1946, pp. 20–21.

Solomon, Maynard. "Marx and Bloch: Reflection on Utopia and Art." *Telos* 13 (Fall 1972), 68–85.

Shurter, Robert L. "The Utopian Novel in America 1888–1900." *South Atlantic Quarterly* 34 (1935), 137–44.

Smith, Goldwin. "Prophets of Unrest." *Forum* 9 (August 1890), 599–614.

Sparks, E. E. "Seeking Utopia in America." *Chatauquan* 31 (May 1900), 151–61.

Stern, Herman I. "Who Are the Utopians?" *Nationalist* 31 (October 1890), 165–71.

Suvin, Darko. "Defining the Literary Genre of Utopia: Some Historical Semantics, Some Genealogy, a Proposal and a Plea." *Studies in the Literary Imagination* 6, no. 2 (Fall 1973), 121–45. (Reprinted in his *Metamorphoses of Science Fiction.*)

———. "The Riverside Trees, or SF and Utopia: Degrees of Kinship." *Minnesota Review* 3 (1974), 108–15.

———. "Science Fiction and the Genealogical Jungle." *Genre* 6 (1973), 251–73.

———. "SF Theory: Internal and External Delimitations and Utopia (Summary)." *Extrapolation* 19 (December 1977), 13–15.

———. "The State of the Art in Science Fiction Theory: Determining and Delimiting the Genre." *Science Fiction Studies* 6 (March 1979), 32–45.

———. " 'Utopian' and 'Scientific': Two Attributes for Socialism from Engels." *Minnesota Review* 6 (Spring 1976), 59–70.

Ulam, Adam. "Socialism and Utopia." In *Utopias and Utopian Thought,* ed. Frank E. Manuel. Boston: Beacon, 1967, pp. 116–34.

Wagar, W. Warren. "Utopian Studies and Utopian Thought: Definitions and Horizons." *Extrapolation* 19 (December 1977), 4–12.

Weinkauf, Mary S. "Five Spokesmen for Dystopia." *Mid-West Quarterly* 16 (January 1975), 175–86.

———. "Edenic Motifs in Utopian Fiction." *Extrapolation* 11 (December 1969), 15–22.

Westlott, Marcia. "Dialectics of Fantasy." *Frontiers: A Journal of Women Studies* 2 (Fall 1977), 1–7.

Wheatley, Richard. "Ideal Commonwealths." *Methodist Review* 75 (July 1893), 581–97.

Wild, Paul. "Teaching Utopia." *English Journal* 55 (March 1966), 335–75.

Williams, Raymond. "Utopia and Science Fiction." *Science Fiction Studies* 5 (November 1978), 203–14.

Selected Unpublished Material

Bleich, David. "Utopia: A Psychology of a Cultural Fantasy." Ph.D. diss., New York University, 1968.

Bibliography

Browning, William Gordon. "Anti-Utopian Fiction: Definition and Standards for Evaluation." Ph.D. diss., Louisiana State University, 1966.

Burt, Donald C. "Utopia and the Agrarian Tradition in American, 1865–1900." Ph.D. diss., University of New Mexico, 1973.

Flory, Claude. "Economic Criticism in American Fiction 1792–1900." Ph.D. diss., University of Pennsylvania, 1936.

Quissell, Barbara Carolyn. "The Sentimental and Utopian Novels of Nineteenth-Century America: Romance and Social Issues." Ph.D. diss., University of Utah, 1973.

Ransome, Eilene. "Utopus Discovers America or Critical Realism in American Utopian Fiction, 1798–1900." Ph.D. diss., Vanderbilt University, 1946.

Rooney, Charles J. "Utopian Literature as a Reflection of Social Forces in America, 1865–1917." Ph.D. diss., George Washington University, 1968.

Shurter, Robert LeFerre. "The Utopian Novel in America 1865–1900." Ph.D. diss., Western Reserve University, 1936.

Thal-Larsen, Margart Wilson. "Political and Economic Ideas in American Utopian Fiction, 1868–1914." Ph.D. diss., University of California, 1941.

Selected Bibliographies on American Utopianism

Adams, Raymond. *A Booklist of American Communities.* Department of English, University of North Carolina, Chapel Hill, 1935, mimeographed.

Baden, Anne L. *Memorandum on List of References on Utopias to be Added to the List of 1922.* Washington, D.C.: U.S. Library of Congress, 15 July 1931.

Bailey, J. O. Bibliography to *Pilgrims Through Space and Time: Trends and Patterns in Scientific and Utopian Fiction.* New York: Argus, 1947, pp. 325–33.

Beauchamp, Gorman. "Themes and Uses of Fictional Utopias: A Bibliography of Secondary Works in English." *Science Fiction Studies* 4 (March 1977), 53–63.

Beiller, Everett Franklin. *The Checklist of Fantastic Literature: A Bibliography of Fantasy, Weird and Science Fiction Books Published in the English Language.* Chicago: Shasta, 1948.

Bentley, Wilder. *The Communication of Utopian Thought: The Bibliography.* San Francisco: Author, 1959.

Catalogue of Books on Socialism, Free Thought, Economics, History, Hypnotism, Hygiene, and American Fiction. Chicago: Charles H. Kerr, 1900.

Clareson, Thomas. *Science Fiction Criticism: An Annotated Check List.* Kent, Ohio: Kent State University Press, 1972.

Crawford, Joseph H., Jr., James J. Donahue, and Donald M. Grant. *"333": A Bibliography of the Science-Fantasy Novel.* Providence, R.I.: Grandon, 1953.

Dameron, Louise. *Utopias: Bibliography.* Rev. ed. Baltimore: Enoch Pratt Free Library, 1938.

Forbes, Allen. "Bibliography of American Utopias 1884–1900." *Social Forces* 6, pp. 188–89.

Hellman, Florence S. *List of References on Utopias (Supplementary to Typewritten List of 1922).* Washington, D.C.: U.S. Library of Congress, 22 November 1926.

———. *A List of References on Utopias (Supplementary to the Typewritten Lists of 1922 and 1926).* Washington, D.C.: U.S. Library of Congress, 31 January 1940.

Bibliography

Lewis, Arthur O. "The Anti-Utopian Novel: Preliminary Notes and Checklist." *Extrapolation* 2 (May 1961).

List of References on Utopias. Washington, D.C.: U.S. Library of Congress, 19 September 1922.

List of References on Utopias: Additional References. Washington, D.C.: U.S. Library of Congress, 15 August 1935.

Meyer, H. H. B. *List of References on Utopias.* Washington, D.C.: U.S. Library of Congress, 1922.

Negley, Glenn. *Utopian Literature: A Bibliography.* Lawrence: Regents Press of Kansas, 1977.

Negley, Glenn, ed. *Utopia Collection of the Duke University Library.* Durham, N.C.: Friends of Duke University Library, 1965; supplement, 1967.

Negley, Glenn, and J. Max Patrick. "Selected List of Utopian Works, 1850–1950." In *The Quest for Utopia: An Anthology of Imaginary Societies.* New York: Henry Schuman, 1952, pp. 19–22.

Roemer, Kenneth M. "American Utopian Literature (1888–1900): An Annotated Bibliography." *American Literary Realism* 4 (Summer 1971), 227–54.

———. Bibliography to *The Obsolete Necessity, 1888–1900.* Kent, Ohio: Kent State University Press, 1976.

———. "Short-Title Bibliography." In *America As Utopia.* New York: Burt Franklin, 1961. [Includes "Supplementary List of Utopian Works: A Sample of Titles Recently 'Discovered' by Teitler and Sargent."]

Rose, Lisle A. "A Bibliographic Survey of Economic and Political Writings, 1865–1900." *American Literature* 15 (1944), 381–410.

———. "A Descriptive Catalogue of Economic and Politico-Economic Fiction in the U.S." Ph.D. diss., University of Chicago, 1936.

Sargent, Lyman T. *British and American Utopian Literature 1516–1975.* Boston: G. K. Hall, 1977.

Utopias: Additonal References. Washington, D.C.: U.S. Library of Congress, 27 April 1938.

Wright, Lyle H. *American Fiction 1876–1900: A Contribution Toward a Bibliography.* San Marino, Calif.: Huntington Library, 1966.

Edward Bellamy: Primary Works

The Blindman's World and Other Stories. With a Prefatory Sketch by W. D. Howells. Boston: Houghton Mifflin, 1898. [Includes reprints of fiction cited below.]

"Christmas in the year 2000." *Ladies' Home Journal* 12, no. 2 (January 1895).

"The Cold Snap." *Scribner's Monthly Magazine* 10 (September 1875).

"Deserted." *Lippincott's Magazine* 22 (November 1878).

Dr. Heidenhoff's Process. New York: D. Appleton, 1880.

The Duke of Stockbridge. New York: Silver Burdett, n.d.

"An Echo of Antietam. *Century Magazine* 38 (July 1889).

Edward Bellamy Speaks Again. Kansas City: Peerage, 1937. [Includes reprints of periodical articles and pamphlets cited below.]

Equality. New York: D. Appleton-Century, 1897.

Bibliography

"First Steps toward Nationalism." *Forum* 10 (October 1890).

"Hooking Watermelons." *Scribner's Monthly Magazine* 14 (September 1877).

"How I Wrote *Looking Backward*." *Nationalist* (May 1889).

"How I Came to Write *Looking Backward*." *Ladies' Home Journal* 11 (April 1894).

"*Looking Backward* Again." *North American Review* 150 (March 1890).

Looking Backward: 2000–1887. New York: Grosset and Dunlap, 1898.

"Looking Forward." *Nationalist* 2 (December 1889).

"A Love Story Reversed." 1888. Reprinted in *The Blindman's World*, pp. 192–236.

Miss Ludington's Sister. Boston: James R. Osgood, 1884.

"Old Folk's Party." *Scribner's Monthly Magazine* 11 (March 1876).

"The Outcome of the Battle of Standards." *Boston Globe*, 16 July 1893.

Plutocracy or Nationalism, Which? Pocket Library of Socialism, no. 18 Chicago: Kerr, 1889.

"A Positive Romance" *Century Magazine* 38 (August, 1889).

"Pott's Painless Cure." *Scribner's Monthly Magazine* 17 (February 1879).

"The Programme of the Nationalists" *Forum* 17 (March 1894).

The "Progress of Nationalism in the United States." *North American Review* 154 (June 1892), 742–52.

The Religion of Solidarity. Yellow Springs, Ohio: Antioch Bookplate, 1940.

Selected Writings on Religion and Society, ed. Joseph Schiffman. New York: Liberal Arts Press, 1955.

Six to One: A Nantucket Idyll. New York: Putnam, 1878.

Springfield Daily Republican. Editorials and book reviews, August 1872–December 1887.

"A Summer Evening's Dream." *Lippincott's Magazine* 20 (September 1877).

Talks on Nationalism. Chicago: Peerage, 1938.

"To Whom This May Come." *Harper's New Monthly Magazine* 78 (February 1889).

"Two Days' Solitary Imprisonment." 1878. Reprinted in *The Blindman's World*, pp. 104–28.

"A Vital Domestic Problem—Household Service Reform." *Good Housekeeping*, 21 December 1889.

"Why I Wrote *Looking Backward*." *Nationalist* 2 (May 1890).

Edward Bellamy: Biography and Criticism

Aaron, Daniel. "Bellamy—Utopian Conservative." In *Edward Bellamy Novelist and Reformer*. Schenectady, N.Y.: Union College Press, 1968.

Austin, H. "Edward Bellamy." *National Magazine* 9 (October 1898), 69–72.

Baxter, Sylvester. "The Author of *Looking Backward*." *New England Magazine* 1 (September 1889), 92–98.

———. "Edward Bellamy's New Book of the New Democracy." *American Monthly Review of Reviews* 16 (July 1897).

———. "What Is Nationalism?" *Nationalist* 1 (May 1889).

Becker, George. "Edward Bellamy's Utopia, The American Plan." *Antioch Review* 14 (1954), 181–94.

Bibliography

Bell, Fred W. "Edward Bellamy and 'The Bellamy Plan.' " *Theosophist* 55 (August 1934).

Biscoe, J. Foster. "Attitude of the Press." *Nationalist* 1 (October 1889).

Blau, Joseph. "Bellamy's Religious Motivation for Social Reform: A Review Article." *Review of Religion* 21 (March 1957), 156.

Bleich, David. "Eros and Bellamy." *American Quarterly* 16 (Fall 1964), 445–59.

Boggs, W. A. "Looking Backward at the Utopian Novel." *New York Public Library Bulletin* 64 (1960), 329–36.

Bowman, Sylvia. "Bellamy's Missing Chapter." *New England Quarterly* 31 (March 1958), 47–65.

———. "Edward Bellamy." *American Literary Realism* 1 (Fall 1967), 7–12.

———. *Edward Bellamy Abroad: An American Prophet's Influence.* New York: Twayne, 1962.

———. *The Year 2000: A Critical Biography of Edward Bellamy.* New York: Bookman Associates, 1958.

Dawes, Anna L. "Mr. Bellamy and Christianity." *Andover Review: A Religious and Theological Monthly,* 15 April 1891.

Dewey, John. "A Great American Prophet." *Common Sense* 3 (April 1934), 7.

Earnshaw, Marion Bellamy. *Edward Bellamy Today.* Chicago: Peerage, 1936.

"Edward Bellamy." *Good Housekeeping,* 21 December 1889.

Franklin, John H. "Edward Bellamy and the Nationalist Movement." *New England Quarterly* 11 (1938), 739–72.

Fuson, Ben W. "A Poetic Precursor of Bellamy's *Looking Backward.*" *Extrapolation* 5 (1964), 31–36.

Fussell, Edwin. "The Theme of Sympathy in *Looking Backward.*" Unpublished, Department of English, University of California, San Diego, 1980.

Garrison, William Lloyd. "The Mask of Tyranny." *Arena* 1 (April 1890).

Gilman, Nicholas P. "Bellamy's *Equality.*" *Quarterly Journal of Economics* 12 (October 1897), 76–82.

———. "Nationalism in the United States." *Quarterly Journal of Economics* 4 (October 1889), 50–76.

Gronlund, Laurence. "Nationalism." *Arena* 1 (January 1890), 153–65.

Gutele, G. "Analysis of Formal Education in Edward Bellamy's *Looking Backward.*" *History of Education Quarterly* 4 (December 1964), 251–63.

Hawthorne, Julian. "A Popular Topic." *Lippincott's Magazine* 45, (June 1890), 883–88.

Higginson, Thomas. "Edward Bellamy's Nationalism." *Our Day* 5 (April 1890).

Higgs, William. "Some Objections to Mr. Bellamy's Utopia." *New Englander and Yale Review* 52 (March 1890), 231–39.

Howells, William Dean. "Editor's Study." *Harper's New Monthly Magazine* 77 (June 1888), 154–55.

———. "Edward Bellamy." *Atlantic Monthly* 82 (August 1898), 253–56.

"The Late Mr. Bellamy." *Critic* 32 (28 May 1898).

Levi, Albert W. "Edward Bellamy, Utopian." *Ethics* 55 (1945), 131–44.

Levin, Harry. "Some Paradoxes of Utopia." In *Edward Bellamy, Novelist and Reformer.* Schenectady, N.Y.: Union College Press, 1968.

Bibliography

MacNair, Everett. *Edward Bellamy and the Nationalist Movement 1889–1894.* Milwaukee, Wis.: Fitzgerald, 1957.

Madison, Charles A. "Edward Bellamy: Social Dreamer." *New England Quarterly* 15 (1942), 444–66.

Morgan, Arthur E. *Edward Bellamy.* New York: Columbia University Press, 1944.

———. *Nowhere Was Somewhere: An Exploration of the Utopian Tradition, with a Discussion of Thomas More and the Inca Civilization.* Chapel Hill: University of North Carolina Press, 1946.

———. *The Philosophy of Edward Bellamy.* New York: King's Crown, 1945.

———. *Plagiarism in Utopia: A Study of the Continuity of the Utopian Tradition, with Special Reference to Edward Bellamy's "Looking Backward."* Yellow Springs, Ohio.: Author, 1944.

Peebles, H. P. "The Utopias of the Past Compared with the Theories of Bellamy." *Overland Monthly,* 2d ser. 15 (June 1890), 574–77.

Quint, Howard. "Gaylord Wilshire and Socialism's First Congressional Campaign." *Pacific Historical Review* 26 (1951), 327–40.

Sadler, Elizabeth. "One Book's Influence, Edward Bellamy's *Looking Backward.*" *New England Quarterly* 17 (1944), 530–55.

Schiffman, Joseph. "Edward Bellamy's Altruistic Man." *American Quarterly* 6 (1954), 195–209.

———. "Edward Bellamy's Religious Thought." *PMLA* 68 (1953), 716–32.

———. "Mutual Indebtedness: Unpublished Letters of Edward Bellamy to William Dean Howells." *Harvard Library Bulletin* 12 (1958), 363–74.

Schindler, Solomon. "What Is Nationalism?" *New England Magazine* 7 (September 1892).

Shipley, Marie A. "Bebel's Bricks or Bellamy's?" *Liberty,* 21 June 1890.

———. *The True Author of "Looking Backward."* New York: John B. Alden, 1890.

Shurter, Robert L. "The Literary Work of Edward Bellamy." *American Literature* 5 (1933), 229–34.

———. "The Writing of *Looking Backward.*" *South Atlantic Quarterly* 38 (1939), 255–61.

Smith, Goldwin. "Prophets of Unrest." *Forum,* 9 August 1890, pp. 599–614.

Walker, Frances A. "Mr. Bellamy and the New Nationalist Party." *Atlantic Monthly* 65 (1890), 248–62.

Walker, Robert H. "The Poet and the Robber Baron." *American Quarterly* 13 (1961), 447–65.

Warner, Charles Dudley. "Editor's Study." *Harper's New Monthly Magazine* 96 (1897).

Willard, Frances E. "An Interview with Edward Bellamy." *Our Day,* 10 October 1889.

Zornow, William Frank. "Bellamy's Nationalism in Ohio 1891–1896." *Ohio State Archaeological and Historical Quarterly* 58 (April 1949) 152–70.

Selected Reviews of Edward Bellamy

"Bellamy's Utopia." the *Nation* 65 (26 August 1897).

Flower, B. O. "The Latest Social Vision: A Review of *Equality.*" *Arena* 18 (1894). Reprint. Boston: Arena, 1897.

Bibliography

Ford, Mary H. Review of *Looking Backward*. the *Nationalist* 1 (November 1889), 352–57.

Harris, W. T. "Edward Bellamy's Vision." *Forum* 2 (October 1889), 199–208.

Higgs, William. Review of *Looking Backward*. *New Englander and Yale Review* 2 (March 1890), 231–39.

Howells, William Dean. Review of *Miss Ludington's Sister*. *Century Magazine* 28 (August 1884).

———. Review of *Looking Backward*. *Harper's New Monthly Magazine* 77 (June 1888).

"*Looking Backward*." *Atlantic Monthly* 61 (June 1888).

"*Looking Backward*." *Los Angeles Times*, 18 March 1894.

"*Looking Backward*." *Nation* 46 (29 March 1888).

"*Looking Backward*." *Saturday* 24 (March 1888).

"*Looking Backward*." *Science*, 20 July 1888.

Morris, W. "*Looking Backward*." *Commonweal*, 22 June 1889, p. 194.

"A New Utopia." *New York Tribune*, 5 February 1888.

William Dean Howells: Selected Primary Works

"Are We a Plutocracy?" *North American Review* 158 (1894), 185–96.

"Editor's Study." *Harper's New Monthly Magazine* 78 (June–November 1888), 154–55.

"Editor's Study." *Harper's New Monthly Magazine* 80 (January 1890), 323.

"Edward Bellamy." *Atlantic Monthly* 82 (1898), 253–56.

"Equality as the Basis of Good Society." *Century Magazine* 29 (November 1895), 63–67.

Letters of an Altrurian Traveller, in *The Altrurian Romances*, ed. Clara Kirk and Rudolf Kirk. Bloomington: Indiana University Press, 1968.

The Life in Letters of William Dean Howells, ed. Mildred Howells. 2 vols. Garden City, N.Y.: Doubleday, Doran, 1928.

"Mr. Howells on Mr. Bellamy." *Critic*, n.s. 29 (June 1898).

My Literary Passions. New York: Harper and Brothers, 1895.

Preface to Edward Bellamy *The Blindman's World and Other Stories*. Boston: Houghton Mifflin, 1898.

Through the Eye of the Needle, in *The Altrurian Romances*, ed. Clara Kirk and Rudolf Kirk. Bloomington: Indiana University Press, 1968.

A Traveller from Altruria (1894), in *The Altrurian Romances*, ed. Clara Kirk and Rudolf Kirk. Bloomington: Indiana University Press, 1968.

Selected Criticism of William Dean Howells

Arms, George. "Further Inquiry into Howells' Socialism." *Science and Society* 3 (Spring 1939), 245–48.

———. "Howells' Unpublished Prefaces." *New England Quarterly* 17 (1944), 580–91.

———. "The Literary Background of Howells' Social Criticism." *American Literature* 14 (1942), 260–76.

Bibliography

Arvin, Newton. "The Useableness of Howells." *New Republic,* 30 June 1937.

Bennett, George N. *The Realism of William Dean Howells, 1889–1920.* Nashville, Tenn.: Vanderbilt University Press, 1973.

Brooks, Van Wyck. *Howells, His Life and World.* New York: E. P. Dutton, 1959.

Cady, Edwin. *The Realist at War: The Mature Years of William Dean Howells, 1885–1920.* Syracuse, N.Y.: Syracuse University Press, 1958.

Carrington, George C. *The Immense Complex Drama: The World and Art of the Howells Novel.* Columbus: Ohio State University Press, 1966.

Carter, Everett. *Howells and the Age of Realism.* Philadelphia: J. B. Lippincot, 1950.

Cooke, Delmar Cross. *William Dean Howells: A Critical Study.* New York: E. P. Dutton, 1922.

Cooperman, Stanley. "Utopian Realism: The Futurist Novels of Bellamy and Howells." *College English* 24 (1963), 464–67.

Crider, Gregory. "Howells' Altruria: The Ambivalent Future." *Old Northwest* 1 (1975), 405–410.

Dietrichson, Jan W. *The Image of Money in the American Novel in the Gilded Age.* New York: Humanities Press, 1969.

Eble, Kenneth E., ed. *Howells: A Century of Criticism.* Dallas, Tex.: Southern Methodist University Press, 1962.

———. "The Western Ideals of William Dean Howells," *Western Humanties Review.*2 (Autumn 1957), 331–38.

Firkins, Oscar W. *William Dean Howells: A Study.* Cambridge, Mass.: Harvard University Press, 1924.

Fox, Arnold B. "Howells' Doctrine of Complicity." *Modern Language Quarterly* 13 (March 1952), 56–60.

Getzels, Jacob Warren. "William Dean Howells and Socialism." *Science and Society* 2 (1938), 376–86.

Gibson, William M. *William Dean Howells.* Minneapolis: University of Minnesota Press, 1967.

Grattan, C. Hartley. "Howells: Ten Years After." *American Mercury* 20 (May 1930), 42–50.

Hough, Robert L. *The Quiet Rebel: William Dean Howells as Social Commentator.* Lincoln: University of Nebraska Press, 1959.

Kirk, Clara Marburg. *William Dean Howells and Art in His Time.* New Brunswick, N.J.: Rutgers University Press, 1965.

Lynn, Kenneth. *William Dean Howells: An American Life.* New York: Harcourt Brace, 1971.

Sokoloff, "William Dean Howells and the Ohio Village: A Study in Environment and Art." *American Quarterly* 11 (1959), 58–75.

Taylor, Walter Fuller. "On the Origin of Howells' Interest in Economic Reform." *American Literature* 2 (1930), 3–14.

Vanderbilt, Kermit. *The Achievement of William Dean Howells: a Re-interpretation.* Princeton, N.J.: Princeton University Press, 1968.

Wagenknecht, Edward. *William Dean Howells: The Friendly Eye.* New York: Oxford University Press, 1969.

Bibliography

Walsh, Harry. "Tolstoy and the Economic Novels of William Dean Howells." *Comparative Literature Studies* 14 (June 1977), 143–65.

White, Morton, and Lucia White. *The Intellectual versus the City.* Cambridge, Mass.: Harvard University Press, 1962, pp. 102–22.

Wright, Conrad. "The Sources of Mr. Howells' Socialism." *Science and Society* 2 (1938), 514–17.

Selected Reviews of William Dean Howells

Bellamy, Edward. Review. *New Nation* 2 (1892), 701–02.

————. Review. *New Nation* 3 (1893), 458.

Kirk, S. "America, Altruria, and the Coast of Bohemia." *Atlantic Monthly* 74 (1894), 701–04.

Review of *A Traveller from Altruria. Athenaeum* 7 (July 1894), 29.

Review of *A Traveller from Altruria. Critic* 21 (1894), 434.

Review of *A Traveller from Altruria. Dial* 12 (1894), 154.

Review of *A Traveller from Altruria. Harper's Bazaar* 27 (1894), 475.

Review of *A Traveller from Altruria. Nation* 59 (1894), 107.

Review of *A Traveller from Altruria. New York Daily Herald,* 23 September 1894, sec 6, p. 14.

Review of *A Traveller from Altruria. New York Daily Tribune,* 30 September 1894, p. 14.

Index

Index

Index